Studies in Mathematics Education Series

Series Editor
Dr Paul Ernest
School of Education
University of Exeter
Exeter

Understanding in Mathematics

Studies in Mathematics Education Series: 2

Understanding in Mathematics

Anna Sierpinska

 The Falmer Press

(A member of the Taylor & Francis Group)
London • Washington, D.C.

UK   The Falmer Press, 4 John Street, London WC1N 2ET
USA   The Falmer Press, Taylor & Francis Inc., 1900 Frost Road, Suite 101, Bristol, PA 19007

First published in 1994

A catalogue record for this book is available from the British Library

Library of Congress Cataloging-in-Publication Data are available on request

ISBN 0 7507 0334 2 cased

Jacket design by Caroline Archer

Typeset in 10/12pt Bembo
Graphicraft Typesetters Ltd., Hong Kong.

Printed in Great Britain by Burgess Science Press, Basingstoke on paper which has a specified pH value on final paper manufacture of not less than 7.5 and is therefore 'acid free'.

Contents

Contents

List of Figures

Acknowledgments

My thanks go primarily to my dear friend Anna Sfard, for having had the patience to go through the first version of the manuscript, offering most helpful remarks and suggestions. I am very grateful to Professors Zbigniew Semadeni and Waclaw Zawadowski for their perceptive comments and constant encouragement. I am also indebted to my colleagues at the Concordia University in Montréal, especially to the late Nicolas Herscovics for our unforgettable conversations on models of mathematical understanding, and to Joel Hillel and Bill Byers, for the many interesting and fruitful discussions we have had concerning the problems of teaching and learning mathematics at the undergraduate level. Last but not least, I wish to say *thank you* to all the students that have participated in my research as subjects or collaborators, trying hard to teach me something about understanding of mathematics.

The writing of this book was partly supported by FCAR grant #93 ER-1535 and SSHRC grant #410-93-0700.

I dedicate the book *To my Parents*.

Anna Sierpinska
Montreal, Canada
March 1994

Preface by Series Editor

Mathematics education is established worldwide as a major area of study, with numerous dedicated journals and conferences serving national and international communities of scholars. Research in mathematics education is becoming more theoretically orientated. Vigorous new perspectives are pervading it from disciplines as diverse as psychology, philosophy, sociology, anthropology, feminism, semiotics and literary criticism. The series Studies in Mathematics Education consists of research contributions to the field based on disciplined perspectives which link theory with practice. It is founded on the philosophy that theory is the practitioner's most powerful tool in understanding and changing practice. Whether the practice is mathematics teaching, teacher education, or educational research, the series will offer new perspectives to assist in clarifying and posing problems and stimulating debate. The series Studies in Mathematics Education will encourage the development and dissemination of theoretical perspectives in mathematics education as well as their critical scrutiny. It aims to have a major impact on the theoretical development of mathematics education as a field of study in the 1990s.

The first book in this series was *The Philosophy of Mathematics Education* by Paul Ernest, which can be said to have lived up to the above description. The next volume to be published will be *Mathematics, Education and Philosophy: An International Perspective*, an edited collection containing chapters by Valerie Walkerdine, Dick Tahta, Brian Rotman, Sal Restivo, Thomas Tymoczko, Ernst von Glasersfeld, Reuben Hersh, Philip J. Davis, Ubiratan D'Ambrosio, David Pimm, John Mason, Paul Ernest, Leslie P. Steffe, Michael Otte, Stephen I. Brown, Anna Sfard, George Gheverghese Joseph, Paul Dowling, Stephen Lerman, and others. Exciting and powerful future volumes for the series by Barbara Jaworski, Ernst von Glasersfeld, Jeffrey Evans and Paul Dowling are in preparation, and will be published or be in press by the end of the year.

The present volume is the second in the series. In it Anna Sierpinska tackles what might truthfully be described as the central problem in mathematics education: understanding in mathematics. Her inquiry draws together strands from mathematics, philosophy, logic, linguistics, the psychology of mathematics education, and especially welcome to an English-speaking audience, continental European research. She considers the contributions of the social and cultural contexts to understanding, and draws upon a wide range of scholars of current interest, including Foucault and Vygotsky. The outcome is an important insight into both understanding and mathematics, valuable both for the teacher and the mathematician. All in all, an important and appropriate contribution to the series.

Paul Ernest
University of Exeter
February 1994

Introduction

My concern with the question of understanding has its sources in the practical problems of teaching mathematics and such basic and naive questions as: how to teach so that students understand? Why, in spite of all my efforts of good explanation they do not understand and make all these nonsensical errors? What exactly don't they understand? What do they understand and how?

My first approach to these questions was empirical: observations of students while discussing mathematical problems, trying to make sense of them, communicating their understanding to others. The problems given to the students were such that, to solve them, the students had, in fact, to construct a new (for them) mathematical concept. The difficulties they encountered, the tentative understandings of a still very unclear situation were often quite close to those experienced by mathematicians in the past. Students' difficulties thus acquired a more universal meaning and significance, depending not so much on their lack of mathematical experience, or abilities, or idiosyncrasies of their still immature thought, but on the nature of the mathematical concept itself, and on the culture in the frame of which it developed.

This is where Bachelard's concept of epistemological obstacle turned out to be very useful. Students' thinking appeared to suffer from certain 'epistemological obstacles' that had to be overcome if a new concept was to be developed. These 'epistemological obstacles' — ways of understanding based on some unconscious, culturally acquired schemes of thought and unquestioned beliefs about the nature of mathematics and fundamental categories such as number, space, cause, chance, infinity, . . . inadequate with respect to the present day theory — marked the development of the concept in history, and remained somehow 'implicated', to use Bohm's term, in its meaning.

It is then on these obstacles that research concentrated: a 'hunt' for epistemological obstacles started at the same time as an effort of precisation, of a better explication of the term was undertaken. The question was posed: on what grounds do we claim that a student's thinking suffers of an epistemological obstacle? Is an epistemological obstacle an error, a misunderstanding, or just a certain way of knowing that works in some restricted domain but proves inadequate when the domain is transcended? Or is it an attitude of the mind that allows to take opinions for facts, a few cases for evidence of general laws, . . .?

The term of epistemological obstacle was invented by the French physicist and philosopher Gaston Bachelard. He used this notion for the purposes of his polemics with positivism in science. Scientists, he said, do not function in the way prescribed by the neopositivists. Nature is not 'given' to us — our minds are never virgin in front of reality. Whatever we say we see or observe is biased by what we already know, think, believe, or wish to see. Some of these thoughts, beliefs and knowledge can function as an obstacle to our understanding of the phenomena. Our generalizations can be biased by our tendency to found all knowledge on a few all-explanatory laws or principles like 'all bodies fall' or 'light propagates in straight lines', or on all-explanatory metaphors like 'air is a sponge'.

But mathematics is not a natural science. It is not about the phenomena of the real world, it is not about observation and induction. Mathematical induction is not a method for making generalizations. None of the examples of epistemological obstacles that Bachelard gave could apply to mathematics, as Bachelard said himself.

Still, mathematics educators had the feeling that it does make sense to speak about epistemological obstacles in mathematics: every day, they were facing something that seemed to function as an epistemological obstacle in their students' thinking. What they were missing was a theoretical foundation. The transfer from natural sciences to mathematics required some adaptation, and some philosophical reflection on the nature of mathematics. This turned their attention to the works of Lakatos, whose view of mathematics as a quasi-empirical science was vividly exemplified in his reconstruction of the history of the formula of Euler for polyhedrons. This history appears as a 'race through epistemological obstacles' — a sequence of refuted wrong or only limited beliefs about what this or that mathematical object should be, what properties it can have, etc.

This view of mathematics required a rethinking of the teaching and of the judgment of the students' understanding. It relativized their errors. Some of their errors were caused by ways of thinking quite legitimate within a certain frame of mind, a certain context of problems and certain beliefs about what is truth in mathematics. It became clear that at least some of the students' ways of understanding deserve more respect and attention, and that instead of trying to replace the students' 'wrong' knowledge by the 'correct' one, the teacher's effort should be invested into negotiations of meanings with the students, invention of special challenging problems in which a student would experience a mental conflict that would bring to his or her awareness that his or her way of understanding is probably not the only possible one, that it is not universal.

At this point the research programme shifted to the problems of design of teaching situations — 'didactical engineering' as the French call it — that would provide favourable conditions for the students to overcome their epistemological obstacles and thus understand the mathematical contents better and deeper.

I started to almost identify understanding with overcoming obstacles. But then a doubt was born: is all understanding like this? Everyday experience of teaching and introspection suggested a negative answer.

Once again, I was at the beginning of my way. The importunate question: 'what is understanding?' popped up once more.

This time it had to be addressed directly. The first move was to consult philosophers and psychologists. *Gestalt* psychology provided some interesting ideas — especially that of equilibrium or harmony of the 'field of consciousness' which seemed to be the aimed at state of mind in understanding. Piaget's theory of equilibration of cognitive structures developed this metaphor to speak about more complex intellectual processes and not just visual perception. Vygotski's theory of concept development was quite interesting, too. The process appeared as an evolution of those operations of the mind that seemed to play an essential role in understanding: first, generalizations of things, joined later by isolation of features of things and discrimination between them, all topped, at the age of adolescence, by more advanced generalizations and syntheses leading to the formation of systemic thinking and concepts.

Search for hints in the classical philosophical literature (Locke's and Leibniz's *Essays on Human Understanding*) was somewhat disappointing. Works in philosophical hermeneutics were, on the other hand, quite illuminating in some ways, although they were concerned mainly with understanding the written or spoken discourse, rather literary than mathematical. Gadamer's and Heidegger's discussions of the 'hermeneutic circle' evoked the idea of epistemological obstacles and their unavoidability in any effort of understanding. Ricœur's description of the process of understanding a text as a dialectic of successive guesses and validation of guesses quite clearly made the distinction between the roles of understanding and explaining at the same time as it revealed their inseparability and complementarity in interpretive processes.

Dewey's reflections on understanding were very appealing to an educator — Dewey often referred to the teaching practice and to observations of a growing child. But his definition of understanding as 'grasping the meaning' brought forth the need to clarify the notion of meaning. Now, semantics is a huge field. The logical semantical views on meaning originated from the works of Frege and Church were hard to swallow — formal logical views on meaning are unacceptable for those whose main concern is a living and developing child. The epistemological and pragmatic perspectives have to be taken, necessarily.

From this point of view, Husserl's theory of the intentionality of meaning was much better: the meaning of a sign is that to which I direct myself (in thought) in an act of understanding. This definition, however, did not solve the problem: while Dewey defined understanding by meaning, Husserl defined meaning by understanding. We find ourselves bound in a vicious circle.

A way out of the impasse seemed to be provided by Ajdukiewicz's 'Pragmatic logic', where understanding was defined independently of meaning using the category of object as a primitive notion and the notion of meaning was introduced through the relation of 'understanding in the same way'.

Ajdukiewicz's definition was very clear and simple; his notion of meaning — very natural. I finally had the impression of having understood what understanding is all about.

But this was not the end of my problems. Ajdukiewicz's definition was restricted to understanding expressions; meaning was the meaning of an expression. Understanding in mathematics is not confined to understanding expressions. Of course, terms, symbols, formulas, theorems can all be regarded as expressions. But even if we count texts as expressions, is a proof a text? Is a theory a text? And what about understanding concepts? For Ajdukiewicz, a concept was simply the meaning of a name. But my deep conviction was that understanding a concept does not start with understanding its name. So there was work to be done still.

In the chapters that follow I present some results of this work. It is an approach to understanding in mathematics, influenced by Ajdukiewicz's definition, and guided by the aim of finding some mental tools to answer questions like: 'What does it mean to understand such and such notion in mathematics?'

In the context of the teaching and learning of mathematics any question about the students' understanding is at once a question about the level of understanding: understanding is at once evaluated. This is why many existing models of understanding in mathematics consist in a hierarchy of levels, steps or stages. However, it is quite clear that any evaluation of an understanding must be relative. Therefore, what is proposed in the present book is to methodologically separate the questions of understanding and 'good' understanding in building up a model and to admit, as fundamental, the notion of act of understanding. An act of understanding is not defined in terms of its impact on cognition; it is not, *a priori*, judged as valuable or worthless. Axiological issues come into the scene when whole processes of understanding are taken into account. Processes of understanding are seen as lattices of acts of understanding linked by various reasonings (explanations, validations) and a (relatively) 'good' understanding of a given mathematical situation (concept, theory, problem) is said to be achieved if the process of understanding contained a certain number of especially significant acts, namely acts of overcoming obstacles specific to that mathematical situation.

The notion of the act of understanding is central in the whole conception of the book. Thus, the second chapter: 'Components and conditions of an act of understanding' occupies much more space than any of the others. The first chapter plays the role of an introduction to it: it inquires into the various senses and uses of the word 'understanding' in ordinary language, discusses the notion of meaning and relations between the notions of understanding and meaning. It displays the rich background of issues which underlie the question of what is an act of understanding that is considered in the second chapter.

Chapter 3 looks at whole processes of understanding, and the roles therein, of explanations and validations, examples, previous knowledge, figurative speech (metaphors and metonymies), activity (both practical and intellectual). The question of evaluation of understanding is dealt with in Chapter 4. One of the problems raised here is concerned with the relativity of any such evaluation. Two important determinants of this relativity, namely the developmental stage of the understanding subject and the culture, i.e., the system of norms, ways of thinking and communicating, as well as what is considered as scientific knowledge by both the understanding subject and the person who evaluates the understanding, are the object of Chapter 5. It is shown, among others, how the psychogenetic development of understanding is influenced by the implicit functioning of a culture.

The view presented in the book is just one of the many possible ways of looking at understanding in mathematics, biased by my own experiences with mathematics, as a learner — a student of Andrzej Mostowski, Karol Borsuk and Wanda Szmielew; as a teacher; as a researcher both in mathematics and mathematics education, and an enthusiastic reader of Ajdukiewicz's articles and books. Understanding is a very complex issue, both philosophically and practically. But it is also a challenging and fascinating one and sometimes we just cannot resist the temptation of writing about it, although it is clear from the beginning that whatever we say understanding is, it is not because 'whatever we say is words, and what we mean to say is not words'.

This book is not primarily concerned with the word 'understanding' or the concept of understanding, although it might seem so. It is meant to contribute to a better understanding of how real people understand mathematics in real life, not of the 'human understanding' of mathematics. It is not a philosophical treatise. In mathematics education we are trying to understand and communicate on, among others, the problems related to students' understanding. For this we need some clarity on what we are talking and communicating about. This is why, from time to time, we need to make a stop in our usual more or less practical activities and think about the language we are using, about the meanings of such common words as 'understanding' or 'meaning'. This book has been such a stop in my own activities, too long, I am sure, and whether it was at all worthy of making — let the reader judge.

Chapter 1

Understanding and Meaning

We are in a class of the fourth grade. The teacher is dictating: 'A circle is the position of the points in a plane which are at the same distance from an interior point called the centre.' The good pupil writes this phrase in his copy-book and the bad pupil draws faces, but neither of them understands. Then the teacher takes the chalk and draws a circle on the board. 'Ah', think the pupils, 'why didn't he say at once, a circle is a round, and we should have understood.' (Poincaré, 1952)

Understanding

The Word 'Understanding' in Ordinary Language

The word 'understanding' is used in very many forms and expressions in informal speech. We say that a person 'understands' something, we speak of a person's 'understanding' of something, and of the various 'understandings' people may have. We also speak of 'mutual understanding', of understanding somebody's utterance or somebody's writing, of understanding a word, an expression, a concept, a phenomenon. We qualify understanding as 'good', 'deep', 'poor', 'complex', 'significant', 'full', 'incomplete', 'intuitive', or 'wrong'. We sometimes speak of 'some' understanding to say that this understanding is not yet very elaborate.

It is often claimed that the word 'to understand' is highly ambiguous (Kotarbinski, 1961, p. 128). Indeed, it is certainly not the same mental and emotional experience to understand the phenomenon of sunset and to understand a poetic description of a sunset. It is not the same to understand the sun as a bright sphere that travels across the sky from dawn to twilight and to understand the sun as the star around which gravitate the Earth and other planets of our planetary system. In this case we speak of two 'ways of understanding' or two different 'understandings' of one and the same thing.

'Understanding' can be thought of as an actual or a potential mental experience, as Kotarbinski pointed out (*ibidem*). For example, when we say that a person, who knows his or her multiplication tables, understands the thought that '7 times 9 is 63', we may mean that the person actually, at this moment, thinks of '7 times 9' and '63' and considers them as equal, or that he or she is capable of so doing at any time, having reflected upon it already in the past.

There are, then, actual mental experiences, which we might call 'acts of understanding' and there is 'an understanding' which is a potential to experience an act of understanding when necessary. 'Understandings' thus seem more to belong to the sphere of knowing: they are the 'resources' for knowing.

An act of understanding is an experience that occurs at some point in time and is quickly over. But, especially in education, we also speak of understanding as a cognitive activity that takes place over longer periods of time — then we sometimes use the term of 'process of understanding' in which 'acts of understanding' mark the significant steps while the acquired 'understandings' constitute props for further development.

Understanding . . . What?

Acts of understanding, understandings, processes of understanding can all differ by that which is understood: an expression of language, a diagram, a concept, a theorem, a theory, a judgment, somebody's thought, a phenomenon, a situation, a problem . . .

In the context of mathematics, we often speak of understanding 'mathematical concepts' in general or of understanding specific mathematical concepts such as number, quantity, volume, function, limit of a sequence, linear independence of vectors etc. However, other things are mentioned as objects of understanding as well.

Let us consider, as an example of a text concerned with cognition in the mathematical field, the 1991 article of James G. Greeno, and find the various uses the author is making of the word 'understanding' and its derived forms. Let us start with the question: what appears there as 'objects of understanding'?

In the first instance of the use of the word 'understanding' in the article, it is associated with 'patterns': 'understanding subtle patterns'. Later the author mentions understanding of 'concepts, notations and procedures', 'equivalences' (e.g., of 42 and 6•7, 2/3 and 4/6, y = 6 − 3x and x/2 + y/6 = 1, etc.), 'relations among numbers and quantities', 'how mathematics is related to situations involving physical objects, quantities of money and other concrete things', 'problems and situations', 'language', 'language of mathematics', 'instructions', 'the linear structure of positive integers', 'relations between places in the environment that are represented by the symbols on the map', 'meanings [of procedures for manipulating notations]', 'reasonings', 'one's physical position in an environment', 'concepts and principles', 'linguistic representations of concepts', 'theoretical entities and processes', 'the difference between an object and the thought about that object', 'the sequence of numerals', 'mathematical concepts', 'a phrase', 'mathematical questions', 'metamathematical views'.

Figure 1: The pattern of the problem of Luc and Michel

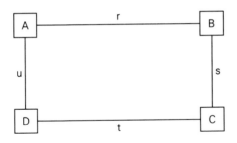

*Confusion Between the Thing I Want to Understand and That on Which
I Base My Understanding*

If I say 'I understand the pattern' (of a class of problems, for example) I may
mean that the object of my understanding is really the pattern, or I may mean
that I intend to understand the class of problems and the perception of some
common pattern in these problems constitutes my understanding of it — the
pattern founds my understanding of the class of problems. In the former case,
I reflect on the pattern itself, which I have previously identified as common
to certain problems. I may say I understand the pattern when, for example,
I have constructed a model of this pattern, identified the basic elements of it.
Then I may be able to formulate problems that follow this pattern and not
only to recognize among some given problems those that satisfy the pattern.

Let us take, for example, the following problem: Luc has $1.45 more
than Michel. Luc doubles his amount of money and Michel increases his by
$3.50. Now Luc has $0.40 less than Michel. What were the initial amounts of
Luc and Michel?

Understanding the problem as having a certain pattern may consist in
perceiving a similarity between this and other problems done in class. This
may allow the use of an analogous procedure to solve the problem. Understanding the pattern itself would probably involve a generalization of the
problem, introduction of variables in place of all the givens and unknowns:
four unknown states A, B, C, D are related by given relations r, s, t, u
between A and B, B and C, C and D, D and A, respectively; to find A and
B. Such understanding could be supported by a representation of the pattern
in form of a diagram, like the one shown in Figure 1.

A pattern of solution would then easily be seen: given are the relations:
$A = r(B) = B + 1.45$; $D = u(A) = 2*A$; $C = s(B) = B + 3.50$; $D = t(C) =
C - 0.40$, whence $D = u(A) = t(C)$, and thus $u(r(B)) = t(s(B))$ which can be
solved as an equation in a single unknown: $2*(B + 1.45) = (B + 3.50) - 0.40$
(Bednarz *et al.*, 1992).

A similar ambiguity may occur with respect to 'understanding a concept'. If the concept is thought of as a certain ready made, existing theoretical

'object' out there, named, defined or described in some way, related to other concepts and interpreted in various situations etc., then understanding it would consist in analyzing this definition or this description, recognizing these relations and these interpretations. The ready made concept would then constitute the object of understanding, i.e., that which is being understood.

But the phrase 'to understand the concept C' can be interpreted also in such a way that something is being understood on the basis of this very concept: something is being brought together as representing a concept, it is generalized and synthesized into that concept C. The concept would then be only formed in the act or process of understanding a situation. Such are the acts of 'thematization' Piaget speaks about; for example, the thematization of the use of geometric transformations into a concept that is fundamental for geometry, allowing the classification of its various domains as 'theories of invariants' of transformation groups.

In the former case the understanding would consist in finding out what 'stands under' the given concept C. In the latter, some situations would be 'taken together' — *'une situation serait com-prise'* in form of a concept.

Thus, when it is said in ordinary language that a certain person has understood something, an X, it may mean that X is indeed the object of his or her understanding, or that he or she has understood something else of which X is seen as forming the 'essence' or the most important feature: he or she has understood something else 'on the basis' of X. The use of the expression 'he or she has understood X' in the vernacular may be confusing in this respect. When discussing the notion of 'act of understanding' in the next chapter the distinction between the object of understanding and the basis of understanding is very much stressed. It seems important to be aware of the difference between 'what is to be understood' and 'on what basis something has to be understood' or 'how do we want something to be understood' in, for example, designing a teaching sequence.

In his article, Greeno used the expression: 'to understand the meaning (of X)'. The definite article 'the' suggests that X has a well determined meaning and what is there to understand is this pre-existing meaning. But in understanding we very often only just construct a meaning of X; then this meaning is a basis of our understanding of X. Dewey considered expressions 'to understand' and 'to grasp the meaning' as synonymous (Dewey, 1971, p. 137). He was thus explaining 'understanding' by 'meaning'. We shall take an alternative point of view and, following Ajdukiewicz, we shall explain 'meaning' by 'understanding'. A meaning of X will be, for us, a certain 'way of understanding' X, an abstraction from the occasional features of an act of understanding and retainment of only certain characteristics of it.

What Our Understanding Consists of? Different Ways of Understanding

Things can be understood in various ways and the understanding may consist of a variety of things. Mathematical examples of different ways of understanding are easily available from research on students difficulties in understanding mathematical notions. Here are some common students' understandings of the limit of function at a point, as described by Williams (1991):

A limit describes how a function moves as x moves toward a certain point.
A limit is a number past which a function cannot go.
A limit is a number or point the function gets close to but never reaches.

In all three cases the understanding consists in identifying a certain characteristic property of the object of understanding (the concept of limit, of function, or just the term 'limit of function at a point').

Understanding may consist of a variety of other things as well. If the object of understanding is a phenomenon then its understanding may consist in finding an explanation of why the phenomenon occurs. One can also understand a practical action by being aware of why this action produces an expected result. There can be many kinds of explanations and therefore different ways of understanding. A person may feel she understands an action because she knows how to perform it successfully. A phenomenon can be understood by recognizing its main components and the relations between them. An understanding of a thunderstorm may consist of an explanation by the laws of physics (electrical discharges, laws of propagation of acoustic and light waves, etc.) or in an identification of a thunderstorm's normal course, effects (rain, thunder and lightning, and the delay between them), states of the atmosphere before and after the storm etc.

Quite a lot of understanding is related to this question 'why' and consists in finding the 'premises', 'reasons' or a 'cause' for something. Kotarbinski uses the following example: 'Jan understood why the selling of the property was a mistake.' He interprets it as follows: 'this means that, through some kind of reasoning Jan has come to the conclusion that the selling of the property was a mistake for such and such reason.' Thus an act of understanding can be a result of some reasoning — reasoning may lead to understanding something.

For some authors, 'understanding' is synonymous to 'understanding why'. It is in this sense that Piaget uses this word in his book on *Success and understanding* (1978). He speaks of understanding a practical action (e.g., building a house of cards or putting a set of dominoes in a row so that pushing the first one would make all the others fall down); in this context, to understand an action means to understand why it works (leads to success) or why it does not work. In fact, Piaget is very demanding with respect to understanding. 'Understanding how' to make something, how to perform a practical action, what to do to attain a certain result, is not understanding at all. Understanding, for him, belongs to the realm of reason: it must be based on conceptualizations and such connections between these conceptualizations that are implicative and not causal. Understanding focuses neither on the goals that the action is expected to attain, nor on the means that can be used to reach them; it goes beyond the information given and aims at the 'determination of the reasons without which successes remain mere facts without signification' (*ibidem*, p. 222). Earlier in the book, in the introduction to the final conclusions, Piaget uses the terms of 'notional comprehension' and 'explicative and implicative processes of comprehension' (*ibidem*, p. 213). Piaget does not speak of any understanding but specifically of an understanding based on such conceptualizations that allow to explain why a certain action has been successful and to imply why certain possible actions would be or would not be successful. For us here, 'understanding' will not a priori mean such 'notional' or 'reasoned' understanding. We shall not impose other norms on an act of understanding except such as we subjectively feel necessary for a mental experience to be called this name.

What an understanding of other peoples' behaviour and products of this behaviour, for example, live speech or written texts, consists of, has been a long-standing problem in hermeneutics and philosophy. For some philosophers (like Dilthey), understanding in this context meant empathy — feeling and thinking as the author feels and thinks. Others, (like Ricœur, 1976), proposed that a text, or any discourse for that matter, distances itself from the author, acquires a meaning of its own and the reader has to reconstruct this meaning for himself.

What 'Stands Under' Understanding?

Several pieces of information are needed to make a statement about an act of understanding less ambiguous. One should know what is the 'object of understanding', i.e., what is being understood; and on what basis is this object being understood (a reason?, an explanation?, a know-how? empathy?), as well as what are the operations of the mind that are involved in the act of understanding.

In asking a person whose intention it is to understand something what does his or her understanding of this something consist of, the expected reply is normally a description of that on which his or her understanding is based and of the operation of mind he or she has been using to make the link between this basis and the object of his or her understanding (for example, the person has identified the reasons of a certain action).

There seems to be a large variety of theoretical views on what can actually constitute a basis for understanding. Understanding expressions was traditionally regarded as based on either images or imagined feelings, situations, etc. or conceptual representations (Ajdukiewicz, 1974). Jerome S. Bruner (1973) based understanding of concepts on three kinds of mental representations: those that could be mediated through actions (enactive representations), those that could be mediated through pictures (iconic representations) and those that could be mediated through symbols or language (symbolic representations). Cognitive scientists preferred to think that understanding of any kind of discourse consists in retrieval from memory of mental 'frames', 'scripts', or 'schemas' which function very much like procedures in a software (Minsky, 1975; Davis, 1984).

A style of speaking (or maybe even thinking) that has gained some popularity in the past few years is embedded in the 'environmental' or 'ecological' metaphor. Concepts, it is said, cannot be thought of in isolation from whole domains of concepts, facts and procedures in which they have their meaning and which constitute, so to say, their 'natural environment'. Therefore, it is impossible to speak of understanding of a concept without speaking at the same time of the understanding and knowledge of its environment — its conceptual domain. Coming to know a conceptual domain thus resembles 'knowing one's way around in an environment . . . and knowing how to use its resources as well as being able to find and use those resources for understanding and reasoning. Knowing includes interaction with the environment in its own terms — exploring the territory, appreciating its scenery and understanding how its various components interact'(Greeno, *ibidem*, p. 175).

In physical environments, understanding and reasoning is based on building the so-called 'mental models' of the reality and simulating the behaviour of real objects in them, imagining situations, just as they might happen in reality and not constructing representations, symbolic or iconic or other and manipulating them according to some more or less formal rules. Greeno claims that the activity of knowing, understanding and reasoning in abstract conceptual environments is analogous to that in physical environments such as a town, a kitchen or a wood workshop. Abstract concepts are treated as real objects that can be combined and decomposed; it is simulation of operations on these objects that is performed rather than formal manipulation according to laws and rules. It is a very poor understanding, Greeno says, if a person, asked to calculate mentally '25•48' represents to himself or herself the paper and pencil algorithm and tries to do it in his or her head. A better understanding occurs if the person treats 25 and 48 as objects that can be 'combined' and 'decomposed': 48 is 40 and 8 and 40 is 4 times 10; 25 times 4 is 100; 100 times 10 is 1000; now, 25 times 8 (which is 4•2) is 2 times 100, 200. So the result is 1200.

Sometimes the objects in the model can be particular graphic representations or diagrams; when we think about functions, for example, we often replace functions by their graphs which can then be translated, reflected, added, etc., in our minds.

'Thought experiment' is an older term that denotes a kind of mental modelling. A thought experiment simulates some physical activity, allows the making of inferences and the understanding of how certain things are related without actually performing this activity.

Greeno uses the term 'affordance' borrowed from Gibson (1986) to name the role that various objects and relations in mental models play in reasoning, and implicitly also, in understanding. In a situation of understanding, an affordance is something that comes in handy as a basis for understanding. Greeno gives a nice example of perception of an affordance in a geometrical situation (which, by the way, could also be used as evidence of the role that the *Gestalt* 'insights' — sudden re-organizations of our field of consciousness — play in understanding).

> A young friend of mine was working on a problem assigned in her geometry course to prove that the lines that connect the midpoints of adjacent sides of a parallelogram form another parallelogram. A hint had been given to draw the diagonal of the parallelogram and she recognized that if she could prove that each midpoint connector is parallel to the diagonal, they are parallel to each other. Her initial efforts to get that proof were unsuccessful. I suggested focusing on the triangle formed by the diagonal and the two sides of the parallelogram and covered one half of the figure with my hand. My friend then saw a different pattern, recognized that the line connected midpoints of the sides of the triangle and remembered the theorem that this line is parallel to the base. The example illustrates perception of a feature of the situation that would not be an affordance unless the person knew the pattern of inference involving midpoints of sides of a triangle and that requires a particular attentional focus for it to be perceived and used. (Greeno, *ibidem*)

An affordance here in this situation is the configuration satisfying the assumptions of a certain well-known theorem about the line that connects the mid-points of the sides of a triangle. The situation which is first understood as one quadrangle in another quadrangle is then understood as two diagrams for this theorem: two triangles with connected midpoints of sides.

Notations, or symbolic representations, are another example of things that 'provide affordances' for mathematical thinking, understanding, and reasoning. They have played an important part in the historical development of mathematics: Viète's algebraic notation, Descartes coordinates, Leibniz's notation of derivatives and integrals are some well-known examples of how the development of representations can give rise to whole new branches of mathematics and new ways of thinking in mathematics. Leibniz is known for his strong belief in the power of good notation. He dreamt of reducing all scientific knowledge to a kind of formal calculus. Such a calculus would enable scientists to solve any problem, any controversy, in an unambiguous way. This dream turned out to be unrealistic but Leibniz's notation for derivatives and integrals remained efficient and handy, suggestive of properties of the operations themselves; it really 'opened the way to discoveries' and 'facilitated the work of the mind' (Juszkiewicz, 1976, p. 274). For Leibniz a symbol should not be chosen arbitrarily; it should be a small story about the thing symbolized, it should 'represent the deepest nature of the thing' (*ibidem*). Then the symbol can be an affordance for the understanding of the thing.

Synonyms of Understanding

Besides speaking of understanding explicitly we sometimes use more round-about ways of expressing ourselves. For example, 'it makes sense to me' could be replaced without much change of meaning by 'I understand it'. 'Successful communication' between two parties is very much the same as mutual under-standing between them.

'I interpret this as meaning this or that' — 'I understand this as. . . .' Of course, the meanings are not exactly the same, there are subtle differences. 'Interpretation' is both understanding and validation of understanding — a slight shift from the traditional attitude in hermeneutics which made a strong separation between the sciences of understanding and the sciences of explain-ing. 'Successful communication' can assume more than 'mutual understand-ing' which may remain on the level of empathy. Communication means that some information has been exchanged and one can expect actions that will be undertaken accordingly by the communicating parties.

'Seeing' in English seems to be the same as 'understanding': what do we mean when, in a conversation, we say 'I see'? We probably refer to some kind of internal 'seeing' of what the other person has in mind.

Understanding is also implicit in expressions containing 'seeing as . . .' or 'recognizing something as. . . .' These expressions give account of a certain way of understanding; they can describe what kind of concept a person has of something. Greeno reports that 'seeing-as' has become a scientific term related to Hanson's theory of patterns of discovery (Hanson, 1961). Hanson gives the following examples: 'One can see the sun as a disk that travels across the sky. One can also see the sun as a very large, very distant body that is visible part of the time because the planet we are on constantly rotates' (Greeno, *ibidem*, p. 182). But earlier than that, 'seeing-as' was raised to the level of a concept and a philosophical problem in Wittgenstein's *Philosophical Investigations*. One of the questions posed by Wittgenstein was that of the distinction between seeing and seeing-as or seeing an aspect. The latter is closer to interpreting and imagining.

> Do I really see something different each time, or do I only interpret what I see in a different way? I am inclined to say the former. But Why? — To interpret is to think, to do something; seeing is a state.
>
> Now it is easy to recognize cases in which we are *interpreting*. When we interpret we form hypotheses, which may prove false. — 'I am seeing this figure as a . . .' can be verified as little as (or in the same sense as) 'I am seeing bright red'. So there is a similarity in the use of 'seeing' in the two contexts. Only do not think you knew in advance what the *'state* of seeing' means here! Let the use *teach* you the meaning . . .
>
> The concept of an aspect is akin to the concept of image. In other words: the concept 'I am now seeing it as . . .' is akin to 'I am now

having *this* image' . . . One can use imagining in the course of proving something. Seeing an aspect and imagining are subject to the will. There is such an order as 'Imagine *this*', and also: 'Now see this figure like *this*'; but not: 'Now see this leaf green'. (Wittgenstein, 1958, p. 213e)

Ricœur evokes Wittgenstein's distinction in relation to the role that metaphors play in understanding: contrary to what can be thought, figures of speech are not there to give a 'picture' of something but to draw attention to some important aspect: 'to figure is always to see as, but not always to see or to make visible' (Ricœur, 1977, p. 61).

This distinction between 'seeing' and 'seeing as' is important in mathematics whose very nature does not allow for 'seeing' its objects, but always to 'see them as'. Let me quote the somewhat bitter words of Poincaré:

What is understanding? Has the word the same meaning for everybody? . . . [Some] will always ask themselves what use it is. . . . Under each word they wish to put a sensible image; the definition must call up this image, and at each stage of the demonstration they must see it being transformed and evolved. On this condition only will they understand and retain what they have understood. These often deceive themselves: they do not listen to reasoning, they look at the figures; they imagine that they have understood when they have only seen. (Poincaré, 1952, pp. 118–9)

'Conceptual representation' in mathematics education is used in a sense that is closer to 'seeing as' than to 'seeing'. But also the term 'conception' is used which has a somewhat different meaning. While a conceptual representation is defined as expressible totally in words, a 'conception' may be very intuitive, partly visual and not necessarily logically consistent or complete. A person who has a 'conception' of, for example, the mathematical concept of limit, 'has some notion' of it, has *some* understanding' of it not necessarily on the most elaborate level. Williams, for example (*ibidem*), distinguishes 'having a conception of limit' from 'having a model of limit', which has to be closer to the mathematical meaning of limit. Williams requires, for a person to have a 'model' of limit, that he or she be able to distinguish, to some degree, true statements from false statements about limits; that he or she be able to make inferences about the concept; that he or she 'have some sense' of what constitutes truth in mathematical analysis; that statements and assertions 'have meaning' to the person and that this meaning does not diverge too far from 'the accepted mathematical meaning'.

To 'have some sense' of something, for this something to 'have meaning' for a person, are again expressions that refer to understanding. To 'have a sense' of something Is yet another expression. Greeno's 'number sense' is a certain way of understanding numbers and quantities, but also of reasoning with them, of coming to know them.

'Grasping the meaning' is used as another synonym — we already mentioned it by quoting Dewey. In understanding, something is 'caught', something almost palpable — the meaning (indeed, Husserl, for example, considered meaning as an object — an ideal object, but an object all the same). Colloquially we express the same idea in asking our partner in conversation: 'Got it?' as if we were throwing something at him or her and he or she was supposed to catch it as a ball.

Adjectives Associated with Understanding

To say that a person 'understands' something is, as we have seen, a highly ambiguous expression. In order to make themselves more clear people use all kinds of adjectives. If we take again the text of Greeno, we find the following qualifications of 'understanding': 'holistic and configural' understanding is opposed to 'rule-based procedures'; a 'cultural understanding' is specific to, and shared in, a culture; 'conceptual' understanding (close to 'seeing as'); 'spatial' understanding (for example, the understanding of numbers based on relative sizes of things, position of numbers on the number line, etc.).

Let us talk a little about 'cultural understanding'. An ethnic community may develop certain ways of understanding or interpreting words, facts, situations, or phenomena that may differ from understandings common in other cultures. The works of anthropologists as well as sociologists of science have brought to our awareness how different, contrary to what Kant might have thought, the intuitions of time and space of people living in different cultures are. Professional communities also develop their own 'standards' or 'ideals' of understanding, or 'cognitive norms'.

The view on learning (and teaching) the notion of number that Greeno presents in his paper is grounded in the more general framework of the so-called 'situated cognition'. As understanding is involved in cognition, one can probably also speak of 'situated understanding'.

> The basic form of situated cognition is an interaction of an agent within a situation, with the agent participating along with objects and other people to co-constitute activity. The agent's connection with the situation includes direct local interaction with objects and other people in the immediate vicinity as well as knowing where he or she is in relation with more remote features of the environment . . . We construct mental models that provide us with situations in which we can interact with mental objects that represent objects, properties and relations and that behave in ways that simulate the objects, properties and relations that our models represent . . . The concepts and principles that a person *understands, in this sense*, are embedded in the kinds of objects that he or she includes in mental models and in the ways in which those objects behave, including how they combine and

separate to form other objects and how they are interrelated by proximity and path connections in the conceptual domain. (Greeno, *ibidem*, p. 200)

'Situated understanding' would therefore be an understanding that is 'concrete' and 'contextual' in the sense that it is grounded in simulated actions on objects, embedded in certain 'situations' rather than in formal inferences from general and abstract statements, even though these 'objects' may be of very abstract nature like, for example, functions or function spaces, and the 'situation' — a highly elaborate research problem of functional analysis.

In speaking about understanding in communication between people, Greeno uses adjectives such as 'shared' and 'mutual' understanding. Such 'shared' or 'mutual' understanding is 'reached' through discussions and 'negotiation of meaning' of terms used in the discussion. In order for such understanding to be established, participants must 'refer' to the same kinds of objects in the mental models they build of the discussed situation. If the situation is mathematical and the objects are abstract objects then one (and sometimes the only) way to decide whether the two people are approximately thinking about the same thing is to use some representations of these objects: symbols, diagrams, graphs and maybe more formal definitions.

In educational practice evaluative qualifications of understanding are frequent. For example, Greeno speaks of 'adequate' understanding of mathematical notation which he opposes to 'mindless manipulation of symbols'. For him, an understanding is 'adequate' if operations on symbols are projections of mental operations on objects in a mental model.

There are also other adjectives that Greeno uses with understanding, such as: '*significant implicit* understanding of many concepts and principles' and '*intuitive* understanding of quantitative relations of comparison, change and combination'. 'Implicit' and 'intuitive' understanding seems to be opposed to 'more articulate and more complex understanding'.

Activities of the Mind That Accompany or Complement Understanding

Greeno often enumerates 'understanding' along with 'reasoning'; also 'knowing', 'perceiving', 'using', 'solving', 'speaking', 'insights' and 'beliefs' can be found in the proximity. Exactly how reasoning and understanding can be complementary is not discussed in the paper of Greeno — this is not the kind of question he asks himself.

We sometimes speak of 'understanding a reasoning'. So a reasoning can be understood. Can an understanding be 'reasoned'? Or must it? In some languages (for example, in Polish) the word 'understanding' (*rozumienie*) is derived from 'reason' (*rozum*). In these languages understanding is or should always be somehow 'reasoned'. However, this ethymological sense is very much lost now, and, even in Polish, expressions like 'intuitive understanding' are commonly used.

There are many questions concerning the notion of understanding, of which the relation between understanding and reasoning is but one. We shall examine it more thoroughly in later chapters. Now let us give some attention to the relations between understanding and meaning.

Meaning

Few concepts have caused as much trouble in philosophy as the concept of meaning. There is a long history of attempts to encapsulate it into theories from which it always seemed to be able to slip away. The reason for this may lie in the unavoidable self-referential character of any theory that would pretend to speak of meaning in a more general way: any definition of meaning has meaning itself, so it refers to itself as well. Rarely, therefore, was meaning considered in its full generality; different philosophers have occupied themselves with meanings of different things, and they focused their attention on different aspects of meaning.

They were probably right in doing so, for, as Austin says (1961, p. 23) while a question like 'what is the meaning of the word "irrational number"' is a sensible one, a question like 'what is the meaning of a word', or, worse even, 'what is meaning' is nonsense. Austin caricatures the effects of our drive to asking such 'nonsensical questions' in the following humourous way:

> To show up this pseudo-question, let us take a parallel case . . . Suppose that I ask 'What is the point of doing so-and-so?' For example, I ask Old Father William 'What is the point of standing on one's head?' He replies in the way we know. Then I follow this up with 'What is the point of balancing an eel on the end of one's nose?' And he explains. Now suppose I ask my third question 'What is the point of doing *anything* — not anything *in particular*, but just *anything?*' Old Father William would no doubt kick me downstairs without the option. But lesser men, raising the same question and finding no answer, would very likely commit suicide or join the Church. (Luckily, in the case of 'What is the meaning of a word?' the effects are less serious, amounting only to the writing of books). (Austin, *ibidem*, p. 27)

In my case, the effects of asking myself the question 'What is the meaning of *anything?*' were of this less serious kind. I wrote the pages below.

What Has Meaning?

There are a few 'grammatical' questions that one can ask about any predicate like 'has meaning'. The first is 'what is it that has meaning'? To this, the most natural answer seems to be 'the sign'. If anything has meaning, it is a sign. Or, a sign is what has meaning. This makes the concept of sign very comprehensive. If we think it is right to say not that a concept *is* a meaning (of a name) but that a concept *has* meaning then we agree with Charles Sanders Peirce that even concepts are signs (Peirce, 1984, p. 439). For Peirce, who, as Ogden and Richards (1946) say, has accomplished the most elaborate and determined account of signs and their meaning — a sign is a representation: it represents or replaces something for someone ('A sign is an object which stands for another in some mind', Peirce, 1986, p. 66). In this sense a sign is a triadic relation: a representation is a mediation between two elements by a third one. Ogden and Richards were inspired by this idea when they proposed their famous 'triangle of meaning' (*ibidem*, p. 11), used, in mathematics education, by, among others, Steinbring (e.g., 1993) as a basis for the study of how the mathematical meanings are constructed in the reality of mathematics classes.

The notion of the meaning of sign has been studied in general, but sometimes attention focused on the meaning of some specific kinds of signs: phenomena (things, persons, features, events, that can refer to something, mean something, express something, evoke feelings, induce actions, etc.), objects in a situation (an object acquires meaning by being an affordance in a problem situation), parts of a whole (the meaning of an element lies in the function it plays in the structure of a whole), names, expressions, sentences, questions, utterances, language as a system, as well as thoughts and propositions.

Where Is Meaning to Be Found?

Another 'grammatical' question about meaning is 'where is meaning to be found'? Philosophers differ in their views on this matter: is the meaning of a sign in the head of the person for whom the sign represents something (a 'picture' in the mind, a 'mental accompaniment' of an expression), or is it in the object represented — in its distinctive features (the connotation of a name given to this object)? Or is the meaning in the sign? Peirce: the meaning is in the sign.

The latter, 'antipsychologistic' stand was taken by Peirce, and this was still quite revolutionary in his time. For Peirce all knowledge is mediated by signs, and cognition is a system of contents, not of subjective mental experiences. The crucial idea here is that the meaning of a sign is determined by the place of this sign in a whole system of signs. The meaning of a sign can only be interpreted by another sign, its 'interpretant'.

> [a sign] has an *Object* and an *Interpretant*, the latter being that which the Sign produces in the Quasi-mind, that is the Interpreter, by determining the latter to a feeling, to an exertion, or to a Sign, which determination is the Interpretant. But it remains to point out that there are usually two Objects, and more than two Interpretants. Namely, we have to distinguish the *Immediate Object*, which is the object as the sign himself represents it, and whose Being is thus dependent upon the Representation of it in the sign, from the *Dynamical*

Object, which is the Reality which by some means contrives to deter-mine the Sign to its Representation. In regard to the Interpretant we have equally to distinguish in the first place the *Immediate Interpretant*, which is the interpretant as it is revealed in the right understanding of the Sign itself, and is ordinarily called the 'meaning' of the Sign; while, in the second place, we have to take note of the *Dynamical Interpretant*, which is the actual effect which the Sign, as a Sign, really determines. (Peirce, 1906)

For Peirce, a sign has an inner possibility of being interpreted before anyone actually interprets it — this he names the *Immediate Interpretant* of the sign, and says that this is what is ordinarily called the meaning of the sign. The *Dynamical Interpretant* refers to actual individual acts of interpretation. Peirce distinguished also the *Final Interpretant*, that to which all actual inter-pretations converge.

Peirce viewed language as one system of signs among others; his perspec-tive on meaning was very broad. Verbal languages are built on symbolic systems, but there are other kinds of signs besides symbols. Peirce spoke of indices, icons and symbols, and many intermediate kinds of signs (Peirce, 1955, pp. 98–119). In indices the relation between the mark (*signans*) and that which it signifies (*signatum*) consists of their actual existential contingency. For example, high temperature and flushed complexion are signs of an illness — they indicate an infection. Marks of animals on the snow indicate their recent passing. The relation between *signans* and *signatum* that accounts for icons is that of resemblance: for example the picture of a car resembles the actual car it depicts. In symbols, there is no factual contingency nor resemblance be-tween *signans* and *signatum,* there is only an 'imputed quality' which links the two component sides of the sign. In this sense, for example, the graph of a function represents the function in a symbolic, not iconic, way. Peirce, how-ever, saw more iconic aspects in mathematical inscriptions than we would generally admit. For example, concerning algebraic expressions, he said:

When in algebra, we write equations under one another in a regular array, especially when we put resembling letters for corresponding coefficients, the array is an icon. Here is an example:

$$a_1x + b_1y = u_1$$
$$a_2x + b_2y = u_2$$

This is an icon in that it makes quantities look alike which are in analoguous relations to the problem (Peirce, 1955, p. 107).

Let us note that Peirce is not saying that the system of equations with which he is illustrating his point is an icon. He only says that it is an icon in some respects. In general, a sign is never just an icon, or just a symbol, or just an index; all three aspects coexist and this is true also of mathematical expressions.

The Meaning Is in the Language As a System

The notion of meaning has most often been looked at in the context of language or languages only. Some philosophers looked at language as a system and either studied the formalized languages constructed in logic and mathematics, or attempted to build idealized models of ordinary languages. Others conceived of language as an activity, a view more common in psychology than in philosophy.

Frege adhered to the former view: he regarded language as a symbolic system. In fact the model language for him was that of pure mathematics from which he excluded even geometry. His attitude led him to reduce the world of reference to but two elements: the logical values of Truth and Falsity. Meaning could thus be assigned only to sentences, not to words standing alone; the sense of a sentence laid in the conditions under which it could be considered as true. Mathematics was thereby brought down to logic (Dummett, 1991). Logical empiricism radicalized Frege's views by identifying meaningfulness with verifiability, and meaning with a method of verification: what decides about the meaning of an expression is the existence of criteria that allow to decide whether simple sentences that contain it are true or false. For example, the word 'red' is meaningful in English, but the word 'ked' is not, because we are not in possession of a method that would allow us to decide, in appropriate conditions, whether 'ked' can be applied to a given object or not (Ajdukiewicz, 1946).

Ajdukiewicz proposed a theory of meaning in the 1930s (e.g., 1934) which he abandoned later due to its limitations: it applied only to the so-called 'closed and connected languages', and did not explain the link between meaning and reference. Meaning in this theory was an attribute of a language as a whole — it was a global approach to meaning. The notion of meaning was based on that of 'directives of meaning' of a language, of which Ajdukiewicz distinguished three kinds: axiomatic, deductive and empirical. The axiomatic directives give a set of sentences that have to be accepted as true in the given language; the deductive directives give rules that allow the acceptance of certain sentences as true on the basis of other sentences accepted as true; empirical directives determine which sentences can be accepted as true on the basis of which empirical data. Thus a language was fully defined by a class of signs and a 'matrix' of directives of meanings formed of these signs and empirical data. Having such a notion of language, Ajdukiewicz was able to define when two expressions have the same meaning. He distinguished two cases: synonymity, when the two expressions belong to the same language, and translation, when the expressions belong to different languages. For example, an expression E is said to have the same meaning in language L as an expression E' in language L' if there exists a 'translation' R, or an isomorphism of the 'matrices' of the languages L and L', according to which E and E' correspond to each other: E' = R(E). The relation of 'having the same meaning' is an equivalence relation; its classes of abstraction were called 'meanings'.

Within this perspective, it was irrelevant what two languages were speaking about; they could be translated one into another provided their matrices were isomorphic. But matrices described only the abstract structure of the languages, ignoring what their expressions could be referring to. One can very well invent two languages, one speaking about the heat and sand of the African desert, and the other about the cold and snow in the North of Canada, but such that their matrices are perfectly isomorphic; then a sentence about a snowstorm would have the same meaning as a sentence about a sandstorm.

While retaining the general idea of defining meaning by abstraction on the basis of an equivalence relation, in his later works Ajdukiewicz took a much less formal approach to language, and managed also to take into account the denotation of expressions. However, philosophers continued attempts to construct the notion of meaning in idealized models of ordinary languages. One result of these efforts is the so-called theory of interpretation which relativizes the notions of extension and intension of an expression to the context of its use in a 'possible world', developed, among others, by Kripke, Montague, and Scott in the 1960s.

The Meaning Is in the Language As a Social Practice

Wittgenstein was close to such 'global' and logical views on language in his *Tractatus*, but his later works (The *Blue and the Brown Books*, and *Philosophical Investigations*) reflect a completely different view. While in the *Tractatus*, language appeared as a uniform system, a logical picture of reality, in *Philosophical Investigations*, Wittgenstein claims that there is no one language but rather a multitude of languages that can be recognized as such by a kind of 'family resemblance'. The methodology that he proposed to study the different languages used by people was that of 'language games': models of different uses of language for different purposes and with different means. Language is thus viewed more as an activity, a social practice, where meanings of phrases are characterized by the use that is made of them, not by the associated mental pictures and not by sets of distinctive features of objects denoted by these expressions (Wittgenstein, *The Blue Book*, p. 65). The question 'What do you mean?' is, Wittgenstein says, just another way of asking 'How do you use this expression?'. He would speak of the 'grammar of an expression' as of the rules that govern the use of it. Some sentences are grammatical, some are not: in learning to distinguish this, we learn the meanings of words in a language. For example, a question 'Has this room a length?' is ungrammatical; in answering such a question we would say, shrugging our shoulders: 'Of course it has!' and this, Wittgenstein remarks, would not be an answer to a question, but a grammatical statement. On the other hand, a question like 'Is this room 15 feet long?' is a sensible question — the word 'length' would be used in it according to its grammar.

Wittgenstein was against looking at language as a calculus proceeding according to strict rules (*The Blue Book*, p. 25). It is only in mathematics, he would say, that the meaning of terms can be given by a set of defining criteria. In the practice of ordinary life and language we recognize things and give them names on the basis of 'symptoms' rather than definitions. For example, we say 'this man has tonsillitis' because we observed that he has an inflamed throat, which is a usual symptom of tonsillitis; if we said it because we checked his blood and discovered the bacillus of angina in it, we would have based our diagnosis on the defining criterion of tonsillitis. In this case, the defining criterion exists, but there are many other cases where such criterion does not exist. Consider such expressions as 'expecting someone to come' or 'pain'.

> In practice, if you were asked which phenomenon is the defining criterion and which is a symptom, you would in most cases be unable to answer this question except by making an arbitrary decision *ad hoc* . . . For remember that in general we don't use language according to strict rules — it hasn't been taught us by means of strict rules, either. We (the philosophers), in our discussions constantly compare language with a calculus proceeding according to strict rules. This is a very one-sided way of looking at language. In practice we rarely use language as such calculus. For not only we do not think of the rules of usage — of definitions, etc. — while using language, but when asked to give such rules, in most cases we aren't able to do so. We are unable clearly to circumscribe the concepts we use; not because we don't know their real definitions, but because there is no real 'definition' to them. When we talk of language as a symbolism used in exact calculus, that which is in our mind can be found in sciences and mathematics. Our ordinary use of language conforms to the standard of exactness only in rare cases (*ibidem*, p. 25).

Joining Frege in his contempt of the formalist position which denied all meaning to mathematical signs, Wittgenstein agreed that there must be something that gives life to the 'complexes of dashes' on paper. He suggested that this something that gives life to a sign — usually called its meaning — must be its use (*ibidem*, p. 4). It cannot be a picture in the mind, for a picture in the mind is just another sign, and a sign added to a sign cannot make the sign more alive. Suppose we replace the picture in the mind by a painted picture: 'why should the written sign plus a painted image be more alive if the written sign alone was dead? — In fact, as soon as you think of replacing the mental image by, say, a painted one, and as soon as the image loses its occult character, it ceases to impart any life to the sentence at all (*ibidem*, p. 5).'

The reason, however, why mathematics educationists seem to be so much attracted by Wittgenstein's later view of language and meaning is not that they have forgotten that in mathematics most terms have their precise definition but rather that they have in mind the language as practised in the mathematics classroom which is not the more or less formalized language of mathematics found in textbooks or research papers.

The language of the mathematics classroom is a very complex structure. The context in which students learn mathematics is a multidimensional one, where the meanings are determined not only by words written in a book or uttered by the teacher. The meaning of a problem, for example, depends on the roles that the students and the teacher assign themselves in the given situation. It will be different, if the problem was posed by one or more students, than if the problem was assigned by the teacher. The meaning will also depend on the intention of the teacher: whether the problem is meant to introduce the students to a new topic and different approaches are allowed; or whether it is meant to check the students' ability to apply a certain method, and the students have to give proof of their knowledge. Each of these situations determine a different 'didactical contract'. The proof, which, for a research mathematician is a means for ascertaining the truth of a theorem, can turn, in a specific kind of didactical contract, into an activity of 'showing a proof', as students often put it, namely showing that one has mastered a technique. Balacheff (1986) remarks that

> most of the time the pupil does not act as a theoretician but as a practical man. His job is to give a solution to the problem the teacher has given to him, a solution that will be acceptable in the classroom situation. In such a context the most important thing is to be effective. The problem of a practical man is to be efficient, not to be rigorous. It is to produce a solution, not to produce knowledge. (Balacheff, 1986)

The social situation of institutionalized learning changes the meanings of mathematical terms. It brings the language of the classroom closer to ordinary language, but not in an unambiguous way. We have to deal with so many different languages in the classroom: the language of mathematical formulas, and the language we talk about them, the language in which we evaluate the students' performance and the language of logical values. The student utters a false statement, and the teacher says: 'wrong', as if he or she were the judge, and the student committed a mischief. Lacombe draws our attention to this shift of meaning whereby mathematics becomes a kind of law rather than discursive knowledge (1984). In the context of jurisdiction, even the most neutral mathematical terms can acquire unintended emotive meanings. These emotive meanings can be a source of anxiety for some sensitive students.

Both the mathematical language and the ordinary language are subject to certain rules of sense and rationality but these rules can be different in each case. The mathematical language relies on definition, deduction, *tertium non datur* and *modus ponens*, while the ordinary language is governed by use, context, implicature and presupposition (see Bar-Hillel, 1971; Grice, 1981). These registers interfere in many subtle ways in a mathematics classroom, and, indeed, the first thing a child has to learn at school is to move within the fuzzy boundaries, to recognize signals that warn it which register is being used at a given moment. These signals are not anything conventionally and explicitly laid out, they are not transparent, although it may seem so to the teacher. They are to be found in the tone of the voice, in an expression (like 'now' uttered loudly), in other things. Too many mistakes in the identification of such signals are another source of anxiety, uncertainty, loss of self-confidence, and, eventually — 'school failure'.

Ordinary words mean something different in mathematics. Yet, especially in the elementary school, they are used inadvertently by teachers as if there was nothing to explain. Children have to guess by themselves that a *big number* is not a number that is written with huge marks on paper, and a *low number* is not one written at the bottom of the page. The *horizontal* and *vertical* refer not to directions in the surrounding space but to the direction of the sheet of paper. A *vulgar fraction* has nothing to do with swearing, *volume* can refer to the amount of liquid one can pour into a container, and not to the 'knob on the television set'. 'Make' as in 'to make a cake' means something different than 'make' in 'two times two makes four', etc. (Durkin and Shire, 1991, p. 74).

Aside from the social-contextual, emotive and sometimes the vernacular meanings, mathematical terms have their so-called descriptive meaning (Ogden and Richards, *ibidem*). At some level of education, this meaning starts to be given explicitly by definition. But even then, the meanings are not learned this way. Students will notice the subtle assumptions of the definition only by entering the practices of speaking, using the term, asking questions, solving problems. Sometimes, the uses of a term may carry meanings not intended by the modern definition: these meanings are preserved through the process of metaphorization that terms normally undergo as they are transferred from the vernacular into the scientific language, and interfere in the grasp of the intended meanings (Skarga, 1989).

Wittgenstein says: 'Essence is expressed by grammar' (*Philosophical Investigations*, Part I. 371), and 'Grammar tells what kind of object anything is' (*ibidem*, I.373). This seems to be true not only of the ordinary language but of the mathematical language as well. Knowing the definition of a term without knowing its grammar will not be very helpful in understanding it. For the grammar of a word establishes the category it belongs to: whether it is a set, or a subset of a larger set, or an element of a set, whether it is a mapping, or a property, what are the objects with respect to which it is relativized, etc. For example, in linear algebra, we say that a subspace is *contained* in the vector space, and not that it *belongs* to it, which indicates that a subspace is a subset of vectors and not just one single vector. When we ask for a kernel, we must specify of which linear mapping it is a kernel of: *kernel* is always a *kernel of* a mapping. We can legitimately ask for the *kernel of a linear mapping* or a linear operator; we cannot ask for a *kernel of a vector space*. We can ask for the *kernel of a matrix*, but *matrix* would have to be regarded as *representing a linear mapping*. More literally, one should ask for the *nullspace of the matrix* which is the same as *the solution space of the homogeneous system of equations $AX = 0$*, where A is the matrix in question. *Linear independence of a set of vectors* is the correct form, not *linear independence of vectors*, although it is often used this way, for reasons of simplicity. We often observe students using mathematical terms and phrases in an ungrammatical way. We say then that this student 'has not understood' the theory: we state a problem of understanding.

Another example: how is the meaning of the term *function* expressed by its use? What are the questions we can ask about a function? What are the questions we can ask about a set of functions? *How* can a function be? Or, what adjectives can we use with the noun 'function'? (Defined/non-defined, defined in a point/ in an interval/ everywhere; increasing, decreasing, invertible, continuous in a point/ in an interval; smooth; differentiable in a point/ in an interval; integrable . . ., etc.). *What* can a function *have?* (Zeros, values, a derivative, a limit in a point/ in infinity; etc.). What can be *done* with functions? (Plot, calculate the values in points . . ., calculate a derivative, an integral, combine functions, take sequences, series of functions, etc.). How do we *verify* that a function is . . . (continuous, differentiable . . . in a point; increasing in an interval . . .)? What can functions be *used for?* (Representing relations between variable magnitudes, modelling, predicting, interpolating, approximating, . . .).

In mathematics, terms have their definitions which are usually very general, but they also have their *primary meanings* and *secondary meanings*, which specify which examples are more 'typical' than others. This part of the meaning cannot be grasped from just the definition, one must study the use of the term. For example, a sequence is a function, but a sequence will not be a typical example of a function. The definition of a rectangle does not specify the ratio between the width and the length, but a rectangle with this ratio very small or very large will not be a typical example of a rectangle.

The ambiguities that occur within the mathematical register are lifted not by reference to definitions but by the context, like in ordinary language. For example, a *polynomial* can be a vector — sequence of numbers almost all equal zero, or a function: this depends on whether we speak of a vector space of polynomials or about the characteristic polynomial of a linear operator, or the vector space of continuous functions on a closed interval. *Multiplication* is used in *multiplication of two numbers*, *scalar multiplication* of a number by a matrix, *multiplication of polynomials* as vectors, or as functions, etc. The *multiplication sign* is sometimes written down explicitly, sometimes not. When there is no sign between two symbols, it does not mean, however, that there is an implicit sign of multiplication there (for example, dx does not mean d times x, but how would one know the meaning of this symbol without being socialized into its traditional use?)

The Ecological and Functional Approaches: The Meaning Is in the Environment
While many psychologists locate the meaning in the 'head' of the cognizing subject, some tend to stress the role of the environment, both physical and social. The well-known adage of those working in the so-called Gibsonian tradition is: 'Ask not what's inside your head, ask what your head is inside of' (Mace, 1977). Greeno, referred to in the previous section, was inspired by this perspective. Besides the role of direct perception of the physical environment

in cognitive development, and the ability of the nervous system to 'tune itself to objectively existing coherent information structures' (Neisser, 1991), interpersonal perception is stressed as well. This view can be traced back to the works of Vygotski, and, later, Bruner, who postulated that language is acquired by the child in a process whose crucial moments are those of 'joint attention' of the adult and the child while they are engaged in a shared activity.

Young children, Neisser writes, learn names of objects not as proper names but at once as categories. The object whose name is learned is perceived as an affordance for action in a certain class of situations. In a further stage the name itself becomes an affordance in situations of communication: it is understood as a symbol which can successfully stand for an object.

> It appears, then, that the acquisition of the first vocabulary depends on the child's (and the parent's) ability to coordinate interpersonal perception and object perception effectively. It is in episodes of joint attention that the child comes to distinguish spoken words from other human noises — to treat them, correctly, as signifying intentional states. The parent is using the word as a symbol for the object and the child knows it . . .
>
> To become aware of the symbolic function of the word is to perceive, simultaneously, both the object itself and the speaker's inferential intent. What is involved is not perception in Gibson's sense, but it's perception all the same . . .
>
> What does the child know when he or she mastered a simple noun? 'Cup' is not a proper name of a single object; it refers to a whole taxonomic category. What defines that category from the child's point of view? . . . It has gradually become clear that the so-called 'classical theory' which treats a category as a set of objects defined by the presence of certain distinctive features, is deeply flawed. It does not do justice to either the perceptual or the intellectual aspects of categorization. On the perceptual side, categories such as cup are indicated more by an object's overall appearance and its affordances for action than by any set of specific features. For this reason some members of a given category are invariably more central and 'prototypical' than others. On the intellectual side, assigning an object to a category — especially a natural kind, such as tree or dog — implies much more than just the presence of a few defining attributes; it typically involves a rich web of beliefs about an extended domain of experience. (Neisser, 1991)

Relations Between Understanding and Meaning

Philosophers differ also in the way they relate the notions of understanding and meaning: some explain understanding by meaning, others explain meaning by understanding. All agree that understanding is a mental experience:

understanding is always 'in the head'. While the meaning is public, at least for some authors, understanding remains private. The confrontation of understandings through social interactions and communications are only steps in a personal process of understanding; they can give an impulse for a change in understanding, but whether the change will be introduced or not remains a individual problem.

In order to be consistent in making the link between meaning and understanding, one should admit that the object of understanding is the same as the object of meaning: it is the sign, broadly understood. When we speak of 'understanding a concept', or 'understanding a thought', then either we think, with Peirce, that concepts and thoughts are signs, or we make a distinction between epistemological objects such as concepts or thoughts and semiotic objects such as signs and we regard these expressions as *'un abus de langage'*: We intend to say that a concept or a thought are the basis of our understanding, and what we aim at understanding are signs that represent these thoughts or concepts for us.

When understanding is explained through meaning it is usually by saying that understanding is the grasp of meaning (or sense). For some philosophers belonging to this trend understanding has the same goal as cognition: to know the truth. This was certainly the case for neo-positivists. Was this also the case of Frege? If understanding a sentence is knowing the conditions of its truth, do we also have to know whether these conditions are fulfilled? There has been a suggestion to extend the Frege-style approach to meaning in such a way that understanding be distinct from cognition (Danto, 1969). Suppose truth is considered as but one class of 'positive semantic values', and sentences but one class of 'semantic vehicles', while the 'descriptive meaning' of a semantic vehicle is a rule that specifies the conditions under which this semantic vehicle bears a positive semantic value. For example, we can assume that a concept has a positive semantic value if it is instantiated; a name when it has a bearer, a picture when it has an original that it truly depicts, a sentence when the conditions of its being true are specified. Thus a sentence has the same descriptive meaning whether it is true or false, and one can normally understand a sentence S without knowing that S. Hence, 'understanding does not entail knowledge, as meaning does not entail truth' (*ibidem*).

The distinction between reason and intellect or cognition based on logic and empirical observation, which originates in the works of Kant, has been very much discussed in relation to the criticism of neo-positivism. On the surface, this seems to be a purely academic discussion, but it is easy to imagine the detrimental consequences in education of an attitude that reduces all understanding to knowledge. Let us recall the wise words of Hannah Arendt, who said that if people lost their drive to ask the undecidable questions about sense, they would also lose their ability to ask the decidable questions on which all civilization is based (Arendt, 1978). Do we want the teaching of mathematics reduced to just the logical questions of whether a given proposition is true or false? Students have to be able to distinguish the questions about truth and proof from questions about reason and sense of mathematical theories, but the latter questions must be considered as part and parcel of mathematics education, and not rejected as 'metaphysical'.

This more pragmatic attitude is less likely to be forgotten in an approach that attempts to explain meaning by understanding rather than vice versa. This has been the option chosen by Ajdukiewicz in his Pragmatic Logic, where the meaning of an expression was defined, by abstraction, as a certain way of understanding it, a class of 'understandings'. In this approach, the conditions of 'correctness' of an understanding are not set a priori. Some understanding is necessary for anything to start to have meaning; 'good understanding', as we shall precise it in the following chapters, is an achievement which requires a long process involving acts of tentative understanding, reasonings, corrections, shifts of attention, etc.

Ajdukiewicz chose four criteria to decide whether or not two people understand an expression in the same way, or attach the same meaning to it: 1. they apply the expression to the same objects; 2. they use the same method of deciding whether or not the expression applies to a given object; 3. they see the expression as being used in the same grammatical mode, i.e., affirmative, interrogative, or imperative; 4. they attribute the same kind of emotive aspect to the expression (neutral, positive, negative) (Ajdukiewicz, 1974, pp. 10–12).

Explaining meaning by understanding is also characteristic of philosophical hermeneutics, where understanding is an interpretation of that to which the thought is being directed in an intentional act. Such an understanding does not have to be full, it can even be false, but it always consists in some kind of ordering, and inclusion into a network of already established 'horizons of sense'. Understanding discloses a meaning: it is a movement from what the text says to what the text is speaking about (Heidegger, 1962; Ricœur, 1976; Skarga, 1989). The direction of the process of understanding is to some degree determined by what, for example, Foucault (1966) refers to as *'épistémè'*, and Skarga as the 'rules of sense' and 'rules of rationality', that characterize a given historical epoch or culture.

Meaning, Significance, and the Objectivity of Meaning

The word 'meaning' is sometimes used in the sense of 'significance', as when we say that 'this has no meaning for me' or when we speak about the historical meaning of a political event or the meaning of a piece of art. In these uses it means importance or value. For Thomas (1991), works of art such as painting or music have 'significance' rather than 'meaning' — if 'meaning' means reference *and* connotation: 'both pictures and music seem able to refer without attaching any meaning [connotation] to the reference; both suggest significance'. Neither need they 'convey a message'. Beethoven's 9th doesn't 'mean that . . .'.

For Hirsch Jr. (1967) the 'significance' of, for example, an intellectual or other work is a kind of 'response' to this work. This work may have some meaning, but this is not the same as its significance. He explains his understanding of the difference between significance and meaning on the example of an author's rejection of a previous work:

> . . . there cannot be the slightest doubt that the author's later response to his work was quite different from his original response. Instead of seeming beautiful, profound or brilliant, the work seemed misguided, trivial, and false, and its meaning was no longer one that the author wished to convey.
>
> However, these examples do not show that the meaning of the work has changed, but precisely the opposite. If the work's meaning had changed (instead of the author himself and his attitudes) then the author would not have needed to repudiate his meaning and could have spared himself the discomfort of a public recantation. No doubt the significance of the work to the author had changed a great deal, but its meaning had not changed at all. This is the crux of the matter in all the cases of authorial mutability with which I am familiar. It is not the meaning of the text which changes, but its significance to the author. Meaning is that which is represented by a text; it is what the author meant by his use of particular sign sequences; it is what the signs represent. Significance, on the other hand, names a relationship between that meaning and a person, or a conception, or a situation, or indeed anything imaginable . . . Significance always implies a relationship, and one constant, unchanging pole of that relationship is what the text means. (Hirsch, *ibidem*, pp. 7–8)

By saying that the meaning has not changed at all, Hirsch seems to be assuming that a text has a meaning which belongs to the text, and that the meaning of a text does not change from one epoch to another or from one reader to another, contrary to the historicist or psychologistic views. What changes is the significance. In fact, Hirsch makes quite a point of it in his book and argues very strongly that a text must be understood in its own terms if it has to be understood at all. Of course, the meaning of the text is not 'given' to us, we must construe it, but we do not construe it by imposing on the words and sentences of this text the categories of our own idiosyncratic ways of thinking, or of the present day culture, language and thought. Hirsch compares such a situation to trying to understand a Greek text by reading it as if it were in English, not in Greek: this way we would simply understand nothing, he says, because Greek words mean nothing in English. We must learn Greek first, and we must guess or learn the necessary knowledge before or while we are trying to understand a text for which this knowledge is a prerequisite.

The skeptical historicist infers too much from the fact that the present day's experiences, categories and modes of thought are not the same as those of the past. He concludes that we can only understand a text in our own terms, but this is a contradictory statement since verbal meaning has to be construed in its own terms if it is to be construed at all. Of course, the convention systems under which a text was composed may not in fact be those which we assume when we construe the text but this has no bearing on the theoretical issue, since no one denies that misunderstanding is not only possible but sometimes, perhaps, unavoidable. The skeptical historicist goes further than that. He argues — to return to our previous analogy — that a natural speaker of English has to understand a Greek text in English rather than in Greek. He converts the plausible idea that the mastery of unfamiliar meanings is arduous and uncertain into the idea that we always have to impose our own alien conventions and associations. But this is simply not true. If we do not construe a text in what we rightly or wrongly assume to be its own terms then we do not construe it at all. We do not understand anything that we could subsequently recast in our own terms. (*ibidem*, p. 133f)

'Understanding is silent', says Hirsch, 'interpretation extremely garrulous' (*ibidem*). Understanding is silent because it consists in reading the text in its own terms. Interpretation is garrulous because it is a translation into the readers' own terms.

Understanding the text in its own terms does not mean that in reading we are trying to empathize with the author and to see what he or she 'wanted to say' by it. Once written, the meaning of the text objectivizes itself. This problem of 'objectivity of meaning' is one of the main themes of reflection in Ricœur's theory of interpretation (1981).

The 'problem of objectivity of meaning' is also important in mathematics education. It was especially important for those who adhered to the 'constructivist' psychology of learning and tried to promote 'constructivistic styles' of teaching mathematics. One question that always arose, when they were trying to bring their theories to practice, was: what happens if the meanings that the child construes in his or her own activity of resolving all kinds of problem situations are not compatible with the mathematical meanings shared by the community of mathematicians and teachers and that are aimed at in the curricula? What should the teacher do? The message that Hirsch and Ricœur seem to be conveying is that what the child is construing in his or her effort to learn mathematics is not his or her own mathematics but the mathematics that is in the shared ways of doing it and speaking about it, in the problems, methods, theories.

Questions such as those are difficult to resolve not only in theory but also in the practice of communication of knowledge. It is possible that they will remain difficult and unresolved for ever. Maybe all we can do is to become more aware of them.

Chapter 2

Components and Conditions of an Act of Understanding

It is time to penetrate further, and to see what happens in the very soul of a mathematician . . . For a fortnight I had been attempting to prove that there could not be any function analogous to what I have since called Fuchsian functions. I was at that time very ignorant. Every day I sat down at my table and spent an hour or two trying a great number of combinations, and I arrived at no result. One night I took some black coffee, contrary to my custom, and was unable to sleep. A host of ideas kept surging in my head; I could almost feel them jostling one another, until two of them coalesced, so to speak, to form a stable combination. When morning came, I had established the existence of one class of Fuchsian functions, those that are derived from the hypergeometric series. I had only to verify the results, which only took a few hours. (Poincaré, 1952)

In this chapter, we shall be focusing on the act of understanding, on its nature, its components and the mental operations involved in it. We shall pose the question of the internal (psychological) and external (mainly sociological) conditions of an act of understanding. Processes of understanding will occupy us in the next chapter.

We pay all this attention to the act of understanding because it seems that in teaching it is the acts that are the main concern of both teachers and students. We want to make the students acquire certain ways of understanding, certain 'understandings', certain knowledge, of course, but we cannot do this other than by helping them to experience acts of understanding. Moreover, especially today, in the rapidly changing technological post-industrial world the student can never consider himself or herself fully educated. He or she must first of all learn how to learn, how to be prepared for the continuous struggle of understanding, of changing his or her ways of understanding. Therefore an awareness of what an act of understanding may consist of, a reflection about it may be more helpful to the future teacher than all the knowledge he or she might have about the expected, the valued (by today's but maybe not by tomorrow's society) ways of understanding certain particular things and topics in mathematics.

In the following discussion, a certain way of looking at an act of understanding will be proposed. This is, however, (may I remind the reader) only a certain way of looking at understanding, and not a description pretending to be 'complete' or 'faithful' in spite of the occasional use of positive assertions such as 'understanding is this or that'. What comes after the 'is' should be taken as a hypothesis.

What Could Be an Act of Understanding?

My starting point will be a concise definition proposed by Ajdukiewicz (1974). Albeit aware of the various senses in which the word 'to understand' is used in the vernacular, he chose to mean by understanding an act of mentally relating the object of understanding to another object.

Ajdukiewicz applied his definition to understanding expressions only. To understand an expression was intentionally to make a link in thought between this expression and something else, another 'object'. This 'object', for Ajdukiewicz, could be a mental representation: an image or a concept (in the psychological sense).

Here is how Ajdukiewicz introduces his definition:

> The rustle of leaves, the singing of birds, the noise of a passing motorcar we hear. The expressions of language of which we have command we not only hear, but also understand. It is not easy to explain in what the understanding of an expression consists . . . It is very often said that a person understood a given word when the hearing of that word intertwined in his mind with a thought about an object other than the word in question. For instance, a person who knows Latin thinks about the Earth on hearing the word '*terra*'; he thinks that the Earth is round on hearing the statement '*terra est rotunda*'. But it is not always required that the hearing of a word should in a person's mind intertwine with a thought about an object other than the word in question when it is said that the person understood that word. It will be said, for instance, that we understand the word 'whether', as it occurs, e.g., in 'I do not know whether he will be here', even though on hearing that word we do not direct our thought toward an object other than the word in question. We would also say, perhaps, that a soldier understood an order if he did what he was told to, even if the order was formulated in a language which he does not understand in the first of the meanings mentioned above.

As can be seen from these explanations, the word 'understand' is used in different senses. Without going here into any detailed analysis of these various meanings of the word 'understand' we shall bear in mind, in the discussion that follows, the first meaning of that word, namely that a person understands an expression if on hearing it he directs his thoughts to an object other than the word in question. (Ajdukiewicz, 1974, p. 7)

I should like to extend this definition beyond just understanding expressions on the basis of a mental representation. I would replace 'expression' by 'object', and admit that any other 'object' can be used as that towards which our thought is being directed in an act of understanding. The first object I would call 'object of understanding', and the second 'basis of understanding'. For example, my object of understanding can be a mathematical word problem, and in the act of understanding I may recognize the problem as following a certain well-known pattern. This pattern would be the basis of my understanding of this problem.

Ajdukiewicz's definition is interesting because it identifies the main components of the act of understanding. There is, of course, the 'understanding subject' (P) — the person who understands. There is that what P intends to understand — 'the object of understanding' (X). There is what P's thought is being directed to (intended) in the act of understanding: 'the basis of understanding' (Y). And there is the operation of the mind that links the object of understanding with its basis.

The Notion of Object; Mathematical Objects

In generalizing Ajdukiewicz's definition this way there is, of course, the question of what does the term 'object' mean here. In the last chapter, we mentioned that, in order to have a unified theory of understanding and meaning, it is reasonable to assume that the object of understanding is a 'sign', sign being something that represents something for someone. But how do we define 'sign'? If we do it this way: 'whatever is understood (or interpreted) by someone in a certain way, functions as a sign for this someone', then the notion of sign is explained by the notion of understanding; we fall into the error of *petitio principii*. It seems to be safer to leave the term 'object' in the definition of act of understanding as an undefined or primitive term, without replacing it by 'sign'. We can only attempt to explicate what we mean by 'mathematical objects', as we are interested by understanding in the mathematical field.

Questions related to the notion of object are sometimes discussed within the community of mathematics educators. The subjective point of view where one rather speaks of 'conceptual entities' or of a person's object of understanding is debated against the more 'realistic' position which poses ontological postulates. The article of Greeno, referred to in the previous chapter, pleaded in favour of the existence of mathematical objects, whose reality in the world of the mind was compared to that of wood workshop tools in the physical world. On the other hand, Yves Chevallard, the philosophizing didactician, proposed to consider something as an object if it is an object for at least one person: if there is a person who has a relation, an attitude (*un rapport*) to it (1992).

My own position is neither platonic realistic nor idealistic; it is closer to that professed by Popper: brought into being by our definitions, mathematical objects are creations of the human mind. But, embedded in a system of logical necessities and consequences of their relations with other mathematical objects, they may have properties that can be hard to discover, or difficult to prove or disprove. The number of still unsolved problems in mathematics testifies for that.

For a student in mathematics who comes to learn what has already been invented and discovered, mathematical objects have an undeniable reality — it is only sometimes very difficult to enter this reality. They don't think they have the right to create anything — everything is already there, brought into being by God or godlike mathematicians, like the mythological Pythagoras, and Euclid, or more modern but nonetheless legendary Gauss and Lebesgue. Even in the simple situation in a linear algebra class of defining a linear operator T on, say, R^3, by its values on a basis $\{e_1, e_2, e_3\}$ some students find it difficult to accept that they have all this freedom to put whatever they want for $T(e_1)$, $T(e_2)$, $T(e_3)$. They believe these values should follow from some assigned formula. But once they have accepted the initial freedom of definition of values on the basic vectors, there comes a second shock: now the images of all other vectors in the space are completely determined — by the initial assumption that T is linear. Of course, we did not have to assume that, but once we did, we are constrained to abide by this assumption.

Mathematics thus appears as a dialectic game between freedom and restrictions, invention and discovery: between the liberty of initial choices and the confinement within the laws of a deliberately chosen system, between the free creation of objects and the struggle of understanding their properties and significance.

In the history of philosophy we have had such strongly anti-platonic positions as that of J.S. Mill who did not consider definitions of mathematical concepts as referring to some objects in any sense. Objects must have some real existence, and what mathematical definitions postulate does not exist even in our minds. A mathematical point has no dimensions, a mathematical line has no width and is of infinite length. But nobody can imagine a point with no dimensions and nobody can imagine an infinite line with no width.

> The points, lines, circles and squares which any one has in his mind, are (I apprehend) simply copies of the points, lines, circles and squares which he has known in his experience. Our idea of a point, I apprehend to be simply our idea of the *minimum visibile*, the smallest portion of surface which we can see. A line, as defined by geometers, is wholly unconceivable. We can reason about a line as if it had no breadth; because we have a power, which is the foundation of all the control we can exercise over the operations of our minds; the power, when

a perception is present to our senses, or a conception to our intellects, of *attending* to a part only of that perception or conception, instead of the whole. But we cannot *conceive* a line without breadth: we can form no mental picture of such a line: all the lines which we have in our minds are lines possessing breadth . . . Since, then, neither in nature, nor in the human mind, do there exist any objects exactly corresponding to the definitions of geometry, while yet that science cannot be supposed to be conversant about non-entities; nothing remains, but to consider geometry as conversant about such lines, angles, and figures, as really exist; and the definitions, as they are called, must be regarded as some of our first and most obvious generalizations concerning those natural objects. (Mill, 1843)

It is of course curious that Mill did not count mathematical concepts as belonging to the category of 'relations' and instead argued very strongly that they do not belong to the category of 'bodies' (for Mill there were four categories of objects: sensations, souls, bodies, and relations). Indeed, mathematical concepts can be thought of as derived from generalizations and idealizations of relations between bodies rather than of bodies themselves: they belong to the 'transfigural' or even 'trans-operational' level, to speak in terms of Piaget and Garcia (1989). Straight lines do not have width because width is completely irrelevant for co-linearity. It is co-linearity that matters for the concept of straight line and this is a relation between at least three things whose dimensions are irrelevant. If, in passing by two sticks placed vertically we suddenly see only one, then we know we are on the line determined by these two sticks and this can be an important information for the sailor who is about to enter his boat into a harbour and wants to avoid shallow waters (de Lange, 1984).

Kotarbinski refers to the German logician W. Wundt who distinguished a slightly different set of categories of objects: things, features, states, relations. Kotarbinski himself takes a strongly materialistic point of view and does not admit of features as objects. In fact, features are even more abstract than relations: they can be thought of as classes of abstraction of relations. Whiteness, for example, he says is a feature of snow; 'whiteness' being a noun in this sentence, it looks as if there were an object such as whiteness. But this is only an illusion — whiteness does not exist independently from things that are white; these things are objects, but not their feature of being white.

It is possible that whiteness needs some medium to appear; that it is some form of energy and there is no reason why it should not be awarded existence just as any other form of energy whether we are able to perceive it through our senses or not. Let me propose here a more liberal point of view: whiteness can be regarded as an object because we can isolate it as an object of our thinking, of our understanding. In this sense mathematical abstract concepts can be objects for us. Real functions defined on the closed interval [0,1] can be objects. Their whole set can be an object. Geometrical transformations can be objects; these objects can form groups, which are again objects, this time of group theory. Even the general concept of function can be an object if someone is able to consider it this way. Also judgments (theorems, conjectures, etc.), reasonings (proofs, explanations) can be regarded as objects.

However, we must be aware that, especially in mathematics, objects are being often only constructed in acts of understanding. Abstract concepts and relations cannot be communicated in an ostensive way. Therefore, what, *a posteriori*, is identified by the understanding person as his or her 'object of understanding', might not have been very clear from the beginning; the 'contour' of this object need not be clear in the first acts of understanding it. It can be vague and blurred. The person may not be able to say what it is that he or she intends to understand. It is only understanding that may lead to some clarification and identification of this object. But still it seems that without a feeling of there being 'something' to understand it is difficult to speak about any act of understanding to have occurred at all.

When Do We Consider We Have Understood? Constraints Regarding the Basis of Understanding

In Ajdukiewicz's definition it looks as if absolutely any object (from the range of representations, for Ajdukiewicz) could be the basis of understanding. But do we, in our intention of understanding make no choice between the possible objects Y to which we link our object of understanding X? Or do we guide ourselves by some criteria? When do we feel we have understood?

Order and Harmony

Order and harmony in our thoughts, the feeling that 'it fits' is probably the most obvious criterion. We know this feeling by introspection: the common act of recognizing something consists in classifying it, putting it orderly among other similar objects, by naming it, for example, when we come across an inscription like '$y = 2x + 3$' and say to ourselves 'Oh! a linear function'.

Even the most primitive acts of understanding require this feeling of order. For example, our undergraduate students' understanding of a mathematical notion may be based on mere memory that they have already heard that name or seen that theorem or formula. But, this memory cannot be isolated: the object is remembered within a certain context. The student remembers at least in what course he or she has heard or seen it.

Order and harmony in our 'field of consciousness' was very important in *Gestalt* psychology: tendency to equilibrium in the field of consciousness is this field's basic feature. This idea reappears in Piaget's theory of equilibration of cognitive structures (1975a). Assimilation and accommodation are two operations of the mind that ensure the equilibrium of these structures.

Also in hermeneutics, interpretation or 'extraction of the sense' of a text or utterance consists in introducing an order:

Sense is always a result of an ordering, whether this is an ordering of words in a sentence, or an ordering of actions or phenomena. If we cannot see this order we feel a lack of sense . . . Since sense is . . . closely related to understanding, then something has a sense if it was already somehow understood, but understanding itself is never just a innocent looking at something. From the very start it is rooted in the world, filled with memories, included in a multitude of horizons of sense. Hence, . . . there can be no sense in what appears as unrelated, inconsistent with respect to these horizons. For something to acquire sense, it must become embedded into this tissue of already constructed senses, or, having torn it apart, it must rebuild it anew. Using the Wittgensteinian expression, we can say that a word has some sense [for us] if it enters into a [language] game that is already known. An utterance has a sense if its message can be included into a game of other messages in such a way that we can say that it obeys the same rules. (Skarga, 1989, p. 167)

Understanding on the Basis of a Unifying Thought
The criterion of 'finding a unifying principle', a relation that 'founds' what we want to understand does not apply, perhaps, to all acts of understanding. However, when it comes to understanding abstract concepts, theorems, theories, it certainly starts to play an important role.

This idea of understanding as 'taking together', conceiving of something as a unity is quite important for Leibniz (*New Essays on Human Understanding*): understanding does not mean just forming 'aggregates of things'; the crucial question is what founds the aggregate as a whole.

Philalethes: The 'composition' of simple ideas to make complex ones is another operation of our mind. This may be taken to cover the faculty of enlarging ideas by putting together several of the same kind, as in forming a dozen out of several units.

Theophilus: This unity of the idea of an aggregate is a very genuine one: but fundamentally we have to admit that *this unity that collections have is merely a respect or relation*, whose foundation lies in what is the case within each of the individual substances taken alone. So the only perfect unity that these 'entities by aggregation' have is a mental one, and consequently their very being is also in a way mental, or phenomenal, like that of a rainbow . . .

Theophilus: It may be that 'dozen' and 'score' are merely relations and exist only with respect to the understanding. The *units are separate and the understanding takes them together*, however scattered they may be. However, although relations are at the work of the understanding, they are not baseless and unreal. The primordial understanding is the source of things; and the very reality of all things other than simple substances consists only in there being a *foundation* for the perceptions or phenomena of simple substances. (Leibniz, 1765, BK II, Ch. xii)

The French word *comprendre*, 'to understand', has its roots in exactly this idea of 'taking together' as a unity. So there must be something that founds this unity, and the perception of this something is exactly what our understanding consists of. Isn't this what happens, in fact, when, for example, we understand the phenomenon of rainbow on the basis of the principle of dispersion of sunlight by refraction and reflection in drops of rain water? Or, when numbers are understood as constructions based on the ideas of quotient structure and equivalence relations. Integers are obtained as equivalence classes of a relation between pairs of natural numbers: $(a,b) \sim (c,d) \Leftrightarrow a + d = b + c$. Then, for example, the class $[1,2] = \{(1,2), (2,3), (3,4), \ldots\}$ can be denoted by '-1'. Likewise, rationals are obtained as equivalence classes of an analogous relation between pairs of integer numbers: $(a,b) \sim (c,d) \Leftrightarrow ad = bc$. It was Cauchy's dream to think of reals as classes of abstraction of a relation between sequences of rationals. This idea, however, suffered of a *petitio principii* and had to be amended (Boyer, 1968, p. 606).

Reduction to Something Simpler or More Fundamental? Systemic Understanding (from Without the Object of Understanding) and Experiential Understanding (from Within)

Scientific understanding has often been characterized as one that reduces complexity, unifies, simplifies, bases everything on a few general laws. This 'reductionist' view of scientific understanding has not satisfied all philosophers. Maslow, for example, has introduced the concept of 'suchness understanding' to contrast it with the reductionist understanding that he said belongs rather to the category of 'lawful explanation' (Maslow, 1966). The 'suchness understanding' (of a situation, for example) refers to experiencing this situation 'as such', in all its richness and variety of aspects. 'Suchness' refers to experiencing a situation from within, without trying to classify it, without looking at its 'system properties'. 'Suchness understanding' in science refers to 'comprehensive experience, in which the only scientific requirement is to accept what exists (*ibidem*, p. 79). The experienced suchness is completely alien to any kind of definition and especially the 'rigorous' definition, because any definition is abstraction and generalization and these do not apply to 'suchness': 'An experience of redness or of pain is its own definition, i.e., its own felt quality or suchness. It is what it is. It is itself.'

So ultimately is any process of classifying, that is always a reference to something, beyond the suchness of an experience. Indeed, this holds true for any abstracting process whatsoever, which by definition is a cutting into the suchness of an experience, taking part of it and throwing the rest away. In contrast the fullest savouring of an experience discards nothing but takes it all in. So for the concepts 'law' and 'order' — these, too, are system properties, as are also 'prediction' and 'control'. Any 'reduction' is a happening within a theoretical system. (Maslow, *ibidem*, p. 81)

The question arises however: is it at all possible to experience the above described 'suchness understanding'? Are we at all able to *isolate* a situation (pain, redness, continuity of a function) and experience (savour) it from within without conceiving of it as a system already? Can we isolate it without 'throwing away' what does not belong to this situation? And even if we were able to live the suchness of an experience — would we then feel as if we had understood it? Don't we *a priori* expect that understanding selects and introduces order — and Maslow assumes that suchness contradicts order?

Fortunately, Maslow acknowledges that 'suchness' and 'abstraction' are complementary rather than contradictory and 'cannot be split apart without damage' (p. 87). Choosing one at the expense of the other can only generate either 'a crippled reduction to the concrete' or 'a crippled reduction to the abstract'. The main point of Maslow is that the 'reductionist' view of understanding, which is integrative and driven towards simplification, does not give full account of human understandings (even in the domain of science), many of which are just 'experiential', remaining within the object of understanding, not going beyond it, abstracting and classifying.

> This is the kind of understanding that the sculptor has of clay or stone, that the carpenter has of wood, that a mother has of her baby, that a swimmer has of water, or that a husband and wife have of each other. And this is the kind of understanding that is ultimately impossible for the nonsculptor, the noncarpenter, the nonmother, the nonswimmer, or the nonmarried, no matter what other resources of knowledge may be available. (Maslow, *ibidem*, p. 89)

May I add: This is the kind of understanding that a mathematician has of mathematics and that is ultimately impossible for the nonmathematician?

Understanding and Reaching the Essence of Things; Phenomenalism and Essentialism

Very often we have the feeling that we have not 'really' understood something unless we have reached to 'the essence' of this something. This happens when the motivation of our intention of understanding is guided by a question of the type: 'What is . . .?'. We want to grasp what makes the object exactly what it is: 'the essence of an object is that without which it would not be what it is' — this is how the 'essence' of things was traditionally understood (Kotarbinski, 1961, p. 46).

The notion of essence has been the object of many controversies among philosophers past and contemporary. Very important in the philosophy of Aristotle and the scholastic philosophy of Middle Ages, its significance was undermined by the scientific and matter-of-fact attitudes of the seventeenth-century scientists and philosophers of nature (Kotarbinski, *ibidem*, p. 488). Facts and phenomena, observation and experience was what all scientific knowledge had to rely on exclusively; the questions about the 'internal deep essence' of things, were ridiculed as irrelevant and even senseless. This positivistic attitude reached its apogee in the 1930s, in the works of Schlick and Carnap.

In the frame of this attitude one can sensibly ask for the essence of a general name but not for the 'essence of things': the essence of a word is nothing more and nothing less than what can be logically inferred from its definition.

> The watchword [of the positivistic attitude] was: observe the facts that can be reached by observation, do not enter into vain speculations concerning the unobservable interior of objects; state regularities of co-existence and succession of phenomena; on these regularities base your predictions, and on the predictions — your technology; take all enquiry into the nature of reality and essence of things to be worthless and even senseless enterprises. For Mill, the essence of man was simply 'the set of characteristic features co-noted by the name "man"'. (Kotarbinski, *ibidem*, p. 486)

But it is very difficult to resign from inquiring into the nature and essence of things. We somehow expect more of scientific understanding than of scientific explanation. This dilemma between our scientific and methodological conscience on the one hand and beliefs about there being a reality that with pain and effort it will be possible to discover on the other, is very well rendered by Werner Heisenberg in his book *Der Teil und das Ganze* (1969). Heisenberg found it difficult to put up with the notion of time as 'that what the clock shows' and felt dissatisfied with his understanding of relativity theory. He said that while having understood the mathematical apparatus of the theory, he still had problems with understanding why the moving observer understands by the word 'time' something else than the fixed observer: he understood the theory with his head but not yet with his heart: '*ich habe die Theorie mit dem Kopf, aber noch nicht mit dem Herzen verstanden*' (*ibidem*, p. 48). He could not resign from his naive notion of time which one has whether one wants it or not and which is a useful tool of our thinking:

> If we now claim that this notion of time must be changed, then we do not know any more whether our language and thinking can remain useful tools of orientation. I do not want to refer here to Kant who described space and time as a priori forms of intuition thereby bestowing upon these fundamental forms a claim to absolute, as it was admitted in the earlier Physics. I should only wish to stress that speech and thinking will become uncertain if we change such fundamental notions, and *uncertainty cannot be matched with understanding*. (Heisenberg, 1969, p. 48)

Of course, it is possible to suspend one's scruples about whether or not a given theory 'really' tells us anything about the object it theorizes upon or models. It is also possible to accept that the meanings of the terms in a theory are different from the meanings that we have attached to these same words up till now. After all, the decision whether, in our understanding, we have or have not reached the 'essence' of the matters upon which we reflect, is our personal decision, based on feelings rather than on some rational arguments. The positivists were satisfied with their understanding; Heisenberg obviously was not.

There are also some attempts at coming to terms with phenomenalism, accepting its merits while not completely rejecting the questions for reaching beyond the observable. Such is, for example, the position of Kotarbinski (*ibidem*, p. 489) and also of Cackowski, who, in his account of 'scientific understanding', refers himself to Feynman's metaphor of the world as a huge chess game.

The phenomenon is for the scientists a real and objective event or process and the task of scientific cognition consists in the discovery of the regularities of these processes and the laws of interaction between events. To come to know these laws and rules — means to understand the world of things. This is how R. Feynman understands the 'scientific understanding' of the world:

'What do we mean by "understanding" something? We can imagine that this complicated array of moving things which constitutes "the world" is something like a great chess game being played by the gods, and we are observers of the game. We do not know what the rules of the game are; all we are allowed to do is to *watch* the playing. Of course, if we watch long enough, we may eventually catch on to a few of the rules. *The rules of the game* are what we mean by *fundamental physics*. Even if we knew every rule, however, we might not be able to understand why a particular move is made in the game, merely because it is too complicated and our minds are limited . . . Actually, we do not have all the rules now . . . Aside from not knowing all the rules, what we really can explain in terms of those rules is very limited, because almost all situations are so enormously complicated that we cannot follow the plays of the game using the rules, much less tell what is going to happen next. We must, therefore, limit ourselves to the more basic question of the rules of the game. If we know the rules, we consider that we "understand" the world'. (Feynman, 1965, p. 2–1)

The scientist is not always able to explain a law; this does not mean however that he never asks the question 'why?' This question is asked and often an answer is found. For example, the discovery of intra-atomic structures allowed to explain the 'rules of the game' on the atomic level (the rules of the inter-atomic connections, the rules of the atomic bonds); the subquantum level (quarks) may facilitate the explanation of intra-atomic structures, etc. Science investigates the rules on different structural levels of the world, one of which serves as premises for the explanation ('understanding') of the rules on other levels. Because of these multilevel structures the phenomenalistic attitude of the contemporary science becomes more complicated and may even be doubted. It is however beyond doubt that the contemporary science has developed very much thanks to this phenomenalistic attitude, understood as an protest against the metaphysical essentialism that directed the scientists' attention to absolutely objectless 'essences', 'beings', 'substances'. (Cackowski, 1987, p. 169)

For many mathematicians and physicists, the possibility of mathematizing a part of reality is that which they organize around their understanding of this reality. They feel they have understood something if they succeeded in building a mathematical model of it (Pollak, 1968). Also genetic psychology stressed the role of mathematizing in understanding (Piaget and Garcia, 1989, p. 4). According to Piaget, it requires logico-mathematical structures to but constitute the object of understanding. Mathematization is present in understanding from the very beginning. If we relied only on our senses we would be unable to preserve certain sensations and attribute permanence to other sets of them — this permanence ensures that we constitute them into objects and are able to store them in memory, analyze them, decompose and recombine.

In the controversy between phenomenalism and essentialism mathematics often played the role of a mediator. Starting from Galileo, grasping a physical phenomenon in mathematical terms was a warranty that the scientific investigation will not be reduced to mere recording of facts, making no distinction between the essential and the irrelevant details. But mathematics, too, has had something similar to the controversy between phenomenalism and essentialism which concerned mainly physicists and philosophers. I refer here to the frictions between formalism and . . . platonism or neoplatonism, maybe?

A 'formal' understanding of a mathematical notion consists in understanding its name on the basis of its definition — a certain statement which has a definite logical structure and definite logical links with other statements (theorems and definitions). A definition in this sense is what is observable in a concept — it is its phenomenon. Such an understanding may not be felt as satisfactory. An analysis of just the definition does not answer the questions about how the concept is crucial or marginal for the theory and its applications, what was its role in the development of the theory, what were the problems that the concept helped to solve or understand better. An awareness of all this may seem important for understanding the concept.

Of course, it is very difficult to speak about the 'essence' of a mathematical notion, although the temptation is great, especially for mathematics educators. From time to time an aspect of a mathematical notion is brought up as being important for its understanding and it is proposed that it be stressed in teaching. Functions, for example, were viewed mostly as particular relations in the period of the so-called 'new math' reform in Europe; later, with the trend towards bringing mathematics closer to life, functions were presented as models of relationships between variable magnitudes. A more both multi-faceted and general perspective is offered in seeing functions as, on the one hand, a certain process (when we speak of transformations of elements of one set into elements of another set and when we are actually doing these trans-formations, by hand or with the help of a computer), and, on the other, a certain object (when we consider functional spaces, for example). The concept of function has many aspects and grasping as many of them as possible in teaching should probably be aimed at. The problem is, however, that when we use ordinary language to say something about a function, we necessarily focus the listener's attention on one possible understanding of functions. This means that 'whatever we say a function is, it isn't' — to paraphrase Korzybski's words

> Whatever we say a thing is, it isn't because whatever we say is words and what we mean to say is generally not words. (Korzybski, 1950, quoted and commented by Bohm and Peat, 1987, p. 8)

Components of an Act of Understanding

In this section we shall discuss, in more detail, the basic components of an act of understanding, namely: the understanding subject, the object of under-standing, the basis of understanding, and the operation of the mind that links the object of understanding with its basis.

The Understanding Subject: Who Understands

When we speak generally of the act of understanding as a psychological and actual event, then we think of it as occurring in an individual person at a given time. In this case the understanding subject is the psychological subject: a student in our laboratory, or in our class, or, simply, you or me.

But when we speak of how the understanding of a certain mathematical notion developed in history, and mention certain acts of understanding that occurred in a past epoch, then this notion of psychological subject is no longer adequate. Of course, it happens that a mathematician gives account of a per-sonal experience (like Poincaré did in the motto to this chapter). But, most of the time it appears that a new way of understanding is shared by mathematicians at a given time with nobody in particular being responsible for its invention. The new way of understanding is 'in the air', somehow.

Lubomirski, a Polish philosopher who studied the problem of general-ization in mathematics (1983), was very much concerned with this notion of subject. The perspective on generalization taken in his book was not that of a logician but that of an epistemologist. He studied generalization in its diachronic dimension and therefore he had to deal with 'the generalizing subject' — he who generalizes — and not only with generalizations as results of the mental work of this generalizing subject. Lubomirski's question was how to understand this category when one wants to speak about generalization as a certain cognitive procedure that leads from one mathematical situation to another.

Lubomirski proposes, without pretending to offer a final solution to his problem, to adopt the Piagetian notion of *sujet épistémique* (Beth and Piaget, 1961, p. 328–9) of which, he says, the notions of psychological subject and the so-called social consciousness are certain deformed concretizations. It is in the operational structures of the epistemic subject that are encoded the 'natural logic' of mathematical thinking and, in the historical perspective, the 'mathematically founded objectivity of coming into being of mathematics', as Cavaillès (1962) would say. It is the epistemic subject that takes on the responsibility of the fact that, in various historical epochs, there existed some commonly shared beliefs that nobody has really individually articulated.

In our work, we cannot completely dispense with the idea of the psychological subject when we speak about the actual understandings of mathematics in actual students. After all, in a mathematics class, a teacher has to do not with *sujets épistémiques* but with very concrete people (some of whom may, of course, grow to be Gausses). But, on the other hand, if we want to speak about understanding of some mathematical topic in normative terms, this notion of *sujet épistémique* comes in handy. To be exact, it is not the way 'a certain concrete Gauss' has developed his understanding between one work and another that will give us some guidance as to what acts of understanding have to be experienced or what epistemological obstacles have to be overcome in today's students. We have to know how a notion has developed over large periods of time, and in what conditions (questions, problems, paradoxes) were the great breakthroughs in this development brought about. This, and not historical facts about exactly who did what and when, can be instructive in designing our teaching and facilitating understanding processes in our students.

The Object of Understanding

In introducing the notions of *Gestalt* psychology, it is often pointed out that one important difference between the *Gestaltist* and the classical 'introspective' psychology points of view on consciousness is that in the classical psychology consciousness was a stream of objectless sensations or impressions, whereas in the *Gestalt* psychology, consciousness was always a consciousness of something.

In Locke's 'Essay', understanding 'has ideas', and it 'gets' or 'derives' these ideas from sensations or reflections on operations of our minds. Sensations and reflections are regarded as 'sources' of ideas. We cannot say that what Locke means is that understanding consists in getting ideas 'of' sensations or reflections, which then would be the objects of understanding; rather, ideas are gotten 'from' these two 'sources'. It is not clear, then, what the object of understanding is, and whether it makes sense to speak about such a thing. Understanding, for Locke, was primarily the source of knowledge; an activity of the mind that produced knowledge. This knowledge must have been, for an empiricist, knowledge about the world. We might presume then, that it is the world (whatever this means) that was the object of understanding for Locke.

It is possible that a more accurate description of the classical psychological position would be not to say that psychologists occupied themselves with 'objectless' sensations, impressions, etc., but rather that this object was not specified: the object was 'the world', or 'reality'. Of course, a vague object functions as if there were no object at all.

Such a vagueness of object of understanding can still be observed sometimes in works of mathematics educators, even though a great step had been taken from the time when the discipline of mathematics education was a mere branch of the general discipline of education. The general discipline of education spoke about understanding in general, whatever the object to be understood, and formulated principles of teaching any subject. It has become clear at some point that teaching methods must be content-specific, because very clearly learning is content-specific. Our minds do not function in the same way whether we study mathematics or the history of literature. However, this 'content-specificity' is often applied to mathematics as a whole, or to some domains of mathematics, like 'algebra', for example. 'Algebra' is a very imprecise term. It means one thing for a scholar working in the field of group representations theory, another for a high-school teacher, and still another for a historian who studies the development of algebraic thought from Diophante to Viète. But even in the context of high-school algebra, when a teacher says: 'My students don't understand algebra', it is not clear what exactly it is that they do not understand: the symbolic system, and the often tacit conventions that come along with it, the notion of equation as representing a certain condition on the variables, the notion of variable as opposed to that of unknown, the notion of parameter as opposed to that of the variable . . .?

It would seem that one important aim of the didactical analysis of a subject of teaching is to clarify *what* it is that we want our students to understand when they study mathematics, and *what* exactly it is that they don't understand. We want our students to experience a certain number of acts of understanding in their studious lives. Each such act has an object which the student has to notice, identify as an object of his or her understanding for any conscious thinking on it to start at all.

The problem of objects of understanding is linked as much with the contents of teaching as with the goals of this teaching. It is not the same whether, in the frame of school 'algebra', we set ourselves the goal to teach the students a technique of solving equations or to have them acquainted with various approaches to solving problems, one of which is solution of equations; or whether we want the students to solve problems or to solve them 'by algebra'.

Also, one must not forget that school is an institution into which many children are forced and not chosen by their free will. Therefore, one has to be very careful when speaking about objects of understanding in the frame of institutionalized learning. From teacher to student, the object of understanding can easily change its identity. What is, for the teacher, an 'algebraic method of solving problems' may become, for the student, a mechanical procedure, a school activity that is done to comply with the requirements of the teacher and the school institution. It may have nothing to do with 'methodology' and certainly nothing with answering interesting questions. The student's activity does not always have a cognitive character; very often it is a strategic activity aiming at going through the school and graduating with as little intellectual investment as possible.

In the following section, we discuss some of the possible objects of understanding in mathematics.

Understanding Concepts

The object of understanding in Ajdukiewicz's 'Pragmatic logic' is always an expression of language. It may be an isolated word, or it may be someone's utterance, but it is always composed of words. Now, when speaking of understanding in mathematics, we are concerned not so much with understanding words as with understanding concepts, relations between concepts (sometimes stated in forms of theorems), problems, arguments (proofs), methods, theories, mathematical symbolism, mathematical representations such as diagrams, graphs etc.

But what is a concept? According to Ajdukiewicz a concept (in the logical sense, not in the psychological sense of a mental experience — a kind of mental representation) is just the meaning of a name (*a* meaning, I should say, as a name can have several meanings, and therefore there may be several different concepts related to a given name). The question now is: can understanding of a concept be reduced to the understanding of its name?

A process of understanding a concept may start well before its name is known or invented. Let us consider an example from an experiment, in which two students were constructing for themselves a notion of limit (Sierpinska, 1985b).

Example: **understanding the concept of limit**

Two 16-year-old students have been 'shown', without the use of words, what is the tangent to a curve in a point, by using a ruler fixed in a point (T) on a curve and sliding while another point of intersection with the curve was moving towards T until it identified with T (Figure 2). Then the position of the ruler was marked, and it was declared by the experimenter that this position is the position of the tangent to the curve in the point T. A certain way of

Figure 2:   Demonstration: the tangent to a curve at point T

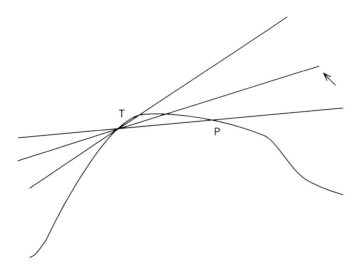

understanding what is the tangent to a curve in a point was thus vaguely suggested. Until now the students would deal with the tangent to a circle only,
understood as a straight line having only one common point with the circle.

The students were then asked to communicate this notion, in writing,
without using drawings, to a couple of other students, in a way that would
allow them to find tangents to given curves in given points.

The task was difficult: the students had to create a language to describe
something that, intuitively, seemed very easy and simple. They had to analyze
a situation given in a synthetic, visual way. Here is a sample of their conversation, in which they attempt to define the procedure of finding the tangent
(students are labelled U1 and U2).

U1:   To find such a line means to come so closer and closer and so
       that . . .
U2:   Exactly. So that . . . what?
U1:   It's like drawing lines through consecutive points.

In a second stage of the same experiment, the students had to develop this
new notion of tangent so that they would be able to compute the formula of
the tangent to the curve $y = \sin x$ at $x = 0$. The students first repeated the
manipulation with a ruler sliding on the sine curve and observed that the point
0 is 'a breakthrough point': as the secant line moves with the intersection
point moving from $(\pi,0)$ through $(0,0)$ and further to $(-\pi,0)$ its angular coefficient first increases and then decreases. They called the value at zero 'the
limit point'. Passing to numerical calculations, the students estimated the
angular coefficients of the secant in the positions of the intersection point P

Figure 3:   Calculating the tangent to y = sinx at x = 0

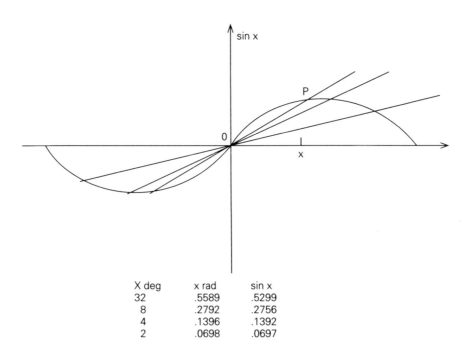

X deg	x rad	sin x
32	.5589	.5299
8	.2792	.2756
4	.1396	.1392
2	.0698	.0697

given by x = 32 , 16, 8, 4 degrees (the students were thinking in degrees, and only later switched to radians). Without even dividing sin x by x to obtain the angular coefficient of the secant, the students conjectured:

U2:   Here the difference slowly becomes smaller and smaller . . .
U1:   Yes, it does.
U2:   It gets smaller and smaller, until . . .
U1:   (whispers) . . . until it becomes one, in the end.
U2:   Yes (firmly). It will tend to one.

The language of the students is full of comparisons and metaphors. 'Tends to one' is an expression metaphorically describing the behaviour of the sequence; it is not a mathematical term yet in their language.

The students have experienced an act of understanding: the object of their understanding was the behaviour of a sequence of positions of a secant OP to the curve y = sin x. They understood it on the basis of a conjecture that, 'in the end' it 'becomes' the line y = x , or that it 'tends' to such a position. This act of understanding brings them closer to understanding the concepts of tangent and limit: it can be considered as a step in the process of understanding the concept of tangent to a curve as the limit of a variable secant, or, more generally, as a step in the process of understanding the concept of limit. [End of example]

Of course, '*the* concept of limit' is *un abus de langage*, because there are many concepts behind the mathematical term 'limit'. It depends on whether we think of the limit of function, in general, or of the limit of a sequence, and whether the sequence is numerical or not; and there are, of course, many degrees of generality of this concept. For example we can define the 'limit of a numerical sequence' in terms of absolute values or in terms of neighbourhoods. The two definitions do not define the same concept; they are logically but not epistemologically equivalent. The second is already one step further into generalization.

If, however we sometimes do speak of 'the concept of limit' in mathematics, we refer to the general idea of something to which some variable thing can be brought as close as we wish. And, in teaching, it is often this way of understanding, this 'general idea of limit', that we wish that our students grasp in the first place. We wish them to discover this idea by themselves, in a way, before being given the name of 'limit' (which has meanings in the vernacular that conflict with the mathematical meaning: Cornu, 1981, 1983). But, of course, we plan that, in further learning, they will become more conscious of the mathematical term of 'limit' and develop more precise mathematical meanings of it, the numerical, the topological, limits of sequences, limits of functions of a continuous variable, etc.

Understanding Problems

Very often, in mathematics, we have to understand 'the problem'. This, again, is an ambiguous term. The 'problem' may be a simple school problem, and its understanding may consist in identifying what is given, what is to be found, and maybe what category of problems does the problem belong to. Here, the problem is given; the aim is to solve it. But sometimes, the aim is to identify the problem: the teacher is saying something, formulating some definitions and facts on the blackboard, proving some theorems; the student has to understand what the questions are that these definitions, facts and proofs are answering. For example, in studying linear algebra at the university level and learning to find all the possible Jordan Canonical Forms related to given characteristic and minimum polynomials, the students must understand what questions have yielded this knowledge, why the canonical forms are at all necessary or useful. For the mathematician who 'works on a problem', understanding it better may result in its reformulation, in the discrimination between the essential and the superfluous assumptions, its generalization, or discovery of an important analogy.

Understanding Mathematical Formalism

Understanding a particular symbolic inscription may be included into the category of understanding an expression. Understanding a formalism, however, may involve deep conceptualizations.

Example: **the formalism of linear algebra**

For a student of linear algebra, the notion of linear independence of vectors acquires meaning in the context of bases of vector spaces. It is linked with the property of 'minimality' of generating sets. Now, to go from this natural idea to the formal defining property of a linearly independent set of vectors, i.e., to saying that the set $\{v_1, v_2, \ldots, v_n\}$ is linearly independent whenever $a_1v_1 + \ldots + a_nv_n = 0$ yields $a_i = 0$ for $i = 1, \ldots, n$, is by no means a straightforward and easy task. A whole chain of acts of understanding is involved in it.

First, one must identify the linear combination as an operation that produces a vector space out of a given set of generators. This act is a specification of a more general idea of generating structures out of a given set of elements by combining them along some allowed rules of combination. This idea can be developed rather early through experiences with various construction toys like LEGO, for example. In vector spaces, the allowed combinations of elements are linear combinations, and the elements (the 'blocks') are called 'vectors'.

Suppose that, with a certain set of vectors, a vector space was generated. Then the question must arise: did we really need all these vectors? Were they all indispensable? Couldn't one or more of them be obtained from others? This is easy to see if one vector is a multiple of another; much less so if a vector is a non-trivial combination of others. Algebra has developed a whole range of techniques for the purpose of answering this question. To understand how these techniques relate to the notion of 'one vector is a non-trivial linear combination of others' or linear dependence of vectors is not at all easy.

A serious obstacle to understanding the formal theory is to conceive of the linear independence as a relation between two vectors rather than as a property of a set of vectors. For example, students would say that the set $\{(1,1,0), (0,0,1), (1,1,1)\}$ is not 'completely' dependent because the first two vectors do not depend on each other. There is an important epistemological threshold here that marks the passing from the school algebra where concrete expressions are manipulated to the algebra that is normally taught at the university: the algebra of structures whose fundamental objects are sets furnished with properties.

The confusion of students with linear independence can be huge. Following is an example that shows what happens when one wants to make sense of the formal definition on the basis of the 'vector-to-vector' conception of the relation of independence. This is the case of an undergraduate student, who, asked to complete the phrase: '. . . is linearly independent' said, in a first movement: 'a linear combination of a span of vectors', thinking maybe, at this point, of the inscription '$a_1v_1 + \ldots + a_nv_n = 0$' that appears in the formal definition of linear independence. This was not a result of a purely perceptual association, however. Believing that linear independence is about one vector being independent of another vector, the student was looking, in the definition, for this one vector that would be independent of other vectors. He thought that it might be the linear combination '$a_1v_1 + \ldots + a_nv_n$'. When he learned that linear independence is a property of a set of vectors, he felt that there is some sort of contradiction there, because, in the definition, this set of vectors seems to be written as one vector — this linear combination! Here is how he recounts his experience in an interview by the end of his second linear algebra course:

> ... I remember last semester that's the problem I had, exactly ...
> Understanding linear independence ... This was really a stupid ques-
> tion, but it was before the last exam, and I asked them what exactly
> linear independence meant because I always thought of it as one vector
> associated with another vector, and now it's a set of vectors being
> associated. So ... but then again it's that set of vectors being written
> as one vector, you know? So you would say it's quite a contradiction
> ... I can't understand like which vector is linearly independent of
> each, like is it the vectors ... Like I know that if all your a's are equal
> to zero then all these vectors have to be linearly independent. But
> then to understand exactly why ... how it works and why it works,
> it took a while, you know ...

The concept of linear independence involves many difficulties of logical character. One difficulty is concerned with conditional statements in general. Students tend to focus on either the premise or the conclusion, usually adding a general quantifier. For example, one student claimed in a discussion over her erroneous proof that 'linearly independent vectors are always zero' thus explaining why she substituted 0 for a linear combination of these vectors: '$a_1v_1 + \ldots + a_nv_n$'. She could have read the definition as: 'for any coefficients '$a_1, \ldots a_n, a_1v_1 + \ldots + a_nv_n = 0$', disregarding the conditional character of the statement completely. Another difficulty is related to the negation of propositions. Linear independence is, logically, a negation of linear dependence and one could say that, well, once linear dependence is understood, the understanding of linear independence should be quite straightforward. But the logical rules of negation do pose a serious problem to many students. Moreover, the acceptance of a definition that is obtained by negating a statement depends on the acceptance of the law of excluded third (*tertium non datur*). However, this law of classical logic is not obvious and may not be accepted by all students. Those who search for truth rather than for consistency do not readily accept the formal aspects of mathematics. Another difficulty is the synthesis of a definition thus obtained by a long chain of translations from an initial 'natural' condition to a symbolically expressed statement. Yet another, a semantic detachment from the initial context of bases in order to be able to consider the property of linear independence as a subject of study in its own right. [End of example]

Understanding Texts
A text (as a whole) can be an object of understanding. Understanding mathematical texts has been identified as a didactical problem by Krygowska

(1969). One of the most striking examples she gives is that of a student who was asked to read and explain how she understands a definition of homothety she has never seen before. The girl starts to read: 'Homothety is . . .', suddenly interrupts and exclaims: 'I don't understand, I don't know what "homothety" means!'. This shows quite clearly that understanding mathematical texts requires a certain awareness of the structure of such texts, of the place of definitions, how they are formulated, what are they composed of (distinction between *definiendum* and *definiens*), etc. Krygowska claims that there are techniques or behaviours that help in understanding mathematical texts and that these have to be explicitly taught and trained in our mathematics classes and not left to the students' own ingenuity.

Mathematical texts and mathematical formalism have their specificities that make their understanding a somewhat different experience than reading, for example, literary texts. While, in reading any text, the interplay between the grasp of the text as a whole and the analysis of the details plays a fundamental role, reading of mathematical texts involves much more of some kind of a 'forward–backward' movement. Especially the more formal mathematical expressions and phrases have to be understood more like two-dimensional diagrams than a linear piece of writing. We can see this on the example of the tiny text which defines the notion of a linearly independent set of vectors, already discussed in the previous section:

$$a_1 v_1 + \ldots + a_n v_n = 0 \Rightarrow a_i = 0 \text{ for } i = 1, \ldots, n$$

This text can read as: 'the only way to write the zero vector as a linear combination of the vectors v sub i is to put all the coefficients equal to zero', or 'a linear combination of linearly independent vectors is zero very rarely; only if all the coefficients are zero'. This interpretation was possible by, first, looking at the text as a whole and noticing the necessity of the condition that is on the right hand side of the sign of implication: in reading, this is rendered by saying: 'the only way . . .' Then one looks back at the left-hand side of the implication and sees it as a decomposition of the zero vector into a linear combination of the vectors v. And now one looks at the right side of the implication and, first, gets a grasp of the whole, noticing that it refers to the coefficients, then reads 'for i = 1, . . ., n', saying 'all coefficients', and ends with reading '$a_i = 0$', again going back from what was written next to what was written first.

Presently, research into the understanding of mathematical texts is given proper attention in mathematics education (Bauersfeld and Zawadowski, 1987; Laborde, 1990; Gagatsis, 1985; Pimm, 1988, 1990, 1992).

The Basis of Understanding

For Ajdukiewicz, an act of understanding an expression is always based on a mental 'representation'. He considered two kinds of such representations:

'mental images' and 'concepts' (in the psychological, not logical sense). It seems that we found our understanding on various other things, as well. For example, on thoughts that are judgments or convictions or just thoughts that things are so and so; let us call this kind of basis of understanding 'thoughts that [so and so]', after Kotarbinski.

There are also other kinds of representations besides mental images and concepts. Psychological research finds some evidence to the effect that our understanding can be based on our ability to do something: on a 'procedural' representation. Such is very often our understanding of numbers and operations on them. We feel we understand because we are able to perform, to count and compute. We have mentioned 'suchness' or 'experiential' understanding which is based on some kind of holistic, non-conceptualized grasp of a situation.

In the following we look in more detail at some of the possible categories of bases of understanding.

Representations As Bases of Understanding
Ajdukiewicz defines representations as instantaneous mental experiences of an individual: 'definite experiences at a given moment in a given person's mind'. In an act of understanding based on a representation of the object that is being understood, the subject does not take any position toward this object and does not evaluate or judge it. The object of understanding is only being matched with some mental image and/or description. If, for example, the object of understanding is the word 'game', someone who is not a specialist in game theory may direct his or her thoughts onto memories of games such as soccer, hockey, tennis, bridge, poker, chess, or solitaire or may categorize the notion of game as an activity meant for entertainment in which something is at stake and in which there are winners and losers.

Ajdukiewicz distinguishes only two kinds of representations: mental images and conceptual representations (or concepts in the psychological — not logical — sense). The notion of 'mental image' encompasses not only visual but also other sensory experiences, auditory, olfactory or kinesthetic. Mental images may also be based on memories of feelings, like pain, or sadness, or joy. A conceptual representation consists of a definition or description of some kind and is, as such, essentially verbal. Such is, for example, the understanding of the word 'square' as a rectangle with perpendicular diagonals.

This categorization of mental representations is very simple, and certainly does not do justice to all the discussions and controversies over this concept in modern psychology (Clements, 1981 and 1982). We shall not enter into the details of these discussions here. Let us only remark, however, that, in reality, representations rarely appear under one of these 'pure' forms.

As Wittgenstein remarked (1958), in ordinary language we are applying a name to an object not on the ground that it satisfies the conditions of the definition of this name but because it has some kind of family resemblance to objects that we have heard called this name. Following this idea, Hofstadter

(1985, p. 547f) has shown how attempts to precisely define a colloquial expression can lead to absurdity. The expression he was analyzing was 'the First Lady' as an example of a name of a role in society. Each definition formulated on the basis of known examples of a 'First Lady' seems to provoke the apparition of other existing or possible examples that contradict the definition.

> . . . something terrible is happening to the concept as it gets more and more flexible [i.e., when its definition becomes more and more general]. Something crucial is gradually getting buried, namely the notion that 'wife of the president' is the most natural meaning, at least for Americans in this day and age. If you were told only the general definition, a gigantic paragraph in legalese, full of subordinate clauses, parenthetical remarks, and strings of 'or''s — the end product of these bizarre cases — you would be perfectly justified in concluding that Sam Pfeffenhauser, the former father-in-law of the corner drugstore's temporary manager, is as good an example of a First Lady concept as Nancy Reagan. (Hofstadter, 1985, pp. 548–9)

In mathematics, an understanding on the basis of 'family resemblance' is very often not sufficient. 'Natural meanings' do not matter that much and this 'terrible thing' is happening all the time. This is not to say that, in mathematics, the definition, in a way, precedes the concept. Important concepts have long histories before a definition is formulated. But, whatever trouble mathematicians may have in finding a definition that would suit everybody's needs and the existing examples, once they have agreed upon a definition, it is binding, and one has to accept all its logical consequences. Let us just recall the history of the concept of function in the nineteenth century. Before Dirichlet and Bolzano, functions were those well behaved relationships that could be represented by almost everywhere smooth curves. After the general definition was introduced allowing absolutely any well-defined relationship between two variables to be a function, mathematicians started to come up with examples of functions that were real monsters to most of their colleagues. At the turn of the century, Poincaré wrote: 'Formerly, when a new function was invented, it was in view of some practical end. To-day they are invented on purpose to show our ancestors' reasonings at fault, and we shall never get anything more than that out of them' (Poincaré, 1952, p. 125). In spite of all this turmoil, the 'natural meanings' of the ancestors were not to be brought back to mathematics.

Students of mathematics normally go through a whole series of such 'terrible things' that put their representations and reasonings at fault. Let us take again the definition of linear independence. One can, in principle, survive for a while on an understanding of linear independence as a relation between two vectors, maybe visualized geometrically in terms of 'not lying on the same line'. But when it comes to the notion of dimension and to understanding why the dimension of the zero vector space is 0, then one has to refer only to the definition to show to oneself that the set composed of only the zero vector {θ} is linearly dependent and that, consequently, the zero space does not have a basis. At this point, one simply cannot do without a strictly conceptual representation of linear independence.

Another category of representations seems to impose itself as one studies understanding of mathematics in younger children. Very often they behave as if their understanding was in their fingers rather than in their minds. In their acts of understanding, the intention of understanding seems to be directed towards an immediate action. It is based on some kind of 'feeling' of an activity which has to be performed here and now. For example, many high-school students just 'know what to do' with an equation: when encountering an equation, for example, $\sqrt{(x-1)} = -5$ they would sit down and try to 'extract the root' by whatever means they can think of. But they may not be able to tell what they are doing, why they are doing it, what is an equation, what is a solution of an equation, and whether it makes sense, in this particular case, to square, subtract, and do all these things they were doing. The kind of representation they have of equations is neither a pure mental image (based on motion, for example), nor is it purely conceptual. We might use the name of 'procedural', a word already used in a similar sense by several authors (Herscovics and Bergeron, 1989) or 'operational' (Sfard, 1991, 1992) or 'process conceptions' (Breidenbach *et al.*, 1992). They are representations based on some kind of schemas of actions, procedures. There must be a conceptual component in them — these procedures serve to manipulate abstract objects, symbols and they are sufficiently general to be applied in a variety of cases. Without the conceptual component they would not become procedures. We may only say that the conceptual component is stronger or weaker.

If the conceptual component is weaker then in an act of understanding our thought is directed to an activity that we cannot express otherwise than by showing how to perform it. If it is stronger then the subject has at least a partially verbalized schema of the activity. A boundary case could be that of one of my linear algebra undergraduate students who defined linear independence of a set of vectors by describing what he would do to check whether a particular set of vectors is linearly independent: 'For the polynomials to be linearly independent they must be expressed as a linear combination then the components are equated. Results are put into a matrix, the matrix is reduced to echelon form. If after being reduced the matrix has all non-zero rows then the polynomials are said to be linearly independent over K.' Or the case of the legendary 12-year-old who thought he understood the formula for the area of the rectangle because 'he got all his answers right'. He probably had a schema for calculating the areas that he could verbalize at least in the form: 'you just take the length and the width and multiply' (Skemp, 1978).

The category of such 'procedural' representations connects to the Brunerian category of 'enactive representations' (Bruner, 1973). For Bruner, a representation is 'a set of rules in terms of which one conserves one's encounters with events' (*ibidem*, p. 316). Hence, it is a way of keeping 'ideas' in memory. A representation needs a medium to express itself, and Bruner mentions three kinds of such media: the enactive, the iconic, and the symbolic. These media are then the key according to which Bruner classifies representations — a classification, let us note, that is remindful of Peirce's typology of signs: indices, icons, symbols.

> A representation of the world or of some segment of one's experience has several interesting features. For one thing, it is in some medium. We may represent some events by the actions they require, by some form of picture, or in words or other symbols. There are many sub-varieties within each of these three media — the enactive, the iconic, or the symbolic . . . [Hence] there are three kinds of representational systems that are operative during the growth of human intellect and whose interaction is central to growth. All of them are amenable to specification in fairly precise terms, all can be shown to be affected and shaped by linkage with tool or instrumental systems, all of them are within important limits affected by cultural conditioning and by man's evolution. They are, as already indicated, enactive representation, iconic representation, and symbolic representation — knowing something through doing it, through a picture or image of it, and through some such symbolic means as language. With respect to a particular knot, we learn the act of tying it; when we know the knot, we know it by some habitual act we have mastered and can repeat. The habit by which the knot is organised is serially organized, governed by some schema that holds its successive segments together, and is in some important sense related to other habitual acts that facilitate or interfere with its learning and execution. What is crucial is that the representation is expressed in the medium of action with many features constrained by the nature of action, for example, its sequential and irreversible nature. An image of the knot carried in your mind or on a page is not the same thing as the knot being tied, although the image can provide a schema around which action can be sequentially organised. An image is a selective, simultaneous, and often highly stylized analogue of an event experienced. Yet it is not arbitrary in its manner of referring to events as is a word. You can recognize an image of something, once having seen the something in question. You cannot recognize the appropriate word by knowing only the event it signifies. Linguistic signification is, in the main, arbitrary and depends upon the mastery of a symbolic code. A linguistic description, therefore, involves knowing not only the referents of words, but the rules for forming and transforming utterances. These rules, like the rules of image formation and habitual action, are distinctive to the medium of language. (Bruner, 1973)

It is clear that this description of representations allows for a wider range of mental experiences than the categorization of Ajdukiewicz, who did not take into account the enactive representations, and in whose conceptual representations only words were allowed.

It is interesting to note, as Bruner suggests, that many acts of understanding may consist not in representing oneself the object of understanding, but in translating from one representation to another, the object of understanding already being some kind of representation in our mind. This may especially be the case in mathematics, whose abstract objects cannot be communicated otherwise than through some form of representation. In the example above of the linear algebra student defining the notion of linear independence, what the boy was doing was translating exactly his enactive-iconic representation of linear independence into a symbolic one (rather faithfully for the time being, to be true).

In his already mentioned work concerning generalization in mathematics, Lubomirski considers what he calls 'mathematical situations'. Generalization is a cognitive procedure that leads the cognizing subject from one mathematical situation to another. This 'mathematical situation' as described by Lubomirski, seems to be a certain representation of the problem at hand, but this representation is neither purely enactive or iconic, nor purely symbolic, and it is rather complex, because it contains 'all those elements of mathematical knowledge . . . that are present at the moment in the subject's consciousness and on which depends the subject's decision about what cognitive activity to undertake and in which way to realize it' (*ibidem*, p. 5). It is possible that a research mathematician works simultaneously with complex systems of representations being flexible enough to go from one set of representational rules to another.

'Mental Models'

Greeno, whose article was extensively quoted in the previous chapter, claims that our knowing, understanding and reasoning are grounded in 'mental models' rather than 'representations'. He presents his view on 'knowing in conceptual environments' as an alternative to the information-processing framework of cognitive science which, he claims, bases knowing on the existence in the human mind of 'representations':

> In the current information-processing framework of cognitive science, knowledge is a set of representations that are stored in the mind, including symbols that represent concepts, properties, and relations as well as representations of procedures for manipulating symbolic expressions. Learning a domain, in this information-processing framework, is the construction of cognitive structures and procedures that represent the concepts, principles and rules of inference of the domain. (Greeno, *ibidem*, p. 174)

This is maybe a slightly oversimplified account of the information-processing view on learning. Information processing in the newest computer environments is certainly not a linear manipulation of built-in procedures the access to which is available only through the strict commands of a formal language. Hyper-languages and multimedia environments, developed in the field of educational technology, work in a way that is very close to what Greeno describes with the help of his 'living in a physical environment' and 'mental models' metaphor.

> In the environmental view knowing a set of concepts is not equivalent to having representations of the concepts but rather involves abilities to find and use the concepts in constructive processes of reasoning. Representations of concepts and procedures can play an important role in reasoning, as maps and instructions can help in finding and using resources in a physical environment. The person's knowledge, however, is in his or her ability to find and use the resources, not in having mental versions of maps and instructions as the basis for all reasonings as action. (Greeno, *ibidem*, p. 175)

Greeno's view of our intellectual lives is very much focused on 'survival' and 'consumption', slightly less on 'production', and of course, very little on just thinking for the sake of thinking itself. This may be an adequate image of knowing but certainly not of thinking in general. For example, even if the notion of infinity — actual infinity — can be thought of as a 'resource' for something, a convenient idealization for solving some of the mathematical theoretical questions — why should we think of it in such a pragmatic way? Isn't understanding just for understanding, reasoning just for reasoning, knowing just for knowing, and not for doing something with this knowledge (like finding and proving a new theorem, publishing a paper, adding it to the CV, obtaining a research grant etc.), something specifically human? Ian Hacking (1975) quotes, in that respect, Aristotle, saying that a man 'who will not reason about anything is no better than a vegetable' (Metaphysics, 1006a), in an interesting argument with Wittgenstein's view on the necessity of proofs. The necessity of proofs lies in the human need of proving and not in the formal need of assessing the truth of theorems. Let me quote this passage here:

> Wittgenstein, in his unfinished 'Remarks on the Foundations of Mathematics' was . . . drawing attention to the undetermined character of mathematical concepts. He went so far as to suggest that a mathematical theorem did not have the marks of necessity until it was proven. But he thought that once the proof was pointed out to us, we would not fail to accept it, except on pain of being called stupid or irrational. That which makes us accept proofs is not our training in mathematical skills and concepts but is a precondition for those skills and concepts, and lies in human nature. It is innate. To be human is to be able to prove a little. (Hacking, *ibidem*, p. 69)

The 'concreteness' of mental models, their being filled with various 'objects' that are being moved around, combined and decomposed, and that, in the course of working with them, become very familiar, is certainly appealing to our understanding and is helpful. However, they may have the tendency to acquire, in our minds, the status of the 'whole truth' about the conceptual domain we are exploring with their help: they actually start to be the whole world. And thus they become obstacles to further exploration. It may even be so that the more we make a mental model function and the better it works, the bigger the obstacle we thus create for ourselves.

For example, the mental model of the domain of numbers and quantities — the 'number sense' — that Greeno proposes to be developed in school-children, is the knowledge of the logistics rather than of arithmetics, the knowledge of the artisan rather than the knowledge of the architect. In this model, numbers are objects very much like wooden blocks of various lengths, and operations are almost physical operations on these blocks. This is all right if the domain of numbers is restricted to positive rational numbers and addition or even subtraction of integers; problems arise with the multiplication of integers whose rules it is difficult to explain without reference to the integers as a structure that extends the structure of natural numbers in a way that preserves the properties of operations in it. It may be difficult, for both the students and the teacher, to get rid, at this point, of the importunate spatial understanding of numbers as blocks. But . . . maybe, in this pragmatic world, it does not make sense to teach all children multiplication in the ring of integers, after all?

'Apperception' As a Basis of Understanding

On the highest levels of abstract thinking, understanding may be based on what the psychologists of the Würzburg School called 'apperceptions'. It is 'apperception', they say, that allows us to understand sentences like 'Thinking is so unusually difficult that many prefer to draw conclusions' (cited in Luria, 1981, p. 21).

The first thing that we identify in this sentence is the opposition that is made there between 'thinking' and 'drawing conclusions': drawing conclusions (in a formal or automatic way) appears as an escape from thinking. We would have thus isolated the logical structure of the sentence, maybe on the basis of such cues as 'so difficult . . . that'. Our understanding is based here on a certain logical pattern. We recognize this pattern because we have some experience with understanding and using sentences like: 'Climbing a mountain is so difficult that many prefer to use a chair-lift'. Usually we pass very quickly over this phase of understanding and go on to wondering why this statement about thinking and drawing conclusions should be true. We may start to ask ourselves questions like: Why should thinking be more difficult than drawing conclusions? Isn't thinking always based on drawing conclusions? etc.

'Thoughts That [So and So]' As Bases of Understanding
Understanding on the basis of some 'thought that . . .' seems to be quite important in scientific thinking. This is the category to which belong acts of understanding that answer our questions about the reasons why things are as they are, why a statement should be true or false, or what results (of experiment, computation, research) can one expect, etc.

A 'thought that [so and so]' need not express a person's conviction or opinion. It may be just a statement one has remembered. For example, in understanding '√2 is an irrational number' on the basis of a thought that '√2 cannot be represented as a ratio of two integer numbers', the thought can, but need not be, a conviction. A person may be convinced of the truth of this thought on the ground of its proof which he or she has understood. Or the person may just repeat, in mind, an argument he or she has memorized. The proof can be understood on the basis of the thought that all its steps seem logically correct. Or, it can be understood on the basis of a thought that synthesises the so-called 'idea of the proof' (*nervus probandi*) and emphasizes all the essential hypotheses. Or, its understanding may consist in perceiving the historical significance of the theorem. In the context of historical considerations, what often comes to mind is that the statement '√2 is an irrational number' is an arithmetical counterpart of the geometrical discovery of the Pythagoreans that the diagonal of a square is not commensurable with its side.

Mental Operations Involved in Understanding

It seems that there are four basic mental operations involved in understanding: identification, discrimination, generalization and synthesis (Sierpinska, 1990b).

Identification
We are speaking here of identification in the sense of discovery or recognition. When I say, for example, that I have identified the object of my understanding, I mean, first, that I have 'discovered' or 'unveiled' it, that is, isolated, singled out from the 'background of my field of consciousness' in which it was, so to say, hidden, and, second, that I have recognized it as something that I intend to understand.

In so identifying an object I am introducing a certain order or hierarchy into what I am presently considering: some things become more important than other things. If there already was a certain hierarchy in my field of consciousness, it can be completely reversed in a new act of identification.

In isolating an object and recognizing it I may or may not be naming it. For example, in perceiving a car crashed against a tree I may or may not think to myself 'Aha, a car crash'. But in any case I would have classified it somehow, put it into a folder, with memories of other crashes I would have seen or experienced. For example, I may say to myself: I have seen something like that before. In this case I identify an object with another object. Instead of giving an object a name I may also be describing it somehow, for example with the help of a metaphor or marking it with the help of a metonymy. If the object is new, this figure of speech can be the root of a name later given to the object. This is how many names in everyday language have come into being.

When I identify an object, I classify it, putting it together with other objects — even if these objects are objects I know nothing about except that I intend to study them.

Classifying is not the same as categorizing. An object included into a class is not a 'particular case' of this class. It is just an element of it. In categorizing, a class of objects is included into another class of objects — the latter is then a generalization of the former. For example, an event (like a particular car crash on the road) can be classified; a phenomenon (of car crashes on icy roads in winter) can be categorized (as a particular case of car accidents).

Identification is the main operation involved in acts of understanding called *einsicht* by *Gestalt* psychologists: acts that consist in a re-organization of the field of consciousness so that some objects that, so far, have been in the background, are now perceived as the 'figure'. Let us have an example of such *einsicht* in mathematics (Sierpinska, 1992c).

Example: **identification of the crucial part of a geometric figure in a proof**

Suppose students have to prove the following fact in geometry (Egret and Duval, 1989):

If O, B, C are non-colinear points in the plane, I is the middle of BC,
D is such that DOBI is a parallelogram and M is the middle of DI
then M is the middle of OC. (see Figure 4.I)

At the beginning of solving this problem, the diagram is probably understood as in Figure 4-II. Only DOBI is identified as a parallelogram. The solution requires that the DOIC part of the diagram be noticed and identified as a parallelogram, as well (Figure 4-III).
[End of example]

Discrimination

Discrimination between two objects is an identification of two objects as different objects. For example, understanding the concept of equation requires a discrimination between the equation as being a condition on some free variables and the equality as a statement which can be either true or false.

The meaning of 'identification' and 'discrimination' is close to what Locke calls 'agreement and disagreement (between ideas)'.

Another faculty we may take notice of in our minds is that of discerning and distinguishing between the several ideas it has. It is not enough to have a confused perception of something in general. . . . How much

Figure 4:   Identification of the crucial part of a geometric figure in a proof

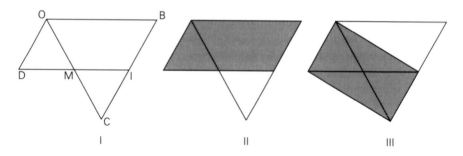

the imperfection of accurately *discriminating* ideas from one another lies either in the dullness or faults of the organs of sense; or want of acuteness, exercise, or attention in the understanding; or hastiness and precipitancy, natural to some tempers, I will not here examine: it suffices to take notice, that this is one of the operations that the mind may reflect on and observe in itself. (Locke, 1690, BK II, Ch. xi)

There can be several degrees of discrimination as there can be several degrees of identification. One is mere perception that two objects are two and not one. Of some such discriminations even 'brutes' are capable, says Locke. Another degree is that when two objects are compared with one another with respect to certain sensible circumstances, contingent to the objects themselves. A still higher degree is when two general ideas are compared from the point of view of abstract relations.

The comparing them with one another, in respect of extent, degrees, time, place, or any other circumstances, is another operation of the mind about its ideas and that is upon which depends all that large tribe of ideas comprehended under 'relation' . . . [The comparing] seems to me to be the prerogative of human understanding ... Beasts compare not their ideas further than some sensible circumstances annexed to the objects themselves. The other power of comparing, which may be observed in men, belonging to general ideas, and useful only to abstract reasonings, we may probably conjecture beasts have not. (*ibidem*, BK II, Ch. xi, sec. 4)

Generalization
Generalization is understood here as that operation of the mind in which a given situation (which is the object of understanding) is thought of as a particular case of another situation. The term 'situation' is used here in a broad sense, from a class of objects (material or mental) to a class of events (phenomena) to problems, theorems or statements and theories.

For example, we may have a mathematical situation related with the Pythagorean theorem. At first, it can be restricted to just the picture of squares built on the sides of a right angled triangle and to the uses of the formula $a^2 + b^2 = c^2$ in various computational exercises. If, at some point, this situation is perceived as a particular case of a situation where the figures built on the sides of a right angled triangle are any similar figures, then we can speak of generalization.

At first sight it would seem that identification and discrimination are operations more fundamental than the operation of generalization which, one would say, belongs already to more sophisticated functions of the theorizing thought. In fact, it is difficult to put a hierarchy on these operations. Generalization can be defined as an 'identification of one situation as a particular case of another situation', but this would only mean that we take the *notion* of identification as more fundamental than the notion of generalization which is derived from it, and not that the *operation* of identification is genetically more primitive or earlier, and generalization can only be developed on its basis. There are many levels of all these operations and they probably develop interactively, the development of one forcing the development of other. We shall see it in more detail through Vygotski's theory of development of concepts in Chapter 5. There are also many forms of generalization, and a fairly comprehensive overview and analysis of them can be found in Dörfler, 1991.

All four operations are important in any process of understanding. But, in understanding mathematics, generalization has a particular role to play. Isn't mathematics, above all, an art of generalization, '*l'art de donner le même nom à des choses différentes*', as Poincaré used to say? In learning mathematics the child is expected to make a particular effort of generalization: from early childhood experiences with numbers of things, to numbers as such, to unknowns, to variables, relations between variables, functions, relations between functions, . . . Any variable is a general term, designating an arbitrary element of a given domain. All algebra is nothing but the study of the generality of our assertions and an attempt towards even more generality.

It is also worthy of noting that the operation of generalization must act on some object: we generalize something — a concept, a problem, a mathematical situation. It is therefore necessary to have identified this something as an object. In guiding our students towards a generalization, very often we forget that the object to generalize may not yet be an object for them. Do they only know what they are supposed to generalize? It might be worthwhile to check whether this object is within their intellectual grasp at that point.

This is not always done. For example, in our linear algebra undergraduate courses, students are led from one generalization to another at a pace that rarely takes into account the normal human possibilities of understanding. The canonical forms of linear operators are introduced before the students have had the time to identify the subtle relationships between linear operators and their matrices, and between the latter and their minimum polynomials. And even if they know something about these relationships they may still not have identified the *problématique* that is resolved by the canonical forms of linear operators. Very often, the canonical forms come in when, for the students, all the previous material is nothing but a set of techniques of solving simple problems of computation or verification. In this situation, the Jordan canonical form, instead of appearing as a major generalization and synthesis, a central theorem of a theory, just joins the existing set of techniques. It becomes reduced, in the students' minds, to a combinatoric procedure of filling in a matrix with the 'Jordan blocks'.

Synthesis

'Synthesis' means for us here: the search for a common link, a unifying principle, a similitude between several generalizations and their grasp as a whole (a certain system) on this basis. For example, after having followed, step by step, a mathematical proof, suddenly we grasp the so-called idea of the proof. The proof becomes a whole, it is no more just a set of isolated logical moves from one statement to another. Czezowski claims that it is also such synthesis that allows one *to find* a proof.

> Proving can be successful only when we are able to grasp the fundamental idea of the proof, called *nervus probandi* thanks to which the proof becomes a coherent system, a well connected whole . . . [For example] the nerve of the proof . . . of the De Morgan law [¬(p&q) ⇔ ¬p ∨ ¬q] is the thought that both the conjunction and the alternative are expressible by implication, and therefore the implication constitutes a kind of link between them which allows us to use the hypothetical syllogism. (Czezowski, 1959, p. 147)

This is an example of a 'local' synthesis in mathematics. But one can also speak of more global syntheses, of grasping, as wholes, vast domains of mathematical knowledge. It is such syntheses that have paved the way to unifications that mathematics has known in the nineteenth and twentieth centuries. These unifications were based on such fundamental organizing ideas as function, mapping, invariant of a mapping, equivalence relation, algebraic structure, quotient structure, category, etc. The so-called abstract algebra, linear algebra, group theory, category theory, etc., are, one can say, by-products of these efforts of synthesis.

It is mainly this kind of synthesis that occupy the mind of Daval and Guilbaud (1945), when they speak of generalization and synthesis as the driving forces of the development of modern mathematical thought. This is also the position of Bachelard. He claims that questions and hypotheses are at the root of any scientific activity and that *'toute hypothèse est synthèse'* (1975, pp. 10–11).

Bachelard (1970) put forward the idea that modern scientific thought is characterized by a certain specific type of hypotheses. These hypotheses are not derived from inductive generalizations of observations of reality or from knowledge given — this kind of view would be based on a kind of positive attitude to reality, observation, experience, and knowledge of our predecessors. The most striking feature of the modern scientific thinking, says Bachelard, is its polemic character: the favourite question seems to be: 'why not?' which leads to 'polemic generalizations' (like the non-Euclidean geometries and non-commutative algebras). However, such an activity would be very futile, indeed, if the thought stopped there. But it doesn't. These generalizations are, in fact, only symptoms of overcoming certain beliefs or points of view which bring about a genuinely new knowledge in form of momentous syntheses such as the idea of Felix Klein of 'geometries of transformation invariants' or the so-called abstract algebra. One should not forget the monumental venture of the Bourbaki group, whose aim was to unify mathematics and reduce the number of its fundamental notions and constructions.

However, this last undertaking can make us suspicious with respect to the value of such unifications: the books of Bourbaki are particularly hard to read; they appear to make understanding more difficult. It seems that there is some limit to the reduction of the number of basic notions, with the help of which others are defined. The smaller the number of such notions, the longer must be the chain of reasonings that explain the relations between notions dependent on these. And the understanding of such relations demand that these reasonings be grasped as a whole.

The idea of understanding in mathematics based on a reduction to a small number of fundamental and very general organizing notions such as set, relation, equivalence relation, group, function was the guiding principle in the so-called 'new math' school reforms in the years 1960–70. It was a shock to all the proponents of the new curricula that not only the children did not understand mathematics better, but their understanding got worse than anything seen so far. It is true that there were many mistakes in the realization of the new programmes, too literal interpretation of certain suggestions, going up to formalization with things that were supposed to be taught in a propaedeutical way, and the like. But the biggest mistake was made in the interpretation of the role of synthesis in understanding: like generalization, a synthesis must be made by the understanding subject himself or herself, not by the teacher. Synthesis as an act of understanding is an act on one's own knowledge. To unify, reduce, generalize and synthesize, there must be something in one's mind that one can unify, reduce, generalize and synthesize. In the reformed programmes the children were expected to synthesize empty sets of knowledge.

One last remark is probably due: we have not included the activity of abstraction as an operation 'involved in an act of understanding'. This may appear as curious — abstraction is seen as belonging to the very nature of mathematical activity. The reason for this omission is that abstraction does not constitute an act of understanding in itself. It is just the act of detaching certain features from an object. But abstraction is not lost in understanding: in fact, abstraction is involved in all and each of the four operations and each of them is somehow involved in abstraction. For example, for the features to be detached, they have to be identified through acts of discriminating between what is important and what can be neglected from some point of view. Also generalizations and syntheses, in creating new abstract objects, necessarily imply abstraction.

Psychological Conditions of an Act of Understanding

The question here is about internal, mental and psychic conditions. It is difficult to say what are the sufficient conditions for an act of understanding to occur, but some necessary conditions seem to be quite obvious.

Attention and Intention

Attention well seems to be a necessary condition of understanding: without attention, without having noticed that there is something to understand, there can be no act of understanding.

Locke says,

> Men . . . come to be furnished with fewer or more simple ideas from without, according as the objects they converse with afford greater or less variety; and from the operations of their minds within, according as they more or less reflect on them. For, though he that contemplates the operations of his mind, cannot but have plain and clear ideas of them; yet, *unless he turn his thoughts that way, and considers them attentively*, he will no more have clear and distinct ideas of all the operations of his mind, and all that may be observed therein, than he will have all the particular ideas of any landscape, or of the parts and motions of a clock, who will not turn his eyes to it, and with attention heed all the parts of it. The picture, or the clock may be so placed, that they may come in his way every day; but yet he will have but a confused idea of all the parts they are made up of, till he applies himself with attention, to consider them each in particular. (J. Locke, 1690, BK I Ch. i)

The mind has to be voluntarily directed towards an object in order to derive an idea of it. It needs awareness of the operations of one's own mind to form ideas of them and start relating them to each other.

In mathematics education, the question of the place of attention in understanding is a very important one. It has been demonstrated by Mason (1982, 1989) how, indeed, understanding of mathematics requires a series of 'delicate shifts of attention'. Mason and Davis (1990) have studied the role of 'noticing' for understanding. For it is not obvious, for a person not yet familiar with a mathematical domain, what to look at, what to attend to. The thought wanders about, sometimes attaching importance to irrelevant details of a symbolic representation. It is very difficult for the teacher to communicate what should be attended to: mathematics deals mainly with relations and these, in general, cannot be pointed to with a finger. What can be pointed to are 'shadows' of things, not the things themselves. Thus, the very object of understanding in mathematics is very hard to communicate. It is difficult to make the students identify this object and maintain an interest in it.

So far we have been speaking of 'attention' in the sense of 'attending to' something: voluntarily thinking of a thing. This links attention with consciousness or awareness. On the other hand, everybody knows stories about 'sudden illuminations', unexpected acts of understanding something of which a person was not thinking of at all at the moment (Hadamard, 1945). Would these stories undermine the thesis of the necessity of attention for an act of understanding to occur?

It does not seem likely. Poincaré, whose biggest discoveries in the field of Fuchsian functions occurred to him while sleeping or taking part in social events, firmly claims that these 'illuminations' would never have occurred to him had he not fully consciously attended to his mathematical problems in the time preceding these events, however not directly in time.

> There is another remark to be made regarding the conditions of this unconscious work, which is, that it is not possible, or in any case not fruitful, unless it is first preceded and then followed by a period of conscious work. These sudden inspirations are never produced (and this is sufficiently proved already by the examples I have quoted) except after some days of voluntary efforts which appeared absolutely fruitless, in which one thought one has accomplished nothing, and seemed to be on a totally wrong track. These efforts, however, were not as barren as one thought; they set the unconscious machine in motion, and without them it would not have worked at all, and would not have produced anything. (Poincaré, 1952, p. 56)

We can speak of conscious work in the sense of purposefully and voluntarily attending to a mathematical problem which is the object of our understanding at that time. This is what Poincaré had in mind. But there is also another kind of consciousness — 'a meta-consciousness' — through which we attend not to the problem itself but to our own ways of understanding it, our going about solving it, etc. How exactly this kind of attention can help in understanding, controlling one's problem solving strategies, etc. is also an important problem in mathematics education (Schoenfeld, 1987).

Attention implies that there is an intention to understand — an orientation towards understanding, grasping the meaning. It seems that without the intention of understanding there can be no act of understanding. On the other hand, is the intention of understanding a sufficient condition for us to say that there has been an act of understanding? It sometimes happens that we very strongly intend to understand something but have trouble in getting the meaning — we feel a blank in our minds — nothing appears where normally the 'basis of understanding' popped up so easily. For example, someone gives us a number (e.g., a street number, like 'sixty-nine hundred Boulevard Décarie') over the phone — in a foreign language — and we can repeat the words but we don't visualize the number as written. Even if we speak this language, we may still count in our mother tongue and feel uncomfortable with names of numbers pronounced in this foreign language. If the information that is being thus given to us on the phone is important, our intention to understand may be very strong indeed. I would be inclined to saying that there has been an act of understanding in such an extreme case: it consisted in identifying the object to be understood.

Question

Not all acts of understanding are preceded by a question. We understand the familiar parts of our mother tongue without questioning ourselves on their possible meanings. But it seems that any act of understanding that brings about a substantial change in what we know, or think, or believe is preceded by a question.

A sensible and interesting question seems to be absolutely necessary in maintaining both the attention that allows us to notice that there is something to understand, and the tension that is required in conducting long reasonings that only can promise the reward in understanding. And only those objects about which we do not know something, about which, therefore, we have a question, are meaningful for us and can become objects of our understanding.

The routine acts of understanding which are not preceded by a conscious 'big' question are called 'ap-prehensions' by Dewey, in contrast to 'comprehensions' which require more reflection. In fact, Dewey speaks about the complementary functions of both 'unquestioned understandings' and those preceded by a question in the processes of knowing. He says,

> All judgment, all reflective inference, presupposes some lack of understanding, a partial absence of meaning. We reflect in order that we may get hold of the full and adequate significance of what happens. Nevertheless *something* must be already understood, the mind must be in possession of some meaning that it has mastered, or else thinking is impossible . . . An increase of the store of meanings makes us conscious of new problems, while only through translation of the new perplexities into what is already familiar and plain do we understand or solve these problems. This is the constant spiral movement of knowledge. (Dewey, *ibidem*, pp. 139–40)

In the Piagetian theory of equilibration the two complementary mechanisms of assimilation and accommodation seem to be analogous to those that are involved in acts of 'ap-prehension' and 'com-prehension', respectively. The mechanism of accommodation is triggered by a mental conflict — an event caused by the discrepancy between information coming from the environment and the existing mental structures. And a conflict is a step towards a question, it predicts a question, prepares the ground for it.

In scientific understanding, the role of questions is deemed fundamental. Bachelard says,

> For a scientific mind, all knowledge is an answer to a question. If there hasn't been a question, there cannot be scientific knowledge. Nothing can be taken for granted. Nothing is given. Everything has to be constructed. (Bachelard, 1983, p. 14)

Social Conditions of an Act of Understanding

For a teacher and a more pragmatically minded mathematics educator, the practical conditions of understanding, various 'aids' to understanding, factors that may help a student to understand mathematics, are more important than speculations about the psychological conditions of an act of understanding to occur. It is obvious that the student must attend to his or her object of understanding, and that he or she must be motivated by some interesting and meaningful question. It is less obvious for the teacher what to *do*, what activities to design, in order to draw the students' attention, to motivate them, engage into the activity of understanding. This is a serious problem and much of mathematics educational research is devoted to it.

However, any solution to this problem must take into account the fact that, in a mathematics classroom, understanding takes place in a social environment that has many different components or dimensions. French didactique has attempted at covering the complexity of this environment in the so-called '*théorie des situations*' (Brousseau, 1986, 1989). Any activity that we design for our students will be altered by the fact that we 'assign' it to them, and they will expect to be evaluated on it. The understanding that students will develop will depend on the kind of 'didactical contract' that will establish itself between the teacher and the students in the given classroom situation. We mentioned this problem earlier in Chapter 1.

Being aware of the mechanisms of didactical contract we can play on some of the variables involved in the institutionalized teaching and construct didactical contracts in which students would be more likely to experience acts of understanding closer to those lived through by mathematicians in their work. Experiments by Legrand (1988), and others, for example, Lampert (1988) have shown that this is not impossible.

Brousseau's theory of didactical situations proposes a certain categorization of these situations. One of them is the 'situation of communication', in which students communicate among themselves, thus verbalizing their mathematical experiences. They also communicate with the teacher, revealing their own understanding of the problem situation; then the teacher enters into a kind of 'negotiation' of meanings with the students which activity sometimes materializes in an 'institutionalization' of the commonly developed knowledge. Unfortunately, this kind of two-way communication is still rather rare in our mathematics classes, and certainly very rare in undergraduate university lecture-rooms. A more familiar situation is that of the teacher who tries to 'communicate' mathematical knowledge to his or her students using all kinds of means and methods of which the verbal language is but one. Diagrams, graphs, tables, and other graphical representations are commonly used and, moreover, believed to have a transparency that researches have shown to be an illusion (e.g., Janvier, 1978). Manipulatives, blocks, pies, and other concrete materials have raised many discussions as well.

Language remains the main means of communication in the mathematics classroom. But, as we mentioned in the first chapter, referring to Wittgenstein, there is no one language but many languages which define meanings of expressions through different uses that is made of them. 'Language' in the mathematics classroom is an incredibly complex notion. There is the language of mathematical symbols and formulas — but the language of the teacher in the classroom is not just based on mathematical symbols; more often than not it is a mixture of the everyday spoken language, didactical jargon and technical mathematical terms. Each of these 'languages' has its own conventions, and these conventions may not be compatible with each other. This is deemed as an important source of students' difficulties in understanding (e.g., Maier, 1986, 1992). Teachers use figurative speech to explain mathematical concepts. Not always successfully. They also use 'body language' like gestures (e.g., large hugging gestures for brackets or sets), noises of various kinds (like bangs), and other ways of capturing attention like highlighting, underlining etc. (Pimm, 1992). It would be interesting to know how these influence students' understanding.

Let us mention below some researches that have been done with respect to the role that various forms, means and styles of communication in the mathematics classroom play in enhancing students' understanding.

The Role of Communicative Activities in Understanding

It is commonly believed that communicative activities enhance understanding in students. Students seem to understand better if they work in groups, participate in discussions where they have to verbalize their understandings, where their understandings are confronted with other students' understandings and where, in defending their own points of view, they have to engage in validations and justifications that make them see better whether or not their understandings are consistent or 'make sense'. In psychology, the value of cooperation with peers (as opposed to asymmetric interactions with adults) was raised by Piaget, and developed by others (Piaget, 1958; Perret-Clermont, 1980). On the other hand, Vygotski and Luria stressed very much the inter-action of a child with adults and how appropriate instructional interventions can indeed enhance the development of the child's spontaneous concepts.

In mathematics education this contention is not taken for granted. There are research projects that test the assumption and confront it with the practice of teaching. Researchers probe the value of classroom discussions and debates (e.g., Pirie and Schwarzenberger, 1988; Bartolini-Bussi, 1990, 1992; Legrand, 1988; Krummheuer, 1991; Richards, 1991; Lampert, 1988), small group dis-cussions (Civil, 1992; Yackel, 1987; Curcio and Artzt, 1992) and other com-municative activities such as writing reports on solving a problem (Morgan, 1991, 1992) or writing journals in the mathematics classroom (Hoffman and Powell, 1989; Oaks and Rose, 1992; Borasi and Rose, 1989; Sterret, 1990; Connolly and Vilardi, 1989). This research brought disillusionment to many of the first hopes and expectations. It is now quite clear that neither discussion or writing will automatically lead to better understanding, that there are many kinds of discussion and writing and many kinds of using this writing of which some give better prognosis about improvement of understanding than others. Researchers now speak of categories such as 'mathematical discussion' (Pirie and Schwarzenberger, *ibidem*), and 'effective discussion' (Civil, *ibidem*; Bartolini-Bussi, 1990). One may write a journal entry as a 'participant' or as a 'spec-tator': one may be using language instrumentally or one may be reflecting, in writing, on the meaning and significance of one's activities (Britton *et al.*, 1975). One may be writing an autobiographical note in one's journal, or build up a narrative, or produce explanations, or just make notes (Oaks and Rose, *ibidem*). It is also stressed that writing journal entries about mathematics classes or problem-solving will not in itself enhance understanding; journals must become objects of comment and discussion — some kind of peer reviewing is proposed — the author must receive feedback on what he or she has written (Hoffman and Powell, *ibidem*).

Many researchers focus on communication as it normally happens in the classroom (and is not designed by a researcher) and reflect on the value for understanding of its different modes, means, and styles. Some seek the rea-sons why very often communication in the classroom fails and try to discover patterns or even rites of communication which in fact have only the appear-ance of communication while, in fact, no communication of ideas, no learning and no understanding (on the conceptual level at least), occurs at all. What happens in the traditional classroom is often a kind of 'routine questioning' in which the teacher expects the students to produce not so much some coherent solutions but only words associated with what the teacher is saying, these words making the teacher believe that the students have understood and the lesson can be continued. The well-known 'funnel pattern' consists in narrow-ing the questions so that the students can only answer what the teacher expects them to answer (Bauersfeld, 1983). The Socratic style questioning has similar effects; the outside observer has the impression that the student has understood; it may also be the teacher's illusion. (However, a kind of 'neo-Socratic method' has lately been developed by Loska (1992) that preserves the main idea of maieutic but leaves the students with a right to choose their own paths of reasoning and to make mistakes). There are other patterns of teacher–students verbal interaction that also give this illusion (e.g., Voigt, 1985; Steinbring, 1993). Atweh and Cooper (1992) describe how, in fact, students are able to avoid learning or understanding and resist teaching by engaging into the 'meaningless rituals' of classroom interactions.

Styles of Classroom Communication

There are different styles of classroom communication between the teacher and the student. One important distinction made of late is that between the so-called 'behaviouristic' and the 'constructivistic' styles of teaching. The first is authoritarian and leaves little room for the students' free and creative activity: the student is supposed to reproduce knowledge rather than construct it himself or herself. The teacher believes that he or she can 'transmit' knowledge by 'telling' the student what he or she has to know and how to understand. The constructivistic style is more symmetric in nature; the teacher will allow the students to develop their own understandings of a new problem situation and will negotiate meanings with the students rather than impose meanings on them. It is generally believed that the constructivistic style leads to better understanding and learning than the 'behaviouristic style' (Cestari, 1983; Perret-Clermont, 1990) but there is an on-going discussion on the actual possibility of maintaining the former style in the practice of everyday institutionalized teaching, and on the details of this style in teaching concrete subject matter. It is generally felt that some things in mathematics just have to be 'told' the students; there is no way of making the students reconstruct some more advanced concepts in mathematics. The discussions and negotiations of meaning can only be done on the meta-level, i.e., on the level of possible solutions, different approaches to a given mathematical question (Dorier, 1991).

What Understanding Is Not

Thus far, in our efforts to understand understanding we have been mainly investigating into the operation of identification: we were trying to say what understanding is. Now the time has come to use our abilities of discernment: we shall attempt to say what understanding is not.

It has already been mentioned in Chapter 1 that sometimes understanding is confused (or deliberately merged) with knowing, and argued that this is perhaps not a desirable thing to do in education. Unfortunately, institutionalized education is framed to develop students' knowledge rather than thinking.

This is a heritage of a long-standing tradition. Thinking, contemplation and understanding for their own sake have not been very highly valued by the modern 'enlightened' times that are concerned mainly with 'results' and 'progress of knowledge'. Any domain of human mental activity had to be organized in the way sciences were: science was the model. The ideal of Hegel's philosophy was to raise philosophy to the rank of science. Are the values of the post-modern era likely to reach our educational systems soon?

Understanding has also to be distinguished from invention or discovery. While any invention assumes understanding, the latter does not necessarily imply the former: there are many straightforward, routine acts of understanding by which we live, make sense of our environment, communicate with others about everyday matters. Only exceptional acts of understanding feel as real discoveries, and these are normally preceded by considerable intellectual effort. Of course, we would expect our students to experience such creative acts of understanding in their learning; otherwise it would be hard to say they learned anything genuinely new. This is probably what Piaget had in mind when he wrote,

> The basic principle of active methods will have to draw its inspiration from the history of science and may be expressed as follows: to understand is to discover, or to reconstruct by rediscovery, and such conditions must be complied with if in the future individuals are to be formed who are capable of production and creativity and not simply repetition. (Piaget, 1975b, p. 20)

Another thing that an act of understanding is not is the activity of reasoning and even less the chain of inferences that lead from the premises to the conclusion. But a reasoning taken as an accomplished whole can play the role of a basis of understanding. In fact, acts of understanding and reasonings can be seen as complementing each other in processes of understanding: this is a view that will be proposed in the next chapter.

There has been a view, held by the so-called 'neo-positivists', and more precisely by philosophers of science related to the deductive-nomological methodology of explanation, that understanding is nothing more than an ability to predict. According to this methodology, the *explanandum* (the sentence describing the phenomenon to be explained) is a logical consequence of the *explanans*, which is composed of two kinds of premises: 1. the class of individual true statements about the specific initial conditions; and, 2. the class of statements representing general laws (and thus also true) (Hempel and Oppenheim, 1948, pp. 567–79). The important thing, in this philosophy, was to explain the phenomena; an understanding of a phenomenon was achieved if the explanation of it allowed to predict its future occurrences:

> The [D–N] argument shows that, given the particular circumstances and laws in question, the occurrence of the phenomenon was to be

expected; and it is in this sense that the explanation enables us to understand why the phenomenon occurred. (*ibidem*)

This position was criticized even by methodologists of the same circle. For example Friedman (1988) argued that,

> Understanding and rational expectation are quite distinct notions. To have the grounds for rationally expecting some phenomenon is not the same as to understand it. I think that this contention is conclusively established by the well known examples of prediction via so-called 'indicator laws' — the barometer and the storm, Koplick spots and measles, etc. In these examples, one is able to predict some phenomenon on the basis of laws and initial conditions, but one has not enhanced one's understanding of why the phenomenon occurred. To the best of my knowledge, Hempel himself accepts these counter-examples, and, because of them, would concede today that the D–N model provides at best necessary conditions for the explanation of particular events. (Friedman, 1988, p. 190)

It is possible to be able to predict future events on the basis of a model which can reflect a complete misunderstanding of the underlying phenomena — such was the case of Ptolemy's astronomy, for example.

By saying that 'understanding is nothing but an ability to predict', we imply that what we mean by 'understanding' is a certain way of knowing. This is not the approach to understanding that is being proposed here. Not only do we discriminate between understanding and knowing, but we also refrain from assuming right from the beginning that understanding is some kind of 'good understanding'. We do not a priori evaluate understanding.

Among the many views on understanding, there is one which identifies an act of understanding with the retrieval of a 'frame' or 'script' from memory, sometimes called the 'computer metaphor approach' (Minsky, 1975; Schank and Abelson, 1977; Davis, 1984). In the domain of psychology of mathematical behaviour in school-children the concept of frame was used to explain some of the common mathematics students' errors. It was regarded as a useful language to think about understanding (or rather misunderstanding). Some researchers have further developed it to allow for an explanation of why a student retrieves a wrong frame in a particular situation (Malle, 1990).

There are several deceiving aspects of his approach. One is that it represents the functioning of the human mind as mechanical, automatical: a 'cue triggers the retrieval of a certain frame from memory' which is then set to function by an input of data. It also reduces the human mind to a logical system, and for a logical system it is not important what is being spoken about, only whether it is grammatically correct or true (in the sense of logical consequence). In particular, mathematics could find itself thus reduced to logic, which is certainly not a view that it would be worthwhile conveying to students. Moreover, in the computer metaphor approach, and cognitive science in general, it is assumed that thinking is always taking place in some language. This brings us to the well-known controversy about whether language and thought are separable or inseparable. Plato, in 'Sophist' wrote that 'thought and sentence is one and the same thing. Only the talk of the soul with itself — this is what we call thought'. Merleau-Ponty (1973) would say that thought cannot exist without the world, outside the sphere of language and communication: it would fall into unconsciousness the very moment it would come into being. But many philosophers contend that there is more to thought than what can be expressed in any language. Bergson said that 'the most living thought becomes frigid in the formula that expresses it. The word turns against the idea. The letter kills the spirit (1975, p. 141)'. There is the well-known testimony of Einstein (Penrose, 1990, p. 548ff). In discussing the matter Penrose says,

> I had noticed, on occasion, that if I had been concentrating hard for some while on mathematics and someone would engage me suddenly in conversation, then I would find myself almost unable to speak for several seconds. This is not to say that I do not sometimes think in words, it is just that I find words almost useless for *mathematical* thinking. Other kinds of thinking, perhaps such as *philosophizing*, seem to be much better suited to verbal expression. Perhaps this is why so many philosophers seem to be of opinion that language is essential for intelligent or conscious thought! (Penrose, 1990, p. 549)

Of course, one could deny the name of 'thought' to the mental experiences that are not expressed or expressible in a verbal form, but it is also possible to assume that such non-verbal things as dynamic diagrammatic representations of algebraic expressions that are being transformed or the consciousness of one's own actions are also thoughts. The consciousness of a mental activity is indispensable for a further more conceptual reflection and thematization of one's mental operations; isn't this the mechanism through which we come to understand and create mathematics? Can we provide a non-human cognitive system with such a consciousness and ability to reflect on its own activity? Can we say that such a system is capable not only of knowing certain things but also of understanding what it is doing?

These are very difficult questions, and the answers, if any, depend on what is meant by 'understanding' or 'knowing' as well as on what is meant by 'computer'. The fast developments of technology nowadays suggest that we be very careful in expressing opinions in these matters. It even may be that these questions are of a philosophical rather than scientific nature, and cannot be decided on the grounds of experiment. This is the message that, willingly or unwillingly, Penrose is conveying in his book on 'computers, minds, and the laws of physics'.

Chapter 3

Processes of Understanding

What is understanding? Has the word the same meaning for every-body? Does understanding the demonstration of a theorem consist in examining each of the syllogisms of which it is composed in succession, and being convinced that it is correct and conforms to the rules of the game? In the same way, does understanding a definition consist simply in recognizing that the meaning of all the terms employed is already known, and being convinced that it involves no contradiction? (Henri Poincaré, 1952).

In this chapter we shall concern ourselves with the process of understanding and the roles played in it of various reasonings, examples, previous knowledge and experience, figurative speech, and, last but not least, activity, practical and intellectual.

The Process of Understanding

Processes of understanding can be regarded as lattices of acts of understanding linked by reasonings. If A and B are acts of understanding, then we may admit that $A \leq B$ (A precedes B) if there has been a reasoning R, in some way induced or inspired by A, that led, on its turn, to the act of understanding B.

For example, let a certain process of understanding start with an identification of an object X as an object worthy of study. Several kinds of questions can arise: like: what is X?; or what is the use of X?; or what can one do with (about, for, etc) X? etc. Let A be the act of understanding based on some (guessed) answer to this question. What then follows is a search for some validation of this guess. The validation is based on a reasoning R. For example, if the question was: what is X? and the guess was: X is Z, then R may consist in proving that X is Z or in verifying whether X is Z. In this case, the result of R is an act of understanding B based on a thought that X is Z, or that X is certainly not Z, or that X is Z under the condition that C, etc. Thus the guess A leads to an understanding B about which there is already more conviction thanks to some reasoning R.

In one process of understanding the relation $\leq$ establishes a partial order.

The unity of a process of understanding is determined by the close relationship of the objects of understanding of the acts of which it is composed.

If, in one process of understanding, two acts A and B are not linked by a reasoning, there always is a third act C such that A and B are linked with C: either both A and B were obtained through reasonings inspired by C, or A and B inspired reasonings that led to C. Thus, acts of understanding and reasonings in one process of understanding constitute quite a dense network (in the ordinary sense of the words).

While, in one process of understanding, the objects of understanding are closely linked to each other, there can be a large variety of bases of understanding. One may even say that a process of understanding something consists of a series of transformations of some initial basis of understanding.

In the following section we try to clarify a little the differences between the various kinds of reasonings involved in a process of understanding.

Reasonings

Ajdukiewicz (1985) counts as reasoning all inference and deduction as well as 'processes of solving mental problems and questions carried out with the use of inference and/or deduction'. Simple reasonings (i.e., those that make use of only one process of inference or deduction) break up into 'spontaneous' reasonings and 'problem-directed' reasonings (*ibidem*, p. 224); the latter, in their turn can be divided into classes depending on the kind of problem they are directed by: proving (when the problem is 'to prove that A'), verifying (when the problem is 'to decide whether or not A') and explaining (when the problem is 'to complete' [a certain sentence], and a possible answer is not given in the wording of the problem; it usually starts with a 'why?').

> Ajdukiewicz understands inference as
> a thought process through which, on the basis of a more or less positive acceptance of premisses, we are led to an acceptance of a conclusion that remained so far unaccepted or accepted less positively by us, and we accept the conclusion to a degree that does not exceed the degree with which we accept the premisses. (Ajdukiewicz, 1985, p. 106)

Deduction is a process similar to inference with, however, a few important differences. First, in the process of inference, the most important thing is the 'acceptance' of something: the goal is to increase the certainty or diminish the doubt. Certainty claims are not so important in deduction. Deduction is more formal; it is explicit and it is based on explicitly admitted rules. Inference leads from accepted *premisses* to *conclusions* that, thereby, become more probable (even if this probability is only subjective). Deduction leads from (hypothetically) admitted *reasons* to *consequences*, that are implied by the reasons according to some well defined rules on the basis of some set of statements admitted as true.

Let us see, as an example, how deduction and inference are involved in a reasoning such as the *reductio ad absurdum*. Suppose that we have to prove to prove a statement p. What we do is the following: we hypothetically assume the statement ¬p and deduce from it a statement q. For the trick to work, q must be false. Our claim that q is false is a result of an inference: we infer that q is false from some accepted premises: definitions, proved theorems etc. Now our accepted premises are: q is false, the implication ¬p ⇒ q is true. From these we infer that ¬p is false (on the basis of the tautology: if q is false then the statement ¬p ⇒ q is true if and only if ¬p is false). This inference has increased our certainty that ¬p is false. This now becomes our accepted premise from which we infer (by the law of *tertium non datur* which we also accept) that p must be true.

The difference between inference and deduction is maybe best grasped in the opposition between the processes of proving and explaining. Ajdukiewicz (1974, p. 223) classifies proving as an inferential reasoning and explaining as a deductive reasoning.

> The foregoing remarks point to a close relationship between proving and explaining. Both when proving a theorem and when explaining a state of things we answer to one and the same 'why?' question. Hence it may be expected that the explanation procedure follows a course which resembles that of the procedure of proving, with the proviso that in the case of an explanation that which is to be explained is known in advance and does not require any substantiation, whereas in the case of proving what is to be proved is not yet known and the proof is to substantiate that.
>
> Let us consider an example to see that it is really so. Suppose a person knows that (a) any physical body which is generically lighter than water does not sink in water but floats on it, (b) ice is generically lighter than water. Now we present to that person the following syllogism:
>
> (a) Any physical body which is generically lighter than water floats on it.
> (b) Ice is generically lighter than water.
>   Hence:
> (c) Ice floats on water.
>
> This syllogism may be said both to be, for the person concerned, an explanation of the state of things described in the conclusion, and a proof of the conclusion. But it may be an explanation, for the person concerned, of the state of things described in (c) *only if* that person knew in advance that state of things to be true, i.e., only if he accepted the statement (c) even before deducing it from statements (a) and (b). On the other hand, this syllogism may be called a proof of statement (c), for the person concerned, only if that person came to accept the statement (c) only by inferring it from statements (a) and

(b), and did not know beforehand whether (c) is true. (Ajdukiewicz, 1974, pp. 442–3)

An explanation of a state of affairs X is therefore a solution of the problem that can be worded as 'why [X] ?'. The answer to this question has the form of '[X] because [Y]'. When I explain a certain fact by referring to some reason of the sentence that states this fact, then I do not at this point only infer this fact from this reason — this fact is known to me independently from this reason. However, I carry out a mental operation which is similar to the operation of inference; namely, in explaining [X] by [Y], I derive the sentence stating [X] from the sentence stating [Y], I perceive the relation of implication between the second and the first, but I do not use this relation to base my conviction about [X] on [Y], because I am convinced about [X] independently from [Y].

Thus, deduction does not serve as a basis for our more positive acceptance of the derived statement. In an explanation of a consequence X on the basis of a reason Y, Y implies X but X is not inferred from Y.

It is worthy of notice that what is explained is a certain *state of things* (a fact, a phenomenon), and what is derived is a statement. For example, in physics, the phenomenon of rain storm is being explained. The phenomenon need not be *inferred* from electrical laws; its existence and its normal course are well known by observation. The question is why it happens and why it happens as it happens.

In fact, an explanation of some state of affairs aims at founding its understanding on a different basis (more conceptual, usually). In the above example of rain storm, a first understanding is probably based on a visual and auditory representation of a rain storm. A second, after an explanation, can be based on a thought that a rain storm is caused by an accumulation of electrically charged clouds.

Proving aims at increasing the degree of firmness with which we accept something as a basis of our understanding.

An act of understanding does not belong to reasonings because neither of its elements contains inference or derivation. It can only be based on a result of a reasoning, taken as a whole, as one single synthesized argument.

Explanation and Understanding

The Role of Explanation in Understanding Mathematics

In distinguishing between proving and explaining, Ajdukiewicz says that what is proved is a statement, and what is explained is a state of things. Therefore, if we wish to speak about explanation in mathematics in Ajdukiewicz's style, we should make it clear what are, for us, these 'states of things' in mathematics. In empirical sciences, a 'state of things' is what is 'ascertained beyond all doubt', by observation, experiment. In mathematics, it can be an existing mathematical theory, and anything that is proved or admitted without proof within this theory.

The quest for an explanation in mathematics cannot be a quest for proof, but it may be an attempt to find a rationale of a choice of axioms, definitions, methods of construction of a theory. A rationale does not reduce to logical premisses. An explanation in mathematics can reach for historical, philosophical, pragmatic arguments. In explaining something in mathematics, we speak *about* mathematics: our discourse becomes more metamathematical than mathematical.

This is what the logical positivistic stand endeavoured to abolish: all informal discourse should be eliminated from mathematics; mathematicians should join efforts to completely formalize all branches of mathematics. Meaning should be reduced to the truth value: FALSE (0) or TRUE (1). In the practice of mathematical research (or any scientific research for that matter), this philosophical stand is difficult to maintain; it is overcome by the drive to find 'reasons' and 'causes' of things, facts, theorems.

> The most important of [the basic instruments of knowledge] is certainly the search for 'reasons', which justify the abstractions and generalizations. Logical positivism has tried from its origin to get rid of this factor and to reduce science to a simple description of phenomena. This was A. Comte's idea. But in reality, every scientific mind, while not always admitting it, asks questions like that. It has often been noted that excellent physicists, while vigorously professing a positivist credo in the prefaces to their writings, contradict this faith in the body of their work by pursuing a bona fide analysis of 'causes'. As one example of this invincible tendency to search for 'reasons', we might cite the evolution of the contemporary mathematical logic. Limiting itself to a purely descriptive language, algebraic logic had long adhered to a purely extensional perspective, hence the 'truth tables', which, in actuality, remain so far removed from any 'truth' that they have led to the truly scandalous paradoxical situation that $p \Rightarrow q$ can be true when there is no actual relation of truth between p and q.
>
> At present we are witnessing the birth of a movement whose aims are to exclude all relations that are not logically necessary as well as significant so that each implication is based on a reason (cf. Anderson and Benlap's logic of *entailment*). Mathematicians, ever since Cournot, have distinguished between demonstrations which simply verify a theorem and those which, in addition, provide the reasons. (Piaget and Garcia, 1989, pp. 271–2)

Indeed, understanding a theorem on the basis of acceptance of the logical soundness of its proof is not the same as its understanding both on the basis of the proof and its 'reasons'. For example, what kind of understanding of the statement that √2 is an irrational number can be derived from its proof by *reductio ad absurdum*? The proof is based on the definition of the irrational number as a number that cannot be represented by a ratio of two integers, and on the property of unique factorization of integers. This does not explain why the fact is so significant. But, if we know how it is related to the discovery of incommensurable line segments by the Pythagoreans, then we can better understand what role it has played in the development of mathematics. Moreover, the proof by itself does not show how incommensurability is related to irrationality; neither does it tell us why the decimal expansion of √2 should be infinite and non-periodical, which is another characterization of irrational numbers. Answers to such questions belong to the explanation of the theorem and go beyond just the proof of it.

Proofs may call for an explanation, as well. Such an explanation can highlight the so called 'idea', or 'this indefinable something that makes the unity of the proof' (Poincaré, 1970, pp. 29–34).

Explanation of an abstract mathematical theory may consist in a construction of its model, in which the variables, rules and axioms of the theory are interpreted and acquire meaning. The model becomes a certain 'reality', ruled by its own 'laws'. In explaining a theory, we deduce its rules, axioms, definitions, and theorems from the 'laws' of the model.

Scientific and Didactic Explanations

The aim of an explanation is to found the understanding on a new basis. Explanations could be classified along the kinds of requirements that are put on this new basis. Explanations which aim at a more conceptual basis of understanding are mostly met in science and this is why we may call them 'scientific'. Explanations which aim at a more familiar basis of understanding (an image or just some previous knowledge and experience) are frequent in teaching, so let us call them 'didactic'.

Scientific explanation is thus opposed to didactic explanation. Far from reducing new knowledge to familiar knowledge, it very often aims at showing how non-obvious certain unquestioned things are. For example, in teaching, the continuity (i.e., the completeness) of the ordered set of real numbers is sometimes explained by reference to the intuitive feeling of 'continuity in the smallest parts' of the straight line, which is used to represent this set. Richard Dedekind (1963) was not very happy with this kind of explanation.

> The way in which the irrational numbers are usually introduced is based directly upon the conception of extensive magnitudes — which itself is nowhere carefully defined — and explains numbers as the result of measuring such a magnitude by another of the same kind. [Dedekind's note: The apparent advantage of the generality of this

definition of number disappears as soon as we consider complex numbers. According to my view, on the other hand, the notion of ratio between two numbers of the same kind can be clearly developed only after the introduction of irrational numbers]. Instead of this I demand that arithmetic shall be developed out of itself. . . . Just as negative and fractional rational numbers are formed by a new creation, and as the laws of operating with these numbers must and can be reduced to the laws of operating with positive integers, so we must endeavor completely to define irrational numbers by means of the rational numbers alone. . . . By vague remarks upon the unbroken connection in the smallest parts obviously nothing is gained; the problem is to indicate a precise characteristic of continuity that can serve as a basis for valid deductions (Dedekind, 1963).

The definition of continuity of real numbers in terms of cuts, proposed by Dedekind, is by no means something 'familiar'. The most surprising thing is the very need to formulate it. For, at first sight, it seems to state an obvious fact. An understanding of this need comes together with an awareness of the non-obviousness of continuity: an awareness of the existence of number domains which are not complete, and of the essentiality of assumptions about the completeness of domain in theorems so intuitively clear as the theorem stating that increasing and bounded sequences are convergent. Thus, in this case, understanding demands not so much a reduction to a more familiar knowledge, as a derivation of a more elaborate knowledge.

Students' Own Mathematical Explanations; an Example

Didactic explanations are used not only by teachers; they can also be used by students themselves. Also the learner can seek explanations that would make the basis of his or her understanding more familiar. The example that follows evokes such a situation. It also shows how proofs and explanations are interwoven in a process of understanding.

Example: **the recurring decimals**

A group of 17-year-old humanities students were shown, on examples, how to convert periodic decimal expansions of numbers into ordinary fractions (Sierpinska, 1987).

$$x = 0.1234123412341234 \ldots$$

Multiply both sides by 10000:
$$10000x = 1234.123412341234 \ldots$$

Subtract the first equality from the second:
$$9999x = 1234$$

Divide by 9999:
$$x = 1234/9999$$

The students were accepting the argument for expansions like the one above (0.989898 . . ., 0.121121 . . ., etc.) but refused to accept that 0.999 . . . = 1 even though it was obtained in an analogous way.

At first the students refused both the reasoning and the conclusion, but later, their attitudes started to differentiate. One student, Ewa, began to accept the proof as mathematically valid, and the conclusion as mathematically correct, but refused to accept it as true 'in reality'.

> Ewa: Arithmetically or algebraically, this is OK, but in reality . . . This will be close to one but it will not be equal one. There will be such a tiny difference, very tiny, but a difference all the same . . . It's like that asymptote to a hyperbola: they never meet . . . The difference gets smaller and smaller, but it never becomes null . . . It reminds me of the upper and lower bounds we were doing last year, remember?

In justifying her opinion Ewa relies on an image of a hyperbola and on reference to an analogy: hyperbola is to its asymptote as 0.9999 . . . is to one. Ewa first identifies a similarity between the relation of the hyperbola to its asymptote and the relation of the number 0.999 . . . to the number 1. The similarity is based on the common feature of 'approaching something' (Ewa understands the number 0.999 . . . as being constructed and not as already constructed: rather as a sequence than as its limit). Then Ewa extends the similarity onto other features of the behaviour of the hyperbola with respect to its asymptote: they never meet. From this she deduces that also the number 0.999 . . . cannot meet the number 1. This is her explanation of what she accepts as a fact: 0.999 . . . ≠ 1.

The only student in this group who finally accepted the equality 0.999 . . . = 1 was Tom. Here is the moment when he changes his mind:

> Tom: Because, no matter how many nines we have here, it will never be equal one.
>
> Teacher: You accepted the argument in case of other numbers. Why not here?
>
> Tom: I don't trust these mathematical proofs. They are just tricks.

There is hesitation in his voice, already. He attempts some modification of the result so that it will be acceptable.

> Tom: Maybe we can say that this zero nine nine is a number the closest to one? Because there is no number closer to one than that. . . . This cannot be equal one unless . . . unless . . . unless we assume that this goes to the very infinity . . . Then it can equal one . . . Because these differences get smaller and smaller, without limit.

Several phases can be distinguished in this short process of understanding:

1   the rejection of the equality $0.999\ldots = 1$ is temporarily suspended and the equality becomes subject to verification;
2   proof of the equality:
    (a)   an act of understanding of the equality based on the identification of a crucial assumption: the number of nines is infinite;
    (b)   inference: 'then it can equal one'
3   acceptance of the equality $0.999\ldots = 1$
4   explanation:
    (a)   act of understanding based on an identification of the main reason: 'Because these differences get smaller and smaller etc.'

(Here Tom stops and the explanation remains incomplete: the step of derivation is not made.)

Instead of pursuing this course of explanation (for example, by assuming the difference $e = 1 - 0.999\ldots$ and showing that, because $0.999\ldots > 0.9$ implies $e < 0.1$, etc. e must be a positive real number smaller than any positive real number, which yields $e = 0$ in the standard analysis) Tom reaches for analogies and metaphors to convince his peers. This decision can be explained either by his explicit mistrust in 'mathematical proofs' or by the constraints of the social situation. Namely, by accepting the equality, Tom found himself in opposition to the rest of the group. Now, what these students need is not an explanation (because they do not believe in the equality) but a proof. So it is a proof that Tom will be looking for. Tom's strategy seems to be the following: Ewa refuted the equality on the basis of an analogy with the hyperbola approaching its asymptote: this was her explanation of the inequality in which she believes. Tom sets to prove that this explanation is not valid because, in fact, the hyperbola ultimately, 'in the end' meets the asymptote. He says: 'If two lines are not parallel then they must intersect. Even if the deviation is minimal, just as here, these lines must intersect somewhere . . . Imagine two people running on these lines . . .'. [End of example]

Examples of Teachers' Didactical Explanations

In the following I discuss several types of explanation: explanations with the help of an example, explanations with the help of a model, with the help of a visualization, and other means. An example of a lesson in which the teacher uses various means of didactic explanations is given in the third subsection.

Didactical Explanation of a Definition or Theorem With the Help of an Example
This kind of didactical explanation can be regarded as an element of an explanation of a theory with the help of a model. In the elementary linear algebra,

for example, theorems formulated generally for arbitrary vector spaces over arbitrary fields, are explained by taking a space R^n for some concrete n, say n = 2 or 3. Sometimes a geometrical model of R^n (a cartesian plane or space) is referred to. Then the theorem is not proved to hold in the model but either its thesis is shown to hold in some concrete case, or the theorem is applied in a concrete case.

Although such a procedure is worthless as a proof, it has some value as an explanation (after all students have no reason to disbelieve the author of the textbook or the teacher, so they do not need a proof to convince themselves of the veracity of the theorem). One aim of such an explanation is to analyze the theorem: to see what values can be assigned to the various variables in its statement, what the thesis means in a concrete case, briefly — to see what the theorem is about. In the case of theorems as complicated as, for example, the Jordan Canonical Form theorem, it is hard to imagine how their mere formulation can be understood without first trying to see how they work in a concrete situation.

Didactical Explanation of a Theory With the Help of a Model

Let us discuss this kind of explanation with the example of the notion of integer number.

Example: **explanations of integer numbers**

Ever since the arithmetic of integers has been introduced into teaching at the elementary level, mathematics educators have had to cope with students' difficulties. Perceiving the source of these difficulties in the abstract and formal character of the structure $(Z, +, \bullet)$, educators have proposed several models (number line models, annihilation models involving, for example, positive and negative quasi-electrical charges, the model of arrows in a two dimensional space). In these models negative numbers and operations on them were interpreted in terms of more concrete manipulations of objects. It was expected that through the use of such models students will have less trouble in the correct application of rules of operations on integers (Freudenthal, 1983, pp. 432–60).

It was clear that an explanation of these rules through their derivation from the axioms and the general idea that we want to have a set of numbers closed not only under addition but also subtraction and that we want this set to be an extension of natural numbers that would preserve all the properties of operations in this smaller set (Freudenthal, 1973), is out of the question with respect to 12–13-year-old children. Such an understanding of integers is possible only when one possesses the concepts of number, variable and group and is capable of thinking of whole sets of numbers as algebraic structures.

Thus, what can be done is to speak about concrete negative numbers, just as, in fact, one speaks about concrete natural numbers, and assign some meaning to them just as one assigns meaning to natural numbers in elementary school (measure of an amount of things, codes of things, positions of things, adding, taking away . . .). The problem is, however, that these meanings of numbers and operations cannot be preserved when extending the set of numbers to contain the negative numbers as well. Adding in the set of integers does not always result in augmenting the amount, and subtracting does not mean that one ends up with something less. It is also not at all clear why, by multiplying two negatives one should get something positive. Authors of the models try to cope with these difficulties, either by proposing to introduce whole numbers through a model that can be further extended to a model of integers in a way that does not reinforce the idea that adding means augmenting, for example (the number line model, e.g., Chilvers, 1985), or by inventing such models of integers that allow to preserve the old meanings of addition and subtraction as augmenting and diminishing (the annihilation model, e.g., Battista, 1983).

Each of these models has features that explain nicely an aspect of integer numbers (not all aspects). For example, the annihilation model implicitly introduces the additive group of integers as the quotient structure obtained from the semi-group of natural numbers by dividing it by the equivalence relation: $(a,b) \sim (c,d) \Leftrightarrow a + d = b + c$. The equivalence class of, say, the pair $(1, 2)$ can be denoted by -1, the equivalence class of the pair $(2, 1)$ is denoted by 1, and 1 and -1 are opposites because they add up to the equivalence class of $(3, 3)$ which is the neutral element of the group, denoted by 0. In teaching, this idea is translated into an enactive representation. Equivalence classes are represented by sets of pairs of counters of two colours, or pairs of counters with plus or minus signs on them. Counters of different colours or different signs annihilate each other. Thus, children are taught to identify pairs such as, for example:

> (2 red, 0 yellow) ~ (3 red, 1 yellow) ~ (4 red, 2 yellow) ~ (5 red, 3 yellow) &c.

or:

> (0 red, 2 yellow) ~ (1 red, 3 yellow) ~ (2 red, 4 yellow) ~ (3 red, 5 yellow) &c.

Adding equal numbers of counters of different colours does not change anything ([n,n] is the neutral element), so such pairs can be used to obtain sums and differences of the newly obtained integer numbers. In this way, rules for adding and subtracting integers are learned.

The annihilation models are particularly appealing for a mathematician because they present a certain general procedure for extending a domain of numbers by taking a quotient structure. How much, however, of this idea is conveyed through manipulating counters to a 13-year-old child, is hard to know. Certainly there is no awareness of an algebraic structure being thus built. The understanding is based on some kind of procedural or enactive representation. But this can be a good start, a foundation upon which a teacher can build a more conceptual understanding later on.

A certain conceptual maturity (which, according to Vygotski, is attained only in adolescence) is necessary to grasp the rules of operations on integers as a certain theoretical, mathematical necessity. In this respect it is interesting to read the confessions of Stendhal (*La vie de Henri Brulard*) about the difficult process of understanding the rule that 'minus times minus is plus' (Hefendehl-Hebeker, 1991).

One of the obstacles in the historical development of the concept of negative numbers was found to be 'an attachment to a concrete viewpoint, that is, an attempt . . . to assign to numbers and to operations on them a "concrete sense"' (*ibidem*; see also Pycior, 1984; Chevallard, 1985b). One may wonder, therefore, whether it is not better to confine ourselves in teaching negative numbers to 12–13-year-olds to reading the thermometer scale, and leave the study of operations to a time when the students are able to make it without assigning a 'concrete sense' to everything they encounter. Of course, one can train the students to perform operations on integer numbers without answering their questions about why they are defined as they are defined (after all, in history, negative numbers were used in mathematical calculations for a long time before they could be theoretically founded and explained). Introducing integers with the help of the number line model or the annihilation model does not answer the question why the rules for operations are defined as they are defined. The only advantage is that the model provides the learner with some concrete images linked with operations (moving to the right by n, annihilating the charge +n with the charge −n) which may consolidate the long-term memory of these rules.

The question is, however, why should we train the students in integer operations at all? What for? As it is, for the time being, 12–13-year-old students are both presented with a model (most often the number line model) and are trained in computation on integers. The most amazing thing is that sometimes, the model — whose aim is only to explain, to give meaning to the mathematical notions being the proper objects of teaching — becomes an object of teaching in itself and its knowledge is assessed on tests. Moreover, new symbolisms grow over the model, which require their own rules to handle them. For example, sometimes integers (concrete integers) are written with signs attached to them in front in superscript: $^+2$, $^-7$. Sequences of additions and subtractions on integers become speckled with crosses and lines up and down. This is exactly a case of a 'didactic transposition' (Chevallard, 1985a) that has gone too far: an alienation of an instrument of didactic explanation. These 'signed numbers' can be confusing, to say the least. Moreover, this symbolism may create an obstacle when learning algebra, where a letter does not necessarily denote a positive number, or a negative number. It is a variable that can assume any value. The minus sign in front of a letter just means that its sign has to be changed: '−' stands, in fact, for the unary operation of change of sign (like the +/− key in calculators). The operation of subtraction becomes obsolete in algebra: we are always adding, except that sometimes we are adding the opposite. [End of example]

Examples of Didactical Explanations During a Lesson on the Limit of a Numerical Sequence

The lesson took place in a class of 17-year-old humanities students in Warsaw. The theme of the lesson was: 'The limit of an infinite sequence' (Sierpinska, 1991).

Example: **explanations of the definition of the limit of a sequence**

In a first phase of the lesson the teacher introduces the notion of 'epsilon neighbourhood of a number'. In explaining this notion the teacher uses two schemas of a didactical explanation:

1   the new notion is derived as a particular case of an already known notion;
2   the definition of the new notion is derived from its model (in this case: its geometrical model).

The teacher starts with an informal definition:

T: We start with the notion of the epsilon neighbourhood of some number, say, number g. An epsilon neighbourhood of a number will be the set of all real numbers that are contained in an interval around this number . . ., an interval the length of which, on both sides, equals exactly this epsilon.

Further the teacher reminds the students the notion of epsilon neighbourhood of a point by referring to 'drawing' graphical representations of such neighbourhoods:

T: Why 'epsilon'? Imagine drawing neighbourhoods . . . We used to speak about plane neighbourhoods, in geometry . . . We spoke about circular neighbourhoods. We drew circular neighbourhoods of points, that is, circles with some radiuses and centres in points whose neighbourhoods we were considering.

The teacher aims at representing the notion of epsilon neighbourhood of number as a special case of the notion of a circular neighbourhood of a point in the cartesian plane. For this, however, one must conceive of straight line as being, in a sense, a special case of the plane, which is possible if both the line and the plane are considered to be special cases of the general notion of an n-dimensional cartesian space. So, what is needed first, is a generalization: the notion of n-dimensional space. This generalization is not done by the teacher in an explicit way: she just calls the number line 'a one-dimensional space', in a kind of metaphorical way:

T: What does such a neighbourhood reduce to in a one-dimensional space? [*T draws a straight line on the board*]. This is the number g.

[*T marks the point g on the line*]. We are considering the neighbourhood with radius epsilon of this point. What does a whole circle reduce to if the universe of my considerations is only this one-dimensional space, this number line, and not the whole plane, hm?

S: [It reduces] to a line segment.

T: To an open line segment, yes.

The thought of the student who answered went into a slightly different direction than the teacher intended: he generalizes to euclidean spaces and not to cartesian spaces, and therefore, what he obtains is a line segment, and not an interval. So now the teacher has to draw the student's attention to numbers, and to suggest that he conceives of the line as a number line:

T: OK And in terms of numbers, such a line segment illustrates . . .?

S: A set.

T: What set? What is the name of such a set?

S: A bounded sequence.

T: Pardon me? [*impatiently*] Come on, now, what does such an open line segment illustrate on the number line?

S: An interval.

T: [*with relief*] An interval, of course! If the radius was epsilon, and I drew the circle from the point that illustrates the number g here, what are the numbers that are there, on the borders of this interval? What values? Can this be established or not?

S: Plus.

T: Here . . . epsilon is positive, because it expresses the length of the radius, so it is clear that it must be positive.

S: $g + \varepsilon$

T: $g + \varepsilon$. And here?

S: $g - \varepsilon$

T: $g - \varepsilon$. Perfect. And exactly such an interval will be called the epsilon neighbourhood of the number g.

It can be seen from the above episode that what the students have to understand primarily in a mathematics classroom is their teacher's intentions.

In the next phase of the lesson the teacher dictates a definition of the limit of a sequence:

T: A number g is called the limit of an infinite numerical sequence if and only if for any positive number epsilon . . . there is a real number k such that all terms of the sequence with indices greater than k . . . belong to the epsilon neighbourhood of the number g.

The students are asked to write this definition 'in terms of quantifiers'. Not without difficulty, a formal definition eventually appears on the board.

$$\lim_{n \to \infty} a = g \Leftrightarrow \forall \varepsilon > 0 \; \exists k \in R \; \forall \; n > k \; |a - g| < \varepsilon$$

The teacher stresses the role of each element of the definition in turn and formulates several informal definitions of the limit:

> To be in the epsilon neighbourhood means to be a number such that its distance from the number g is less than ε.... Here is what it means: starting from an index that is already greater than k, all terms of the sequence will fit into the epsilon neighbourhood of the number g . . . This means that they will be so close to the number g that their distance from this number will be less than the given epsilon. . . . Notice that the definition starts with the words: for every epsilon. This means that epsilon can be chosen as small as we please . . . No matter how small the neighbourhood of the number g is, it will contain a lot . . . an infinite number of terms of the sequence . . . Because k may turn out to be enormous. But even such a k will cut off only the first terms of the sequence. Even if this is a million of terms, those that have to squeeze into the neighbourhood constitute a majority, there is an infinity of them . . . starting from a certain place all terms of the sequence will squeeze into this neighbourhood.

The notion of limit is also visualized with the help of a certain standard graphical representation (Figure 6). This visualization consists in drawing a two-coordinate system, some ten isolated points arranged as if on the curve $y = 1 + 1/x$, $x > 0$. This visualization is not a result of plotting a graph of a sequence the formula of which would be given beforehand.

The teacher compares thus obtained representation to 'a hyperbola that converges to its asymptote', and shows why 1 can be regarded as the limit of the thus represented sequence:

> T: Does this term fit into this chosen neighbourhood? No. This one? Neither. This one? No, but never mind.
>   The 15th term will well fit into the neighbourhood. Say, I establish k equal 14 and starting from the 15th term . . . so only 14 terms did not fit into the neighbourhood. Someone might say, well, this is a big neighbourhood, so one can see it from the last desk, and this is supposed to work for every epsilon. So let us take a smaller epsilon, as small as we please.
> S: And yet there will be an infinite . . .
> T: And yet there will be an infinite number of terms in this neighbourhood. All of them — starting from a certain point.

In the last phase of the lesson the teacher shows, by examples, how to prove, by definition, that a given sequence has a given limit. She also gives a kind of recipe how to do such a proof.

Figure 5:   A visual representation of a convergent sequence

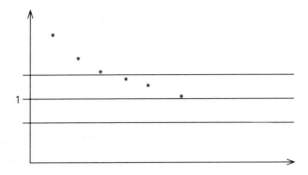

The examples were:

(1) $a_n = 1/n$ $g = 0$
(2) $a_n = (2n - 1)/n$ $g = 2$
(3) $a_n = (n^2 + 1)/3n^2$ $g = 1/3$

The first problem is solved by the teacher with very weak participation from the students. This solution is regarded as a model for solving this kind of problems. The schema of solution is explained by the teacher:

> You write in problem 2 that you have to check the truth of the statement . . . only for a_n you substitute not 1/n anymore but this expression, and for g not zero but 2. And then, under the modulus, please reduce to the common denominator, and transform the inequality in such a way that it determines the n. And then it will be very easy for you to check whether the statement is true. Now, please, do your calculations. [*Silence. T walks around*] . . .
>
> I repeat it once more. When you check the truth of this statement, then the equivalent fact that the given number is the limit of the sequence, is also true. So you substitute the concrete a_n and g and transform the inequality so that it determines the n. And then, it will be very easy to evaluate the logical value of the statement. It is very similar to what we have just done. Jack, work, stop talking.

Roughly speaking, there were three kinds of explanations of the notion of limit during the lesson. In each kind, the reasons were formulated in a certain model: the model of natural language, the model of geometrical representations, the model of an action (of proving that a given sequence has a given limit). The derivation consisted either in a formalization (formalization of a definition of limit dictated in plain words), or in an interpretation of the formal definition in the language of the model. The reasons of the formal definition thus appeared to be either the informal definition using plain words but essentially the same as the formal one, or definitions using some more homely expressions and vivid metaphors (like 'squeezing' of the terms of sequence into a neighbourhood: this gives the idea that the epsilon is small), or the fact that converging sequences behave like hyperbolas that come closer and closer to their asymptotes, or the seemingly sensible activity of transforming the formal definition by plugging in concrete values of certain variables and solving (for k) an inequality with absolute value. These 'reasons' were meant by the teacher to become solid bases of understanding of the formal definition of limit in the minds of the students.

Now, even if the students have adopted as their own such bases of understanding of the notion of limit (and the students' erroneous answers and silences don't leave much hope even for that) the use of these bases for further understanding of mathematical analysis is doubtful. At that point the students have not as yet identified convergent sequences as a special class of sequences among other sequences — and as an object worthy of study — because no sequences other than convergent were considered during the lesson. Also, the significance of the conditions of the definition was not founded on examples of sequences for which the non-satisfaction of one of the conditions leads to the statement of the non-convergence of the sequence. On the other hand, the non-essentiality of the feature of the visual representation which presented a sequence converging 'uniformly', and from only one side of the limit, was not raised. Neither of the explanations attacks the common convictions or representations that students may have with respect to the idea of a magnitude approaching some value with time.

The heaviest reproach is, however, that the teacher's explanations explained nothing because explanations explain states of affairs and, for the students, the definition of limit has certainly not yet become a state of affairs. Not only they are not convinced about it, but they don't even know what it is all about. [End of example]

The Role of Example and the Medium in Which It Is Presented for Understanding

Examples play a role in explanation: if what is to be explained is a general statement, an example obtained by a specification of variables may be used as a reason from which the statement is derived by induction. Thus an example may become a basis for understanding this general statement.

It is a pedagogical adage that 'we learn by examples'. Pedagogues, of course, think of paradigmatic examples in this case. They think of instances that can best explain a rule or a method, or a concept.

The learner is also looking for such paradigmatic examples as he or she is learning something new. The problem is, however, that before you have a grasp of the whole domain of knowledge you are learning, you are unable

Figure 6:   Graphical representation of an iteration of a linear function

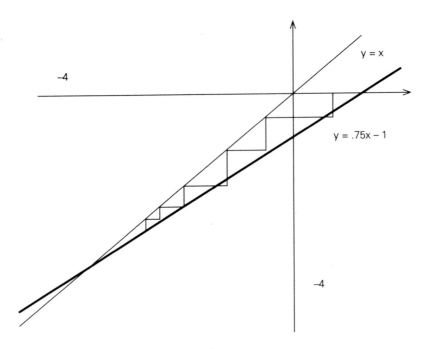

to tell a paradigmatic example from a non-paradigmatic one. So you make mistakes, wrong choices, wrong generalizations (because, of course, you generalize from your examples). Moreover, as the example is normally represented in some medium (enactive, iconic or symbolic), you may mistake the features of the representation for the features of the notion thus exemplified.

Below are some drastic examples of such situations in a couple of 16-year-old students' processes of understanding the notions of iteration of function and attractive fixed point. Disregarding all definitions, the students based their understanding on those of the first examples that they have found most strikingly explanatory (Sierpinska, 1989).

Example: **iteration of functions and the fixed point**

The fixed point of a mapping was defined by the teacher as a point that does not change under the mapping. Examples of the fixed points of an axial symmetry, homothety, a linear function (given by a formula) were given. But then a graphical representation (Figure 7) of the sequence of iteration of an R to R function was shown (dynamically, on a computer screen) and it was said that the x-coordinate of the intersection point of the graph of the function with the auxiliary line y = x represents the fixed point of the function. Some students abbreviated this definition to: 'the intersection point is the fixed point'.

The last example used by the teacher (and investigator) in the introductory session was the following:

Figure 7: *Iteration of a piecewise linear function*

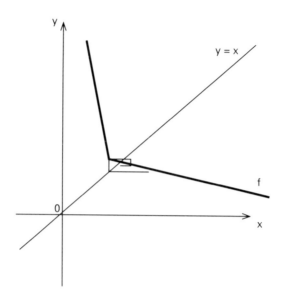

$$f(x) = \begin{cases} -5\,x + 8 \text{ for } x < 9/7 \\ -1/3\,x + 2 \text{ for } x \geq 9/7 \end{cases}$$

The graphic representations of the iterations of this function (Figure 7) with various initial points were dynamically represented on the computer screen.

When the teacher was introducing this example, one student exclaimed: 'No, here, there are two functions!'. This elicited explanations on the part of the teacher that a function need not be given by a single formula in the whole domain etc. This exclamation is, again, a symptom of understanding [the notion of function, in this case] on the basis of examples rather than definitions.

Further, iteration sequences (i.e., x, $f(x)$, $ff(x)$, $fff(x)$ etc.) of the function, starting with x = 1, x = 0.8, and x = 1.2 were studied both in the numerical and graphical settings. The problem given to the students to solve immediately after the introductory session was to find functions with a periodic iteration sequence 2, 3, 2, 3, 2, ... having attractive fixed points in the interval (2,3). As one possible solution was a piecewise linear function, one student was led to believe that the notion of iteration of function is valid only for piecewise linear functions like the one in the above example. He also believed for a moment that the fixed point is the articulation point of the two linear parts. It was easy to make him change his mind because the student was intelligent; the fact that he did think so, shows nevertheless that understanding on the basis of examples is not just the domain of the slow or less able students.

For all five students whose understanding was closely studied in the experiment, at the beginning, iteration of a function was just an activity of drawing little line segments between the graph of the function and the auxiliary line y = x. They did not know where to start from and were unable to reproduce the teacher's actions exactly because they hadn't paid attention to the relation between the iteration sequences and this activity of representing them graphically. All they attended to was the image. They would explain to each other: 'You have an attractive point [they would omit 'fixed'] if you get such a spiral little line, or such stairs'.

This visual representation persisted for a long time in students' understanding of iteration, even though their understanding was becoming more and more analytical. Iteration was understood by most of them as a kind of transformation of a point of the graph of the function, so:

$(x, f(x))$ is transformed onto $(f(x), ff(x))$ which is transformed onto $(ff(x), fff(x))$, etc.

Some students had not even identified the notion of fixed point as an object *per se*, at least at the beginning. They would speak of 'attractive' and 'repellent' points. Each student passed through the period of conceiving of the fixed point as the point of intersection of graphs of f and y = x. And again, this visual representation would be retained in their already analytic concepts of fixed point. For example, two students kept the name of fixed point for the intersection, and the argument x such that $f(x) = x$ was named 'the x-coordinate of the fixed point'. Even these students had trouble in isolating the notion of fixed point from the context of iterations. They would say, at some moment, that the fixed point is a point for which the sequence of iteration is constant. [End of example]

It seems then that 'learning by examples' is a property of our minds that has little in common with the pedagogical expectations expressed in the adage. An example is always embedded in a rich situation that contains more elements, data, information than just those directly related to the object exemplified. The teacher cannot be sure that, from this sea, the students will fish only the bits strictly relevant for the formation of the concept. It is hard, therefore, to understand the teacher's frustration, when, after having prepared the best of examples, he or she finds that the students are still able to commit the most unbelievable mistakes and errors. The method of paradigmatic examples is not really a method of teaching. Rather, it is a way in which concepts are being formed: the examples cannot be transmitted from the teacher's mind to the learner's mind. The latter must construct or reconstruct examples that can be regarded as paradigmatic in some more objective sense. The teacher can only help the learner by organizing situations against which the consecutive tentative forms of these examples can be tested, in which they can be revealed, and in which a change can be discussed and negotiated, if necessary.

Examples are, in understanding abstract concepts, the indispensable prop and the necessary obstacle. It is on the basis of examples that we make our first guesses. When we start to probe our guesses, the fundamental role is slowly taken over by the definitions.

Figures of Speech in Understanding

We may start from the principle that we all take a natural pleasure in learning easily; so since words stand for things, those words are most pleasing that give us fresh knowledge. Now, strange words leave us in the dark; and current words [with the things they stand for] we know already. Accordingly, it is metaphor that is in the highest degree instructive and pleasing. (Aristotle, 1932, p. 206)

Figures of Speech for Understanding and Figures of Speech for Explaining

Books and articles that praise the role of figurative (and, in particular, metaphorical) language in cognition are usually full of polemics with the opponents of figurative speech in scientific communication. For example, Lakoff and Johnson (1980), authors of the popular book *Metaphors we live by*, start by quoting Thomas Hobbes the nominalist, for whom metaphors were like *ignes fatui*, always ready to mislead the traveller at night, and John Locke who said that metaphors serve 'any design but that of naked truth'.

In fact there is no contradiction between the proponents and the opponents of the metaphor. The two parties are only considering two different uses of metaphor.

One is the spontaneous use of metaphor in a problem situation, where something new (a new concept, a new relationship, a new method, a so far unnoticed aspect) is being identified and no language is available yet to speak about it. There is a search for words, names, comparisons in the intention to understand — to ground the emerging 'object' in something. The knowledge about the newly identified something is not ready yet. A metaphor always highlights an aspect of a situation, and thus helps to identify something *as* something. We observe this creative role of metaphor in the making of mathematical objects both by students and mathematicians. One of the mathematicians interviewed by Anna Sfard (1994) said: 'To understand a new concept I must create a metaphor. A personification. Or a spatial metaphor. Or a metaphor of structure. . . . There is, first and foremost, an element of personification in mathematical concepts. . . . For example, yesterday, I thought about some coordinates. I told myself: 'this coordinate moves here and . . . it commands this one to do this and that' (Sfard, 1994).

Mathematical terms and expressions are indeed sometimes very powerful metaphors. We tend to forget about their metaphorical origin and impact on our understanding, as they already belong to the accepted lexicon. Pimm (1988) draws our attention to this phenomenon:

To most people, the statement 'the complex plane is a plane' would be a commonplace one . . . Yet this metaphoric naming and the above identification which underlies it has certain mathematical effects, as can be seen by suggesting that 'the complex line' is an alternative expression for the same set which stresses certain different features and ignores others. Referring to C as 'the complex plane' highlights the two-dimensional (ordered pair) representation of complex numbers $a + ib$ and encourages an approach to complex analysis by means of two dimensional real analysis via 'real and imaginary parts'. The plane metaphor also encourages the seeing 'a complex number as a vector' . . . which offers an effective image for complex addition and subtraction, but one less so for multiplication and division. (Pimm, 1988)

The other use of metaphor is concerned with presentation or explanation of a body of knowledge already in existence.

Simplifying things a little bit, one may say that, in the first case, the metaphor serves *understanding*, and, in the second, that it serves *explanation*. While explaining with the help of a metaphor may improve the understanding of the person who explains (because of the above mentioned reasons), it need not induce the intended understanding in the person to whom something is being explained. This person may focus attention on the irrelevant parts of the image provided by the metaphor or wish to see complete 'isomorphism' between the object and the metaphorical image and thus miss the point. (As, for example, when taking too much to heart the metaphor of 'complex plane', one might forget that complex numbers are primarily a field, and an algebraically closed one).

Locke was very much against the use of figures of speech in communication. He would say that they serve the purpose of covering the ignorance of the speaker and confounding listeners rather than that of clarifying matters. Leibniz had a more balanced view in this respect:

Philalethes: The way to prevent such confusion [caused by the polysemy of words] is to 'apply steadily the same name' to a certain collection of simple ideas 'united in a determinate number and order . . . But this neither accommodating men's ease or vanity, or serving any design but that of naked truth, which is not always the thing aimed at, such exactness, is rather to be wished, than hoped for . . . the loose application of names, to undetermined, variable, and [in blind thoughts — G.W. Leibniz] almost no ideas, serves both to cover our ignorance, as well as to perplex and confound others which counts as real learnedness and as a mark of superiority in knowledge.

Theophilus: These language troubles also owe much to people's straining to be elegant and fine in their use of words. If it will help them to express their thoughts in an attractive way they see no objection to employing figures of speech in which words are diverted slightly from their usual senses. The new sense may be narrower or

wider than the usual one (this is called *synecdoche*); it may be a transferred sense, where two things have had their names exchanged because
of some relation between the things, either a concomitance (*metonymy*)
or a similarity (*metaphor*); and then there is *irony*, which replaces an
expression by its opposite. This is what such changes are called when
they are noticed; but they are rarely noticed. Given this indeterm-
inacy in the use of language, a situation where we want some kind of
laws governing the signification of words . . . what is a judicious person
to do? If he is writing for ordinary readers, he will deprive himself of
the means for giving charm and emphasis to what he writes if he
abides strictly by fixed significations for the terms he uses. What
he must do — and this is enough — is to be careful not to let the
variations generate errors or fallacious reasoning. Thus ancients
distinguished the 'exoteric' or popular mode of exposition from the
'esoteric' one which is suitable for those who are seriously concerned
to discover the truth; and that distinction is relevant here. If anyone
wants to write like a mathematician in metaphysics or moral philosophy there is nothing to prevent him from rigorously doing so;
some have announced that they would do this, and have promised us
mathematical demonstrations outside mathematics, but it is extremely
seldom that anyone has succeeded. I believe that people are repelled
by the amount of trouble they would have to take for a tiny number
of readers: like the question of Persius, *quis leget haec* ('Who will read
this?') with its answer *vel duo vel nemo* ('Either two people or no one')
(Leibniz, 1765, BK II, Ch. xxix, sec. 12)

Bachelard criticized very much the use of familiar metaphors in scientific
explanations of the eighteenth-century physics. For him they functioned as
'epistemological obstacles' to the development of scientific thought by playing the role of all-explanatory devices. Bachelard evokes the metaphor of
'sponge' which was supposed to explain both the properties of the air, and the
properties of the center in which electricity flows. '*Obstacle verbal*' was
Bachelard's name for the attitude of a scientist who satisfies himself with such
explanations (Bachelard, 1983).

Metonymies appear to be less controversial, maybe because they are
less consciously employed, less visible, and are most often used in oral communication. Their importance in communication is paramount: they allow
for an economy in the use of words, if only the speaker and the listener are
'in tune' on a subject. This is important in mathematical communication. The
metonymical use of mathematical symbols is well known: for example, the
name of a value of function, '$f(x)$', for the function itself, the name of a
representant of a class of abstraction for the class of abstraction, e.g., 3/5 for
{ 3/5, 6/10, 9/15, etc.} (Bauersfeld and Zawadowski, *ibidem*). While a metaphor used by someone can be a symptom of his or her act of identification
of a new object, a metonymy can be a symptom of an act of generalization:

as when the metonymical shift of reference goes from a certain class of objects to a larger class of objects. We shall see this on the example of the historical development of the concept of function.

However, metonymies used by our students are not always signs of such acts of generalization. On the contrary, they can be symptoms of certain restricted ways of understanding, even obstacles to generalization. Here are two examples of such a situation. The first comes from an experiment already mentioned above, on iteration of functions (Sierpinska, 1989). The second is from a research on undergraduate students' difficulties with linear algebra (Sierpinska, 1992b).

Example: **the value of a function at a point**

A group of 16-year-old students had to solve the following problem: to find functions (from R to R) that would have an attractive fixed point in the interval (2,3) and a periodic trajectory 2, 3. This last condition means that, if f is the function, then $f(2) = 3$ and $f(3) = 2$. In the students' notes, instead of such conventional inscriptions, the students wrote: 'x(2) = 3 x(3) = 2'. Of course, theoretically, the students might have denoted the unknown function by 'x'. However, their further behaviour suggested that 'x' stood for the argument of function, as usual, and the inscription 'x(2) = 3' was meant to say: 'substitute 2 for x in the formula of the function; you should get 3'. The latter was the expression they used for what is normally worded as: 'the value of the function in 2 is 3'. The inscription 'x(2) = 3' simply better expressed their conception of function as a 'result of a calculation'. This conception of function is maybe a little distant from the formal definition but it seems to be quite close to a more 'constructivistic' definition of function, as worded, for example, by Cauchy, in his 1821 '*Cours d'Analyse*':

> We call functions of one or more variables such quantities that present themselves, in calculations, as results of operations made on one or more constant or variable quantities. (Cauchy, 1821 Cours d'Analyse de l'Ecole Polytechnique, 1e Partie, Analyse Algébrique. De l'Imprimerie Royale. 1821).

[End of example]

Example: **metonymical use of variables in linear algebra**

Metonymies are handy tools of direct communication, as we mentioned before. Used in a written text addressed to someone who has not been there at the moment of its creation, and is unaware of what the author might have been focusing on while writing it, they sometimes look like nonsense, they feel like jokes. One of my linear algebra students had this habit of writing his solutions in such a metonymical way. He was using *ad hoc* notations, for the purposes of the one problem he was solving at the time, regardless of all conventions. His own conventions had very short life; he would switch from one to another within one solution. He would use numbers as variables, but he would also use them as codes. For example, '(5,5,5)' would stand for an arbitrary vector whose all three coordinates are equal: here is what he wrote to show that the set of vectors in the 3-dimensional real space whose all three coordinates are equal forms a subspace of that space:

a = b = c   IS A SUBSPACE
1°   (0,0,0)
2°   (5,5,5)
     (5,5,5)
     (10,10,10)
3°   k(1,1,1)
     k, k, k

Once he used the following inscription:

| 11 | 12 | 13 |
| 21 | 22 | 23 |

to denote an unknown 2x3 matrix: '12' being the code of the entry in the first row and second column. In explaining what is a symmetric matrix he wrote:

1	2	3
4	5	6
7	8	9

adding: '2 is the same as 4, 3 is the same as 7, 6 is the same as 8'.

Indeed, this metonymical style of writing in mathematics was not some kind of deliberate excentricism on the part of this student. Rather, it was a result of an obstacle that we might call 'numerical reckoning' ('*logistice numerosa*') — thus alluding to a pre-Viète way of thinking about variables in algebra that is to be distinguished from 'reckoning by species' ('*logistice speciosa*') developed by Viète in his *Introduction to the Analytic Art* (Piaget and Garcia, 1989, p. 147). In numerical reckoning, the basic element of thinking is the concrete, isolated number; if it does not matter what number it is in a given situation, it can be denoted by a letter or by a randomly chosen numeral, or any symbol for that matter. In the reckoning by species, the basic elements of thinking are the species of numbers or magnitudes, not their concrete representants. Numerical reckoning is satisfied with showing a method on examples; it is not interested in the formulation of a general theory, its goal is to efficiently solve certain concrete problems. Therefore it does not need a system of notations that would be comprehensive, consistent and generally applicable. Any *ad hoc* symbolic means would do to explain how to solve a certain kind of question by example.[End of example]

Construction of a Metaphor As a Symptom of a Creative Act of Understanding

There exists an opinion that the very possibility of learning something radically new can be explained 'only by assuming some operation which is very similar to metaphor (Petrie, 1979). 'The metaphor', says Petrie, 'is one of the central tools in overcoming the epistemological gap that exists between the old and the new knowledge'. (The other tools he mentions are: analogies, models, 'exemplars', i.e., exemplary paradigmatic solutions of problems). A radically new knowledge, according to Petrie, is the kind of knowledge that cannot be attained just through assimilation of new data into the existing mental structures and calls for an accommodation of the latter.

Johnson (1980) agrees, in principle, with Petrie when he says,

> metaphors generate novel structurings of our experience in a way not fully anticipated by our available systems of concepts . . . The new metaphor provides a basis for elaborating new concepts (or relations of concepts), and its adequacy may be judged at least partially by how well it 'fits in with' the concepts already articulated . . . Metaphors lead us to experience the world in novel ways. By causing a reorganization of our conceptual frameworks they institute new meaning. These foundation acts of insight are tied to truth claims because they alter the systems of fixed concepts with which we make truth claims . . . So understood, metaphors may be seen as grounding the concepts that we then use to speak determinately of as objects. The primary role of metaphor is thus to establish those structures we later articulate by means of fixed, determinate concepts (and systems of concepts). (Johnson, 1980, p. 65)

Thus, by structuring, ordering our experience and making it 'fit in with' the existing mental structures, a metaphor is a basis of understanding. An act of understanding based on a new metaphor is a creative act of understanding insofar as it 'causes a reorganization of our conceptual frameworks'. Moreover, an act of understanding based on a metaphor plays a crucial role in the development of our thinking: it prepares the ground for the formation of a concept.

Sometimes the concept obtains a name that bears the traces of the metaphor or metaphors that announced its coming into being. Our language is full of such 'lexicalized' or 'conventional' metaphors. This is also true for the mathematical language. For example, expressions such as '*convergent* sequence', '*limit* of a function $f(x)$ when x *tends to* a' are remindful of the metaphors used by the creators of Calculus and Analysis to describe the newly identified notions. Not yet having explicited the concept of limit as a concept on its own right, Newton used the term what today we call the derivative 'the ultimate ratio of evanescent increments'. He used to explain this notion with the help of the word 'limit', used metaphorically, and the images of movement towards something, of approaching something:

> The ultimate ratios with which the quantities *vanish* are not, strictly so speaking, the ratios of *ultimate increments*, but *limits* to which the ratios of these ever decreasing quantities *approach continually*.

Or, he would write,

> Quantities, and the ratios of quantities, which in any finite time con-
> verge continually to equality, and before the end of that time approach
> nearer to each other than by any given difference, become ultimately
> equal. (Newton, 1969)

All these words: 'ultimate', 'converge', 'continually', 'approach' provide
our minds with images on the basis of which we have the impression of
understanding what Newton is talking about.

Example: **metaphors and metonymies in the historical genesis of the concept of function**

An interesting interplay between metaphors and metonymies can be found
in the historical development of the concept of function. Mathematicians,
astronomers and physicists occupied themselves with relationships between
variable magnitudes from times immemorial, but it is only by the nineteenth
century that the class of all such (well determined) relations was identified as
a definite mathematical object. Newton, whose 'fluent quantities' seem to be
very close to what today we would call continuous functions of time, never
really considered them in isolation from the rates of their changes, i.e., fluxions.
Fluents were the primitive functions of fluxions, which were, on their turn,
the derivatives of fluents (Juszkiewicz, 1976, p. 257).

'*Fluxio*' is the metaphor of the flowing waters of, for instance, a river.
The idea of the flow of time is based on its comparison to a river that flows.
Newton probably first used this image to describe how the time variable
changes: it is characterized by a 'continuous flow' with constant velocity — a
steady 'stream'. Later, the name of 'fluxion' was extended to term the rates of
change of all kinds of quantities that, like time, are characterized by a continuous
flow, and the name of 'time' was given to all uniformly flowing quantities,
i.e., such that their fluxions can be represented as an unity.

> I consider time as flowing or increasing by continual flux and other
> quantities as increasing continually in time and from the fluxion of
> time I give the name of fluxions to the velocities with which all other
> quantities increase . . . I expose time by any quantity flowing uni-
> formly and represent its fluxion by an unity. (Newton, 1967, p. 17)
>
> I shall, in what follows, have no regard to time, formally so
> considered, but from quantities propounded which are of the same
> kind shall suppose some one to increase with an equable flow: to this
> all the others may be referred as though it were time, and so by
> analogy the name of 'time' may not improperly be inferred upon it
> (*ibidem*, p. 73)

In the above, there are two metaphors followed by two metonymies.
First, time is metaphorically called a 'fluent quantity'; this name is then
metonymically extended to denote any continually increasing quantity. On

the other hand, the velocity with which time is changing is metaphorically called 'fluxion', a name which is then metonymically extended to denote the velocity of any continually increasing quantity.

The terms of 'fluent quantities' and 'fluxions' were not adapted on the continent (maybe because of their limited use: motion, its changes and rates of change).

The term of 'function' was born in the geometrical context of analytic investigation and description of curves. In his 1673 manuscript *'Methodus tangentium inversa, seu de functionibus'*, Leibniz was concerned with two mutually inverse problems: 1. for a curve, for which the relation between the abscissas and the ordinates is given by an equation, to find its subtangent, subnormal and other segments linked with a curve; 2. to find the relation between the abscissa and the ordinate when a certain property of the subtangent, subnormal, or some other segments linked with the curve is given. These segments 'linked with the curve' are called 'lines fulfilling some *function* for the curve' (Juszkiewicz, 1976, p. 159). Here, for the first time, the term 'function' appears in a metaphorical use.

Twenty one years later, in 1694, in an article published by *Le Journal des Sçavans* Leibniz used the term 'functions' to denote

> all the line segments that are obtained by producing an infinity of straight lines, corresponding to a fixed point and the points of the curve, and they are: the abscissa AB or Aβ, the ordinate BC or βC, the chord AC, the tangent CT or Cϑ, the normal CP or Cπ, the subtangent BT or βϑ, the subnormal BP or βπ . . . and an infinity of other, the construction of which is more complicated (Juszkiewicz, 1976, p. 159).

This is a sign of a metonymic abbreviation: lines fulfilling some 'function' for the curve are, now, simply, 'functions'. However, the sense in which the term 'functions' was used by Leibniz in this article, did not seem adequate: it diverted the attention from what was most important in the analytical study of curves, namely from the relations between 'the line segments fulfilling some functions for the curve' and focused on these lines themselves. Thus, the point in the discussion between Leibniz and his disciple Jean Bernoulli was not so much the adequacy of the term 'function' but something much deeper: what is more important in the study of curves, coordinates or relations between the coordinates, objects or relations between objects. It became clear that the relations are exactly what distinguishes one curve from the other, and that in classifying these relations one obtains a classification of curves. Before that discovery, mathematicians used the classification of Descartes: curves were divided into mechanical and geometrical and the mechanical curves were excluded from mathematical study. The new principle of classification allowed for the consideration of these curves, as well (Leibniz called them 'transcendental', while the geometric curves of Descartes were called 'algebraic').

This shift of attention together with the conviction that only relations expressible by analytic formulae are worthy of mathematical study had led Bernoulli to the isolation of the concept of a 'quantity in whatever manner formed of indeterminates and constants' which he denoted by 'n' (*posito n esse quantitatem quomodumque formatam ex indeterminatis et constantibus*) (1694 in *Acta Eruditorum* see Cajori, 1929). The word 'function' did not appear in this article. It turned up again three years later, in 1698, when, in a letter to Leibniz, Bernoulli writes that he proposes to use the letters X and the Greek letter x to denote the above mentioned quantities because then 'it is at once clear the function of what' is X or x. In this context, the word 'function' is again used metaphorically, in a way similar to that in which it was used for the first time by Leibniz with respect to subtangents, subnormals etc. But now, the focus is on the dependence of the object that fulfills the function on the objects for which this function is fulfilled. For example, a person Y may fulfill the function of chairman at a meeting of a body of people (just as the coordinates of the points of a curve fulfill a function for the curve); but this function is a function *of* this meeting of a group of people, i.e., this occupation or duty or purpose *depends on* there being a meeting of a body of people; the function of chairman is a function for a group of people. A function as duty or purpose is always a function of and for something, depends on this something.

In further correspondence between Leibniz and Bernoulli, there occurs a metonymical shift of reference and the word 'function' starts to be used as a name of the analytic expression describing a relation of dependence of one variable on other variables (and not as a name of the relation itself) (Juszkiewicz, *ibidem*, p. 166).

The 1718 article of Jean Bernoulli, published in the *Mémoires de l'Académie des Sciences de Paris*, contains an apparently official definition of the term 'function': a function of a variable quantity is a quantity in whatever manner formed of this variable quantity and constants (Juszkiewicz, *ibidem*, p. 160). This meaning of 'function' is, in principle, still preserved in Cauchy's 1821 definition (quoted above).

Now, for the word 'function' to denote an arbitrary well-determined correspondence between two variables as understood, for example, by Lejeune Dirichlet in 1937 ('if a variable y is so related to a variable x that whenever a numerical value is assigned to x, there is a rule according to which a unique value of y is determined, then y is said to be a function of the independent variable x', (Boyer, 1968, p. 600)), a backward shift of attention was necessary: from the way of representing a relation to the relation itself; and — a generalization: from relations expressible analytically to arbitrary relations.

Let me summarize below the 'figurative history' of the concept of function:

1673
Metaphor (giving a 'new' name to an 'old' object):
Object {abscissa, ordinate, subtangent, subnormal, etc.} → Name: 'line segments fulfilling a certain *function* for the curve'

1694

Metonymy (shifting the use of a name to a different object):

Name: 'function' (as the role that abscissa, ordinate, etc. play for the curve) → Object: {abscissa, ordinate, etc.}

— Shift of attention from objects to relations between objects.

— Conviction that only analytically expressible relations are worthy of mathematical study.

— Identification of the concept of a quantity in whatever manner formed of indeterminates and variables.

1698

Metaphor:

Object: a quantity (X) in whatever manner formed from indeterminates (x) and constants → Name: 'the quantity X is a *function* of the variable x'.

1718–1821f

Bernoulli's definition of 'function of a variable quantity':

Metonymy:

Name: 'function' [as a relation of dependence of one variable with respect to another] → Object: an analytic expression representing a relation between variables.

Before 1837

Metonymy:

Name: 'function' [as an analytic expression] → Object: the analytically expressible relation between variable quantities.

1837

Metonymy:

Name: 'function' [as an analytically expressible relation of dependence between variable quantities] → Object: any well-defined correspondence between variable quantities.

[End of example]

The Role of Activity in Understanding

Activity Versus Passiveness of the Mind in Understanding

It is almost tautological to say that understanding is an active rather than passive experience if we want to speak of acts of understanding. An act of understanding happens only in an attentive mind, who is willing to identify objects, to discriminate between them, to perceive generality in the particular and the particular in the general, to synthesize large domains of thought and experience. Our minds are not being passively 'imprinted with ideas of things without'. Understanding does not 'come into us to lie there so orderly as to be found upon occasion' (Locke, 1960, BK II, ch. xi). It needs active construction to even see what everybody seems to see in an effortless and natural way.

It has been reported that persons blind from birth to whom the faculty of seeing has been restored have great difficulty in discriminating even between a square and a triangle.

> One man having learned to name an egg, a potato, and a cube of sugar when he saw them, could not do it when they were put in yellow light. The lump of sugar was named when on the table but not when hung up in the air with a thread. However, such people can gradually learn; if sufficiently encouraged they may after some years develop a full visual life and be able even to read. (Young, 1960, p. 63., quoted in Goldstein and Goldstein, 1978, p. 17)

In their *How we know?* Martin and Inge Goldstein comment that,

> seeing — the sense we think of as most directly putting us in touch with facts — is learned rather than automatic. We see with our minds, not with our eyes, and we are subject to whatever unconscious biases and misconceptions are produced by the training that teaches us to see. We are not arguing a case for disbelieving what we see. We have no choice, really. However, being aware that perception is not passive observation but rather a learned use of our intellectual faculties, however unconsciously it is done, should alert us to the possibility that things need not be what they seem, and that changes in our own thinking may change what we see. (Goldstein and Goldstein, *ibidem*)

These last words bring us to the question of the influence of education and, more generally, culture, on what we attend to, what, therefore, we understand, and how we understand it. These questions will be dealt with in Chapter 5.

Acting Upon an Object in Order to Understand It

According to the psychologists representing the so-called 'activity theory', understanding something requires acting upon it, transforming it, for example, into a subjective representation. The understanding subject is the 'agent' whose relation to the object is mediated by his own activity (Leont'ev, 1981; Davydov and Radzikhovskii, 1985; Davydov; 1990; Bauersfeld, 1990). As a result of the action of the agent on the object, a new object may come into being: the agent would have produced something. In this approach to the role of activity in understanding, the attention focuses on transformation and production of objects (external or mental) as results of the activity of the understanding subject: it is concerned with the changes of reality.

The definition of an act of understanding that was proposed in the previous chapter might be seen as quite compatible with this view, if we consider that the linking of the object of understanding with its basis is an activity that transforms the object. However, our definition is far from suggesting that an act of understanding, a priori, has a voluntary aim to change something. In fact, a better word to use would be 'maps', not 'transforms': in an act of understanding, one object is mapped onto another. Neither would we say that, in an act of understanding an object is being 'produced'. Of course, some of our acts of understanding do change (for us) the world we live in. We start to see the same things in a completely different way. But normally, we don't 'plan' it: we don't try to understand something *in order* to change it. We just try to understand. Period.

On the other hand, when we speak not of understanding in general, but of good or deep understanding, for example, in mathematics, then we think of the possible activities that a student could engage in, indeed, what actions could he or she perform on the object of understanding. We suggest that the student transforms this object. For example, we suggest that a formal definition be deformalized, that an informal statement be formalized, that a general statement be specified, that an assumption be taken away from a theorem, to see if it would still hold, etc. In fact, students tend to be very passive in their processes of understanding, taking things as they are, solving problems as they are given, often strictly following some model solution, never asking themselves questions that are not already in the book. But mathematics has to be understood in an active way because what we have physical access to are only symbols, representations of various kind. It is necessary to scratch a little through them to get to the concepts that are hidden behind.

But this is a different view on the function of the transformation of object in understanding: we transform in order to better understand; an act of understanding in itself is not meant to transform anything. Indeed, what happens in a process of understanding, is that our object of understanding is not the same from one act to another: however, we would not so much transform this object as we would look at something different, a different aspect maybe, or we would look from a different level. For example, we would reflect on our own actions when dealing with our former object of understanding. In understanding mathematics, whose generalizations form hierarchies such that what has been an operation at one level becomes an object at a higher level, this kind of change of object of understanding plays a crucial role.

In this we are closer to the approach of Piaget, for whom understanding is built in a complex dialectic process between action and reflection upon action or in a movement back and forth from an instrumental use of operations through reflexive abstraction to a reflected abstraction for which the first abstraction becomes an object of study.

The action can be a physical action on material objects or it can be a more intellectual activity on symbols of abstract objects as it happens in mathematics (e.g., when we apply a sequence of translations to a geometrical figure to check whether it is congruent to another one, or when we solve a concrete system of equations to find a set of points satisfying certain conditions). Let us consider these two situations in turn.

From a Physical Action to Understanding

The relation between successes in performing concrete physical actions and understanding why these actions were successful was studied by Piaget in his book *Success and understanding* (1978).

It may be worthwhile noting at this point that, although 'understanding' appears in the title of the above mentioned work, throughout the text Piaget speaks of the relationships between 'skill and knowledge', 'action and thought', 'doing and knowing', 'action and conceptualization' (*ibidem*, pp. vii–viii), 'practical success and notional comprehension' (*ibidem*, p. 213) as if referring to one and the same thing. This is somewhat disturbing, as, for us here, 'knowledge', 'thought', 'understanding', 'conceptualization' are far from being synonymous. It also follows from the contexts in which the words 'understanding' or 'comprehension' are used that Piaget has high expectations with regard to the 'states of consciousness' they refer to. Let us then keep in mind that, for Piaget, understanding means conceptualization or conceptual understanding, and understanding an action means 'explicative' and 'implicative' understanding, that is understanding that both explains why a given action was successful and allows for implying whether a planned action can or cannot be successful.

In *Success and understanding* Piaget was looking for the mechanisms by way of which the 'doing' is transformed into the 'knowing', even though there is admittedly a considerable time lag between the two. What he found is that this transformation is done in three steps or stages: in the first, conceptualization lags behind successful action; in the second, the two go hand in hand; in the third, conceptualization overtakes action.

In the first stage, action has an autonomous and cognitive character; one knows by doing. Hence a certain know-how is developed which is self-sufficient for obtaining success within a certain range of activities. The high level of practical skill at this stage contrasts with the low level of conceptualization which concentrates on the external results of the action. For example, in Piaget's experiments, although the subjects were successful in constructing roofs (two cards) or houses of four cards, in their explanations of why they succeeded, they were not taking into account the role of inclinations, i.e., that the two cards support each other in the roof structures or that one card props the other in the figure T. Instead, when asked 'How does it keep up?', they would say, for example, 'Because it touches', referring thereby to the result of their action.

In the subsequent stages, conceptualization and action start to have reciprocal effects on each other. The second stage is the period of transition, where conceptualization and action go hand in hand with each other but are undiscriminated by the subject. While conceptualization already supplies action with its power of anticipation, this anticipation relates only to immediate action — the conceptualization is immediately implemented in action. Or we can say that the results of an action are always experimented in direct action; they are not inferred from assumed premises as it will happen in stage III.

> ... it is not because subjects at level IIA interpret the transmission of movement by the passage of an impetus across the passive or mediating [billiard] balls that they go on to organize their actions so as to tap this impetus and to facilitate its circulation inside the balls (in the way that an engineer familiar with the principles of electromagnetism constructs instruments on the basis of Maxwell's equations). What conceptualization supplies to action is a reinforcement of its powers of anticipation and the possibility, in a given situation, of devising a plan for immediate implementation. In other words, its contribution is to increase the power of co-ordination already immanent in action, and this without the subject's establishing the frontiers between his practice ('What must I do to succeed?') and his conceptual system ('Why do things happen this way?'). Moreover, even in situations where the problems are distinct and where the point is to understand rather than to succeed, the subject who has become capable, thanks to his actions, of structuring reality by operations, nevertheless remains unconscious of his own cognitive structures for a long time: even if he applies them for his personal use and even if he attributes them to objects and events for the purpose of explaining them causally, he does not turn these structures into themes of reflection until he reaches a much higher level of abstraction. (Piaget, 1978, pp. 215–6)

The mental operations that are constructed in the process of reflexive abstraction in stage II are not 'representations' of actions — they are still actions because they produce new constructions — but they are 'signifying' actions and not physical actions: the connections they rely on are of implicative and not causal nature, i.e., they are connections between significations. This opens the way to the conceptual understanding of the action which becomes a fact in the third stage.

In the third stage conceptualization finally overtakes action. This phase characterizes itself by the functioning of the 'reflected abstraction' for which the product of the reflexive abstraction becomes itself the object of reflection and conscious formulation. The subject focuses no more on the results of the action but on its mechanisms; no more on the question: 'What must I do to succeed?' but on the question 'Why do things happen this way?'. Now, the results of an action can be inferred from what the subject knows about its mechanism; they need not be experimented in action. The subject can now programme the whole action: action is guided by theory.

The question is, of course: how the search for reasons of the success of an action can become autonomous to the point of dispensing with all actual objects? (That it can — we know from the existence of, for example, mathematics!). Piaget sees the answer to this question in, on the one hand, the necessary generalization that any explanation of the success normally requires, and, on the other, the recursive character of the construction of operations (*ibidem*, p. 222).

When, in stage III, understanding overpowers action, the subject's attitude towards the success changes: the immediate and concrete success doesn't matter that much anymore; the immediate result or goal of an action does not count. Unlike action, understanding, in the sense of finding reasons, does not have a 'result'. If understanding has a goal, it is that of (re)establishing an equilibrium. In that, understanding is more like a free vector — it admits of a direction, but not of an end point. But this direction can only be identified *ex post factum*, Piaget claims, saying that this indeed resolves the age-old question of objectivity of mathematics: whether it is 'invented' or 'discovered'. The necessity of a new and unforeseen construction can only be shown in retrospect by means of deductive instruments developed at this new stage, not before or during their elaboration. Thus,

> mathematical creations are neither discoveries, because the entities thus constructed did not exist beforehand, nor inventions because their creator is not free to modify them at will — they are constructions with the particular property of imposing themselves of necessity just as soon as they are completed and closed on themselves, but never during their elaboration. In respect of teleonomy they thus provide a typical example of a direction without finalism, which is precisely the characteristic of an equilibration. (*ibidem*, pp. 227–8)

From Instrument to Theme of Thought

By its reference to mathematics, the above quotation already makes a transition to the question of relations between the more intellectual actions on symbolic forms and understanding of these actions. This question is the main subject of Piaget and Garcia's book (1989). The three stages seem to be present in both the psychogenesis of knowledge and the history of science: Piaget labels them with prefixes 'intra-', 'inter-' and 'trans-' (for example: the intrafigural, interfigural and transfigural stages in the development of geometry; or the intraoperational, interoperational and transoperation stages in the development of algebra). The first stage is interested only in particular objects (e.g., geometrical figures or algebraic operations). The second looks at relations between these particular objects. At this stage mental operations reflecting these relations are constructed. The last stage 'thematizes' these operations which have played only an instrumental role in the previous phase, transforming them into objects of reflection. It is at this level that theories come into being.

Examples abound in the history of mathematics of such thematizations or shifts of attention from results of actions and effectiveness of techniques to the study of the 'mechanisms' of these actions and techniques. It is thanks to such shifts that the general notions of function, group, category have been constructed. It is the thematization of transformations in geometry that has led to what is now well known as the 'Erlangen Program'. Another example is provided by the history of linear algebra between the nineteenth and the twentieth century, the former having centered its efforts of techniques of solving systems of equations and finding determinants, the latter developing a theory of linear operators in which determinants are but a kind of invariants of matrix representations of linear operators and a measure of existence of eigenvalues.

The main point of Piaget in both of the mentioned works is that no matter how elaborate the 'thematization', it always has its roots in some more or less concrete activity: any development starts with an action on objects, i.e., on the 'intra-' level, goes through making connections between objects at the 'inter-' level, and, if it culminates with a perception of and reflection on a whole structure at the 'trans-' level, it is only to consider it, at a further stage, as a new 'intra-' level. None of these can be skipped, if a conceptual understanding has to develop: shortcuts are possible in teaching, but not in learning. And this is the ultimate advice that mathematics educators take from Piaget when they pick up his idea of a dialectic process between the instrument of action and object of reflection and develop in various forms and argumentations (see 'dialectique outil-objet' of R. Douady (1986); 'process-object' of E. Dubinsky (1992b), 'operation-reification' of A. Sfard (1992), etc.). The necessity to make this point is urgent both with those teachers who allow their students to reduce their learning to rote memorization of formulas and the activity of 'plugging-in' numbers into them, as with those who, overly concerned with 'meaning' and 'understanding', never let the students actually instrumentally use certain mathematical methods and techniques for the solution of some meaningful problems, but at once demand that they conceptually understand why these methods and techniques work, i.e., they want the students to understand the theory before they could even become aware of the usefulness of its tools. The former never let their students get onto the second and third levels or stages of knowing and thinking; the latter point to their students the highest level while depriving them of the ladder with which they would be able to climb there. As usual, the solution lies somewhere in between.

The Question of Continuity of the Processes of Understanding

In philosophy the question of continuity is posed with respect to human cognition both in its psychogenesis and historical development. Such a question can also be asked with respect to processes of understanding.

If continuity in time of a process of understanding means that small increases in time always produce small changes in the ways of understanding, then processes of understanding are not continuous. Sudden 'illuminations' or sudden changes in the way in which a situation is viewed, when aspects theretofore unnoticed come to the foreground, are facts well documented in psychology and in personal accounts of scientists. These are the moments of a radical change in understanding.

But one can speak of a different kind of continuity, as it is done in philosophy, in the sense that from one kind of cognition to another, or from one historical epoch to another something is preserved, something remains essentially the same. For example, for someone who believes that scientific knowledge is accumulated through ages and nothing essential is rejected or refuted, the historical development of knowledge will appear as a continuous process.

Piaget and Garcia, speaking of the psychogenesis of knowledge, and deriving it from actions which are certainly different from thought, make an explicit distinction between the 'functional continuity' or the stability of the regulatory mechanisms of cognitive development and the 'structural continuity' or the mathematical continuity in time of the results of these constructions. The results can change in a leap fashion: 'this change can include breaks, leaps, disequilibria, and reequilibrations.'

> We have tried throughout to provide support for the hypothesis, formulated in the Introduction, that there exists a certain functional continuity between the 'natural', prescientific and the scientific subject (where the latter remains a 'natural subject' outside of her scientific activity for as long as she does not defend a particular philosophical epistemology). If such a functional continuity exists, we can conclude that the two characteristics we attribute to all knowledge in the field of sciences themselves are even more general than expected: the relative absence of conscious knowledge of its own mechanism and the continuously changing nature of the construction of knowledge. In fact, as the epistemological analysis of scientific thinking finds itself obliged to go back to its prerequisites, which are constituted by the cognitive elaborations of prescientific levels, this recursive procedure confronts us with increasingly unconscious structurings which are increasingly dependent upon their prior history. (Piaget and Garcia, *ibidem*, p. 266)

One can also speak of such 'functional continuity' or continuity of mechanisms in processes of understanding, which, albeit distinct from processes aiming at the acquisition of knowledge, cannot be separated from them in that the two are complementary. At any level, a process of understanding will necessarily imply the operations of identification, discrimination, generalization and synthesis which will be linked by various reasonings; however, these operations and reasonings will present various degrees of sophistication at different levels, and the contents of the acts of understanding will also vary considerably.

All more recent analyses of the question of continuity in science, very much discussed in polemics with neo-positivism, show that the question itself is not well posed. Piaget and Garcia do this in the way described above after having discussed in depth the differences in positions of Bachelard, Popper, Kuhn, Feyerabend and Lakatos and defined their own stand with respect to these authors. Let me mention only their reference to Bachelard, as his epistemology plays a special role in the approach to understanding that is presented in the present book. Bachelard takes the discontinualist stand and stresses very strongly the qualitative differences between 'common knowledge' and scientific knowledge, considering the former, with its 'familiar metaphors' and 'unquestioned opinions' as creating obstacles to the latter. Also the historic development of scientific knowledge characterizes itself by abrupt breaks with previous findings and ways of thinking: the examples of 'non-theories' such as the 'non-Euclidean geometries', the 'non-Newtonian mechanics' etc., serve as a support for Bachelard's thesis (Bachelard, 1970). What changes from one phase to another of cognitive development is the 'epistemic framework'. This framework is a product of both the cognitive system and the socially accepted paradigm of science. Unquestioned and partially unconscious, it becomes 'an ideology which functions as an epistemological obstacle that does not allow for any development outside the accepted framework' (*ibidem*). The rupture that is necessary to overcome the obstacle, extend the framework and answer new scientific questions accounts for the discontinualistic view of the history of science (or any development of human cognition for that matter).

But again, this discontinuity is only in the products of the cognitive system; the mechanisms of functioning of this system may remain fundamentally the same.

Another explanation of the unnecessary controversy between continualism and discontinualism is provided by Cackowski (1979). Considering the question of continuity versus discontinuity between the extra-scientific cognition and the scientific cognition, he presents a model of development of knowledge that shows the illusions of the discontinualism. This model is based on two points.

The first point is that (a) a complete formalization of scientific language is an utopia, and therefore never can scientific knowledge be freed from the impact of the 'everyday thought'; (b) no matter how rigorous and axiomatic-deductive our methods of validation are in a particular domain of sophisticated scientific or theoretical thought, understanding (and, thereby, the search for reasons of the choices of axioms, or of the important questions) ultimately relies on empiric-inductive thinking (Piaget and Garcia, as well as Kuhn would add that understanding relies also on the predominant world view, *Weltanschauung* or ideology which have more in common with society and culture than with the cognitive system itself; however, the social-cultural and the cognitive components cannot be dissociated within a single epistemic framework); (c) the receptive-constructive nature of human thought is capable of overcoming the following oppositions between the everyday and scientific thinking without necessarily completely denying the role of the former in the coming into being of the latter: objectivity — relativity, objectivity of structures — subjectivity of structures, objectivity and interiorization of subjectivity — subjectivity and exteriorization of subjectivity, realism — idealism, centripetal orientation of the 'epistemological vector' (from thing to the mind) — centrifugal orientation of the vector (from 'mind' to objective embodiments of the mind which are the embodiments of conceptual structures created by the mind), primordiality of description in relation to explanation — primordiality of explanation in relation to description.

The second point starts with the assumption that the functioning of the human thought is of an oscillating nature — between the empirical and the conceptual-theoretical levels. If one looks only at one of these levels, there is an illusion of discontinuity, where thought leaps to the other level. In fact, what happens is that the gap on one level of thought is bridged by the thought of the other level:

> . . . the illusions of discontinualism emerge from the fact that a certain link in the development of the means of thought [e.g., language], methods or the object of thought is by-passed. This must occur when one analyses the process of the development of thought solely on the factographic level (flat empiricism). We have already said that the factual processes of thinking take place between the level of abstraction and the empiric-objective level of the concrete. Examining the development of knowledge, of cognition within the framework of either one of those two levels, we shall not discover any continuity, because continuity realises itself along a sine. When at one level of cognition there occurs a gap — there is continuity at another level; thus, the gap is filled but at a different level. This is the way in which we see the model of cognition, in which discontinuity and continuity are dialectically linked . . . The real link which precedes the emergence of abstract thought is to be found not at the level of abstract thought, but at the level of observation, of a technical or social-material experiment and activity. Also the real continuation of abstract thought lies beyond the level of abstract thought and is to be found in the sphere of an observational, experimental, technical or material-social utilisation of an abstract thought. It is only through this transition to the level of the concrete, live utilisation that abstract thought confirms its informational contents, its existence. The situation is similar with facts: they become real scientific facts insofar as they are understood, while their understanding takes place through including them into a theory. (Cackowski, 1979)

Cackowski concludes with some sad reflections on both the real practice in contemporary science and the pedagogical practices. By refusing to 'understand' (which necessarily implies oscillating between different modes of thought) some scientists in fact break with scientific thinking, either reducing their activity to a thoughtless accumulation of facts or to an 'equally thoughtless' non-theoretical formalization. Teaching at the university level (but not only at this level) suffers from the consequences of such attitudes, providing students with highly sophisticated methodologies they don't know what to do with because they don't know what are the questions that these powerful methodologies could possibly answer. By ignoring the unity of cognition, says Cackowski, academic teachers can create insurmountable obstacles to the development of the creative scientific thought in general.

The postulate of unity of cognition should encompass both the dialectic of the empiric-inductive and the theoretic-deductive knowledge and the dialectic of the concepts used as instruments of action and as objects of thought, mentioned at the end of the previous section.

Chapter 4

Good Understanding

How is it that there are so many minds that are incapable of understanding mathematics? Is there not something paradoxical in this?
Here is a science which appeals only to the fundamental principles of
logic, to the principle of contradiction, for instance, to what forms,
so to speak, the skeleton of our understanding, to what we could not
be deprived of without ceasing to think, and yet there are people who
find it obscure, and actually they are the majority. That they should
be incapable of discovery we can understand, but that they should fail
to understand the demonstrations expounded to them, that they should
remain blind when they are shown a light that seems to us to shine
with a pure brilliance, it is this that is altogether miraculous.

And yet one need have no great experience of examinations to
know that these blind people are by no means exceptional beings. We
have here a problem that is not easy of solution, but yet must engage
the attention of all who wish to devote themselves to education.
(Henri Poincaré, 1952)

The Relativity of 'Good Understanding'

When a mathematics teacher says 'My students don't understand [for example]
fractions', this does not mean that these students have not experienced acts of
understanding related to fractions. It only means that they have not understood
them well by this teacher's standards. The students may think they have
understood fractions in a way but, for the teacher, this way was not good
enough. Maybe it was incomplete or superficial, procedural or instrumental,
restricted to concrete examples, rather than general, relational or conceptual,
reaching to the very essence of the notion, etc.

If a mental experience of connecting an object X with an object Y is at
all considered by the understanding subject as an act of understanding the
object X, then, subjectively, the object of understanding has been well understood: Y has to 'fit in with' X. If, on the other hand, Y is not considered as
a sufficient basis for understanding X then the subject would say: 'I don't
understand X.' (Note that the subject would say this also in the case when he

or she cannot match any object Y with the object X that he or she intends to understand. But this may mean also that the subject was trying various objects Y and none seemed to fit.)

The situation changes dramatically if it is not the subject himself or herself but someone else who looks at an understanding. Then we have to do with a normative point of view, which is common especially in the teaching and learning situations, at school, with its curricula, textbooks and examinations. Here, some ways of understanding are higher valued than others.

Note that I am saying 'normative' and not 'objective point of view'. Can we speak of an objectively good or correct understanding of something?

Not in an absolute sense, maybe. But some evaluations can be more objective than others. For example, if we speak of understanding a concept belonging to a certain mathematical theory by a student who is aware that he or she is studying a theory and not revelations about the nature of the world, and who is also (hopefully) aware of the basic notions and assumptions of the theory, and the student's way of understanding this concept stands in contradiction with a result of the theory, then we might rightly judge that this student's understanding of the concept is wrong. This judgment, albeit relative to the theory in question, depends only on the logic of the theory and not on, for example, the mood or the system of values of the judging person. This is why it is 'objective', even if this objectivity is only local.

This does not mean that it would be easy to produce such an objective judgment: how would one practically check that a person's understanding is not contradictory with any statement of the theory? There may be an infinity of them. It is much simpler to prove that a student's understanding is not perfect: one contradiction would suffice. This is why the mathematics educational literature is full of stories of students' 'errors', 'lack of understanding', 'misconceptions', 'misunderstandings', etc. Accounts of good understanding are rare, and those that exist are often poorly justified.

When it comes to understanding not a particular concept of a theory or a particular method but the theory as a whole, when, for example, one asks the question 'what is the point of this theory?', then the evaluation must be more subjective. Here the problem is not so much with the meanings as with the significance, and criteria of significance are not a matter of just the logic. The judgment depends on one's philosophical attitudes towards scientific knowledge, views on the *raison d'être* of the theorizing thought, on the goals of learning mathematics, on one's theory of intellectual development, etc. The judgment of a person's way of understanding will be relative to cultural norms, which are not justified by reference to some logical system but by an appeal to traditional values.

Let me illustrate these problems of relativity with the story of a student having trouble in understanding linear algebra (Sierpinska, 1992b). We shall see here the clash between the subjective feeling of understanding or not understanding and what is considered to be good understanding by teachers. There will be two aspects of this clash: one in which the student does not feel he has understood, but his understanding may be considered as just fine by the teacher, and another, where the student thinks he understood but his understanding is inconsistent with the theory.

Example: **Raf's problems with understanding linear algebra**

Raf (fictitious name) is an undergraduate student, a mathematics major who has successfully completed his first-year courses. He passed the two linear algebra courses with an A and a B but he does not think he understood linear algebra well enough. In an interview a week after the final examinations, he kept comparing Linear Algebra with Calculus which he felt he understood a lot better. There were many reasons for which he thought 'Linear' was more difficult. One of them was that it was hard to see the point of linear algebra, while, for 'Cal', it seemed to be quite obvious. Why was everybody repeating that linear algebra is so important? He asked his teachers about it and what he heard was often: 'if you continue in mathematics, you will see why it is so important.' Some people added that linear algebra is useful in many other domains of mathematics as well as in applications. Raf himself said that 'I can see that if you are using computers and if you have to do, like, applied mathematics, then of course I can see where it comes in handy.' He also said that he finally is starting to understand that linear algebra, 'basically, it's a new form . . . a new way of communicating mathematics'. But he complained about not being told that by the teachers right away, as well as about vectors and matrices, 'how important they are in all other fields, for example, in statistics, . . .' However, he was not happy with these explanations of the importance of linear algebra. The interesting thing was that, when he was arguing for the importance of Calculus, he wouldn't use much stronger arguments — just the applicability of Calculus in engineering. The arguments why Calculus was easier were more convincing: 'In Cal you can visualize a lot more.' In fact, the Calculus course was at a much lower level of synthesis and abstraction than the Linear Algebra course. The students' tasks were mainly to calculate areas, volumes. They didn't have to 'show proofs', like in Linear Algebra. Therefore, there is something else that Raf is not understanding about linear algebra, not just why it is so important.

In the citation below 'I' stands for 'interviewer', '. . .' mark the suspension of voice; '{. . .}' marks an omission of a part of the protocol.

> Raf: . . . it's maybe that in Cal you can visualize a lot more. But in linear . . . It's not that I don't like linear, it's that I don't understand linear. You know, I've like had two courses now and I passed them both but it's not something that I can say that I understand, you know, I know how to do some problems, I know how to do inner product space. I liked that part. But there are some of the problems . . . Until now I still haven't had that feeling where I completely understand what linear algebra is all about . . . Like, I don't see the point of it. {. . .} Everybody keeps saying that linear is so important, it's so

important. I still haven't seen that yet. I still don't understand linear. You know, I can see things. I could now understand more what a vector space is. But last semester I was thinking what do they mean by a vector space . . . What's so different about that space than any other space, you know?

I: And what's so different about it?

Raf: Oh, it's just the axioms that you have to use to remain in the vector space . . . That's what I have come down to realize. It's just a different way of dealing with vectors, in particular, and matrices, in different axioms, eight of them, about addition and multiplication, whatever . . . And if they follow these eight rules you are in a vector space. The same about subspaces. They have to be closed under addition and scalar multiplication and it's in the subspace and that's what I see of it. But the general idea {. . .} why linear is so important . . . Maybe if teachers explained to students right away what was the importance of linear, you know, the underlying importance of it, maybe we would have an easier understanding of it. Like always when we talk about it we find linear is very abstract, you know. {. . .} Like, I understand vectors {. . .} but what I don't understand is their point . . . Like, I don't understand the importance of T-invariant subspaces because I don't understand them. I have a little understanding of that but it's not very strong. You know what I find is difficult {. . .} sometimes teachers {. . .} would go to show us things that are not so difficult but just a little bit too far from us. . . .

The problem of Raf and many other students in his class was that, while they were still at the inter-level of algebraic thinking (in Piaget and Garcia's terminology), the whole course was conceived in terms of the trans-level: it contained strong synthesizing results such as the Cayley-Hamilton theorem, the Primary Decomposition Theorem, the Jordan canonical form of linear operators and matrices. The main objects of study were not operations on vectors in particular vector spaces but operations on whole vector spaces, linear operators, classes of vector spaces, classes of subspaces such as T-invariant subspaces, relating the subspace with a linear operator on the space. In order to understand what is the point of introducing these concepts, one must have a kind of bird's eye view on the whole *problématique* of linear algebra and one must be at the trans-level of algebraic thinking.

Raf, and many other students, had a very hard time understanding the concept of T-invariance. In the interview, when we spoke about it, Raf's understanding appeared as a real mess. Asked to explain what is a T-invariant subspace, he said: 'One that maps onto itself' (1), which seems close (except for 'onto' instead of 'into', and there is no mention of the operator). It turns out, however, that he thinks not so much of subspaces as of vectors being invariant. A vector is invariant if its multiples remain in the subspace: 'any multiples of those vectors will be T-invariant, will still be in the subspace' (2). He also writes: '$v \in W$, $kv \in W$' (3). This sounds as if all vectors in any subspace would be T-invariant, as subspaces are closed under scalar multiplication, anyway. It looks independent of the operator, also. The operator does play some role, however, in Raf's understanding of T-invariance. Asked to write symbolically what he said in (1), he puts: '$T(kv) = kT(v) \in W$' (4). This now looks as if any vector is T-invariant under any linear operator T. But maybe Raf wanted to write rather something like '$T(v) = kv$' which looks more like a definition of an eigenvector. Indeed, Raf somehow associated T-invariance with eigenvectors or vectors that are mapped onto multiples of themselves (which is not so stupid, after all). He said, later, some time after I explained to him that a vector that maps onto a multiple of itself is usually called eigenvector, that he learned it that way from some book: 'When I looked at it [T-invariance] in another book, the way they were describing it, they were using eigenspace, and the eigenvectors, and so that's where I got these ideas . . . You know, always k times v . . . when v is in W then kv is in W'. He repeats here the same kind of expressions he already used in (3), and (2), but maybe he thinks of kv as being the image of v under T.

While T-invariance is defined as a property of subspaces, Raf used to think of it as a property of vectors, which can be a symptom of his being at the inter-level of algebraic thinking and not yet at the trans-level. But, as he said himself, he used to live under the assumption that he understood T-invariance correctly.

> Raf: {. . .} you think you understand and you ask and you are corrected and it turns out that you understood it the wrong way. And I'd go around under the assumption that I understood it the right way.
> {. . .}
> Raf: {. . .} the teacher doesn't notice that the students are having a problem because the students are not speaking up. It's not a fault of either it's just . . . The concepts are sometimes . . . You are learning something, or you are supposed to be learning something . . . I should say I . . . I learn something but it turns out that I am learning it completely wrong. You know? But it works!
> I: For a while.
> Raf: For a while and when you get to a problem, and this doesn't work, and then you have to go back. And in linear that seems to happen a lot more 'cause in Cal you know right away if what you are doing is wrong or right.

It is true that in linear algebra courses, especially if they are done in the chalk-and-talk style, with little conversation with students, the students' understanding is not probed enough. Most of the questions and problems are straightforward exercises (find the matrix representations, find eigenvalues, diagonalize, etc.) or proofs. Neither put into question the students' understanding. In exercises, they can get a correct answer by blindly applying a method shown in a model solution. The proofs do not probe the students' knowledge, either, because many students don't even know how to start doing a proof, so they do not invest any previous knowledge into such an exercise; therefore, when they read the proof written by the textbook's author or teacher — this proof does not contradict any of their assumptions. [End of example]

Various Approaches to Research on Understanding in Mathematics Education

In spite of all the theoretical problems that one may have in defining 'good understanding' in mathematics, the question cannot be escaped: it is important, both for the teachers and the students. It is so important that, in mathematics education, 'to understand' often means 'to understand well', and in many theories of understanding the focus is only on different levels of 'goodness' of understanding, or kinds of understanding, some of which are better that other. Some researchers endeavour to uncover the mechanisms of thought that lead to good understanding; some elaborate on mental activities that enhance understanding, etc.

Generally speaking, one could distinguish three main approaches to the question of understanding in mathematics education. One of these approaches focuses on developing teaching materials that would help the students to understand better. Another concentrates on diagnosing the understanding in students. A third one is interested in the more theoretical issue of building models of understanding. Some of these models are more prescriptive (what are the mental and other activities that have to be performed in order to understand); other are rather descriptive (what is it that people do in order to understand; or how people understand mathematics or particular mathematical topics). This does not mean that any researcher would fit strictly into one of these categories and not in another. Larger research projects normally envisage all three of these preoccupations. It is only particular publications that might fit into a single category.

In mathematics education there is quite a number of publications that explicitly deal with understanding. Some of them are referred to in this book. I shall not undertake the task of classifying them into the three approaches. Maybe I can leave it to the reader. For example, where would you put 'Children's understanding of mathematics: 11–16' edited by K. Hart (1981)?

Let me refer to some Polish authors, less known to the non-Polish speaking audience. For example, Z. Dyrszlag, who has worked on understanding quite intensively in the 1970s, under the supervision of A.Z. Krygowska. He proposed, in his 1972 paper, to assess a student's level of understanding on the basis of well-chosen questions and problems that the student was able to answer and solve. (Such was also the approach used in Hart's book). In Dyrszlag's further papers (1978, 1984), there is a shift from just diagnosis to 'control', the latter meaning not only evaluation but monitoring in the aim of improvement. Control requires a vision of a certain ideal state and Dyrszlag went into some more theoretical considerations, distinguishing, for example, between a descriptive (static) understanding and an operative (dynamic) understanding. He also proposed to determine a person's understanding on the basis of a set of abilities. These 'abilities' were not content specific: they were meant to be applicable to processes of understanding in mathematics in general. However, it can be seen that Dyrszlag had in mind the more advanced formal and rather pure than applied mathematics. This attitude towards mathematics was characteristic of Krygowska and her school. Dyrszlag enumerated altogether sixty-three abilities grouped in twelve blocks that would account for a good understanding. Related, for example, to understanding definitions, there are abilities such as: the ability to find errors in an incorrectly formulated definition; to give examples and non-examples of the defined concept; to produce counter-examples in order to prove that an assumption is essential; to explore limit cases, to write a definition in two different symbolic conventions, etc. With respect to solving problems Dyrszlag speaks of the ability to 'solve inverse problems'.

This ability seems particularly interesting. Concerned with the Piagetian idea of invertibility of mental operations and the concrete operational stage, we recommend that the primary-school child be taught addition of a number together with subtraction of one as two mutually inverse operations. The same with multiplication and division. But we somehow forget about this useful principle when it comes to teaching mathematics at the university. For example, the standard question in the linear algebra courses is: given a linear operator, find its characteristic polynomial. Why not ask the question: given a polynomial, find a linear operator for which this polynomial is the characteristic polynomial; how many different (in what sense?) linear operators can you find? How many non-similar matrices would have a given polynomial as their characteristic polynomial? What if a minimum polynomial was also given? An investigation into such questions has led some (the investigation was optional) of my undergraduate linear algebra students to a better understanding of the canonical forms of linear operators and matrices.

Another Polish didactician, M. Klakla, worked on mathematical understanding within a similar framework, but he interested himself with specific mathematical topics, for example, with understanding quantifiers in mathematical logic (Klakla *et al.*,1992). The first step of the research consisted in a detailed analysis of the teaching material both from the logical mathematical and the didactical points of view. This analysis led to setting up a list of 'aspects of understanding logical quantifiers'. In a second step, test questions were designed such that, to answer them, the student had to be aware of each and all of these aspects. An analysis of the students' responses allowed them to order the targeted aspects with respect to their difficulty (rate of failure). In the case of quantifiers, it was found, among others, that the most difficult thing seems to be concluding from false general statements to existential statements and their negation, as well as from true existential statements to general statements or their negation. Klakla's approach is perhaps a little less 'pragmatic' than that of Dyrszlag in the sense that it focuses rather on the diagnosis than on monitoring students in a teaching process.

Models of Understanding

As we have seen, researchers have different goals in mind as they approach the question of understanding in mathematics. Some of these goals are more pragmatic (to improve understanding), some are more diagnostic (to describe how students understand), some others are more explicitly theoretical or methodological. But whatever the primary goal, some theory of understanding is always in the background, whether explicitly laid out or not.

There are at least four kinds of such theories or models. One kind are those that are centered on a hierarchy of levels of understanding. The Van Hiele model of understanding in geometry belongs here (Van Hiele, 1958; Freudenthal, 1973, p. 125; Hoffer, 1983; Guttiérez *et al.*, 1991). There are other examples, referring to other conceptual domains (Bergeron and Herscovics, 1982, elaborate on levels of understanding functions; Herscovics and Bergeron, 1989, propose a three-tiered model of early understanding of natural numbers; Nantais and Herscovics, 1989, study the difficulties of early multiplication; Peled, 1991, concerns himself with integers). There are general models not referring to a particular mathematical concept, like, for example, the Pirie and Kieren 'recursive model of understanding' (1989).

Other kinds of theories of understanding are those whose main idea is that of an evolving 'mental model', 'conceptual model', 'cognitive structure', and the like. Greeno does not explicitly speak of a 'model of understanding' — he is interested in cognition in general — but in his conception of knowing, understanding (as well as reasoning) is based on mental models, so he would fall into this category. Lesh *et al.* (1983) are speaking of 'conceptual models'. This idea was used and developed by other researchers as well (e.g., Arzarello, 1989). 'Cognitive structure' is, of course, a Piagetian term and several authors do refer to him explicitly in constructing their models of understanding. For example, Dubinsky and Lewin (1986), propose what they call 'genetic decompositions' of mathematical concepts to describe the development of cognitive structures in relation with the learning of these concepts. These 'genetic decompositions', for a particular mathematical concept, the authors say, 'map the way in which students empirically formulate their understandings for the first time', and they 'generate an account of the arrangements of component concepts and cognitive connections prerequisite to the acquisition of these concepts'. Dubinsky and Lewin are aware that their model does not reach to the act of understanding itself, and,

> seems only able to explicate all the prerequisite structures, both necessary and sufficient, for the cognitive act to occur. It can provide the readiness, but the act itself remains inaccessible and idiosyncratic, dependent on the particular way in which a given subject notices and organizes his/her experience. It would seem one never has direct access to cognitive processes . . . but, at best, only to what an individual can articulate or demonstrate at the moment of insight itself. Precisely what occurs at that moment seems as inaccessible as it is essential. (Dubinsky and Lewin, 1986)

A third kind of model views the process of understanding as a dialectic game between two ways of grasping the object of understanding. The dialectic couple can be composed of the concept considered as a tool in solving problems and this same concept viewed as an object of study, analysis, theoretic development: the dialectic of instrument and thematization. For example, R.K. Skemp's opposition between the instrumental and relational understanding, R. Douady's *dialectique outil-objet*, and A. Sfard's operational versus structural understanding in algebra seem to belong to this trend.

The fourth kind could be called the historico-empirical approach. Here, attention revolves around obstacles to understanding encountered both in the history of the development of mathematics and in today's students.

The Historico-empirical Approach to Understanding in Mathematics

This approach is close to that taken by Piaget and Garcia in their *Psychogenesis and the history of science.* However, there are some subtle differences which stem from the different perspectives of epistemology and education. What is relevant to epistemology are the 'mechanisms of development', stages, trends, laws (such as the law of equilibration of cognitive structures, and the functioning of reflexive and reflected abstraction). For Piaget and Garcia, the essential problem is,

> . . . how to characterize the important stages in the evolution of a concept or a structure or even of the general perspective concerning a particular discipline, irrespective of accelerations and regressions, the impact of precursors or 'epistemological gaps' . . . The central problem, in fact, is . . . that of the existence of the stages themselves, and particularly that of explaining their sequence. (*ibidem*, p. 7)

But, from the point of view of mathematics education, what is interesting are exactly these 'accelerations and regressions' and 'epistemological gaps', as well as 'epistemological obstacles' and difficulties because it is assumed that to learn is to overcome a difficulty. That an equilibrium has to be finally attained — this is taken as a banality; the problem is that without first destabilizing the student's cognitive structures no process of equilibration will ever occur, i.e., no learning of something radically new will ever occur. The construction of meaning seems to be determined not by the stages — at least not only by the positive stages of a move towards a change but also by the negative impact of various norms and beliefs and ways of thinking that constitute obstacles to this change. It is thus interesting, for a mathematics educator, that, in the early period of the history of Calculus, mathematicians had some difficulty in discriminating between what we now call the convergent and the divergent series and that Leibniz could argue that the sum of the infinite series $1 - 1 + 1 - 1 + \ldots$ can be considered as $1/2$. It is also quite revealing that Cauchy thought that the limit of a convergent sequence of continuous functions should be a continuous function, and that the concept of uniform convergence was invented to amend the error. The study of the contexts and mental frameworks in which such understandings appeared and were overcome can help both in identifying today's students' difficulties, and in finding ways of dealing with them.

Here we come across another difference between the epistemological and the educational perspective. Epistemology may stop after having defined the 'stages and mechanisms of development' or even after having identified the obstacles to changes of modes of thinking. For a mathematics educator, this is only a starting point. The central problem of education is not so much the description and categorization of the processes of development of knowledge as the intervention into these processes.

Also, at this hour and date, we are much less sure about such concepts as 'development' or 'progress' of knowledge. Epistemological obstacles are not obstacles to the 'right' or 'correct' understanding; they are obstacles to some change in the frame of mind. While we would accept to speak of levels of complexity of thought, and certainly the trans-level involves more complexity than the inter-level, we feel much more reluctant to judge a system of values and categories of thought that go with the former as more 'progressive' than the one that goes with the latter. We have to prepare our students for a lifetime of changes, adjustments of ways of thinking and understanding: if there is anything we have the obligation to prepare students for it is a readiness for a constant revision of these.

The need of 'reorganizations', over which Piaget and Garcia pass rather quickly in their work, is indeed one of the most serious problems of education. In teaching we do not follow the students' 'natural development' but rather we precede it, trying, of course, as far as possible, to find ourselves within our students' 'zones of proximal development'. But we cannot just tell the students to 'now reorganize' their previous understandings, we cannot *tell* them what to change and how to make shifts in focus or generality, because we would have to do this in terms of a knowledge they have not acquired yet.

So we must introduce the students into new problem situations and expect all kinds of difficulties, misunderstandings and obstacles to emerge and it is our main task as teachers to help the students in overcoming these, in becoming aware of the differences; then the students will perhaps be able to make the necessary reorganizations.

The use that educational research makes of historico-critical analyses, such as those of Piaget and Garcia, is much more content-specific and much more instrumental. For mathematics education, general developmental theories are only a means to elaborate on and design the development of particular mathematical concepts and processes. For epistemology, this hierarchy is reversed: general theories are the very goal of its research and the study of particular processes is but a means to attain this goal.

The fundamental assumption that underlies the historico-empirical approach is not that of a parallelism in the contents between the historic and genetic developments of scientific understanding. What is considered as responsible for the similarities that we find between our students' understandings and the historical understandings, is not the supposed fact that the 'philogenesis recapitulates ontogenesis' but, on the one hand, a certain commonality of mechanisms of these developments (Piaget and Garcia, *ibidem*, p. 28), and, on the other, the preservation, in linguistic tradition and the metaphorical use of words, of the past senses (Skarga, 1989).

According to Piaget and Garcia, one of the mechanisms of knowledge development is the 'sequentiality' in its construction. 'Sequentiality' means that 'each stage is at once the result of possibilities opened up by the preceding stage and a necessary condition for the following one (*ibidem*, p. 2). As every next stage starts with a reorganization, at another level, of ways of understanding constructed at the previous stage, the understandings of the early stages become integrated into those of the highest levels. Therefore, the meanings from the early stages are not lost, they are implicated in future understandings, and thus, also, in their history. The second mechanism is one that 'leads from intra-object (object-analysis) to inter-object (analyzing relations or transformations) to trans-object (building of structures) levels of analysis (*ibidem*), which is common to both the individual and the historical development.

Another source of the kinship between students' understandings and those encountered in the history of science and mathematics is found in the bifurcation of ways in which words that have once played the role of fundamental categories of thought change their meaning. One branch of this bifurcation can be called 'rationalization' as when a word or expression becomes a scientific term, included in a theory. Another branch can be called 'metaphorization': the word acquires a metaphorical meaning or the value of a symbol and lives in the vernacular (Skarga, *ibidem*, p. 135). For example, the notion of mass, in physics, has passed from the ordinary meaning of something big or heavy through the Newtonian meaning relating it to force and acceleration, through the mass from relativity theory and to the mass from Dirac's theory. Bachelard describes these stages as stages of rationality: the classical, the relativistic, the dialectic (Bachelard, 1970). But, in the vernacular, we still refer to a body of matter, a 'shapeless mass' or a 'sticky mass' of something, we also speak of a 'mass of people' . . . The same could be said of such categories as number, infinity, cause or chance and probability. Rationalization and metaphorizations are processes that go in different directions. While rationalization breaks linguistic traditions and ontologies that they carry, metaphorization preserves them in ways that are not quite literal, but still bear some of the old emotions and values. Skarga writes,

> This leap into metaphor is not a break with experience, although it could be a result of distanciation from the literal meanings thanks to the verification of experience by scientific methods. It consists in a fixation of very strong primary experiences, together with associations that they awake, filled with emotions and values and a rich tissue of imagery . . . There exist experiences so strong that time cannot destroy them. They become sources of whole theories such as [for example], the theory of elements, and when the theory is abandoned, they express themselves in a network of metaphors, and it is exactly this network that has the power of survival not as a remembrance long forgotten and put aside but as a live word . . . Language is a real treasure-house of thoughts and images of which we are the heirs . . . (Skarga, 1989, pp. 136–7)

'Good Understanding' in the Historico-empirical Approach: Significant Acts of Understanding

Our definitions of an act and process of understanding did not, a priori, presume external evaluation. An act or process of understanding had to be an act or process of understanding for the understanding subject. In speaking of the 'conditions of understanding' we had in mind those conditions under which the understanding subject is able to experience an act that feels like an act of understanding. However, the more normative point of view cannot be avoided, and we shall have to tackle the question of good understanding, even though we know that any definition of good understanding must be relative to some set of norms, whether philosophical or logical.

Considering a single act of understanding of an object X we can evaluate it according to whether the basis of understanding Y is conforming to some accepted or expected way of understanding the object X. We can use the criteria of logical consistency within a theory, or criteria dictated by a certain system of beliefs (about the nature of mathematics, for example, or about the goals of learning mathematics). We can also evaluate it by reference to the subject's internal cognitive system and system of beliefs and use the criterion of internal consistency.

We can speak of the significance of an act of understanding, and not only of the internal or external consistency of its basis. However, in this case we would have to take into account not an isolated act of understanding, but this act as involved in the network of a process of understanding. Also, we would have to have an idea of what we aim at: a vision of an 'ideal' way of understanding of the object in question. Then we could judge whether the subject is 'going in the right direction', whether a given act of understanding brings him or her closer to that 'ideal' vision.

With such a vision in mind, some acts can be considered as more significant or important than others. But how do we judge that one act of understanding is more significant than another? This is where the historical study comes in handy. If we know what were the major breakthroughs in the history (or pre-history) of a theory; what questions triggered sudden new developments; what were the understandings that caused stagnation, then we are able to identify those acts of understanding that are really important.

But in the evaluation of understanding, the developmental stage of the child or student is an important factor. Although the early understandings are implicated in the 'grown-up' understandings, they may not be transparent, and the history of mathematics is the history of grown-up mathematics. Therefore, historical analyses have to be done in interaction with empirical studies of how mathematical concepts develop in children. Thus, an act of understanding can be judged significant, if it marks a transfer to a different level of thinking, for example, from the intra- to the inter- level, or from thinking in complexes to conceptual thinking, if we wish to work within the framework of Vygotskian psychology.

In general, we propose to judge as more important than any other those acts of understanding that consist in overcoming an obstacle, whether developmental, or epistemological — related to the mature scientific knowledge.

Let us take a simple example. When the notion of power zero is introduced by decreeing that $a^0 = 1$ some students will simply add this information to the mathematical rules they remember, without giving much thought to it. Others will accept it as a useful convention allowing to preserve the continuity of the exponential function $y = a^x$. But yet other students will revolt against it by saying that the very inscription a^0 does not make sense, if taking to power n means to multiply a by itself n-1 times. In this case we say that conceiving of power as repeated multiplication is an obstacle to understanding the exponential function.

It seems reasonable to admit that an understanding that is founded on a question or on an identification of something we do not quite understand, is superior to an understanding, unproblematic but banal and often merely verbal of $a^0 = 1$ as a convention and one more rule to remember. It goes deeper into the meaning of this convention, it starts a search for its reasons. In fact, it implies a revision of the notion of power — an overcoming of an obstacle; it involves a construction and not just a memorization of the concept of real power (a^x, x in R).

One doubt that comes up here is that judging understanding in terms of epistemological obstacles makes this judgment even more relative, because, one may say, an obstacle is always an obstacle to a change to a different way of understanding or knowing, and how do we know that this new understanding is better than the old one. However, we must note that something (a belief, a scheme of thinking) functions as an obstacle often only because either one is unaware of it, or because one does not question it, treating it as a dogma. Overcoming an obstacle does not mean switching to another system of beliefs or another persistent and believed universal scheme of thinking but rather in changing the status of these things to 'one possible way of seeing things', 'one possible attitude', or 'a locally valid method of approaching problems' etc.

The Philosophy of Epistemological Obstacles

Why do we think that good understanding has to be achieved through 'overcoming obstacles'? Why do processes of understanding have to be of such dramatic nature? The reasons lie in our assumptions about both the intellectual development of an individual and the historical development of knowledge. The first assumption is that from one level of knowing and understanding to another, there is a need of at once integration and reorganization. Cognition is not an accumulative process. This is assumed to hold both for the psychogenesis and the history of scientific knowledge. This psychological view is in harmony with the philosophy of Bachelard, for whom, to 'find the truth', 'intellectual repentance' is necessary:

> Reflecting on a past of errors, the truth is found in a real intellectual repentance. In fact, one knows always against some previous knowledge, by destroying ill-built knowledge, by overcoming that which, in the mind itself, is an obstacle to spiritualization. (Bachelard, 1983, p. 14)

Thus, new understanding can only partially be built on previously developed ways of understanding. Hence, for example, at school, when we pass from whole numbers to integers, or from arithmetic to algebra, we must leave room for the 'intellectual repentance' — a reorganization of previous understandings. While integers can be regarded as a generalization of natural numbers, we must keep in mind that children's understanding of the latter, as it develops in the first school years, cannot serve as an immediate basis for this generalization. Pupils do not grasp natural numbers as a whole, as a structure equipped with certain operations and which is not closed under some of these operations. But it is only such understanding that can be a basis for the generalization. Quantities of something, amounts of apples and cakes, and operators that tell you how many times you are taking such and such quantity — the usual understanding of numbers by kids that young — cannot serve as a basis for understanding the ring structure of integers. And this is almost what is expected of them, if we think they will find some meaning in the rule 'minus times minus is plus'. Integers are already a first step into algebra which, far from being 'generalized arithmetic', is a methodology of mathematics. Arithmetic, from the point of view of algebra, is already the theory of numbers.

Other assumptions of the philosophy of epistemological obstacles are related to the positivistic illusions of the possibility to build scientific knowledge on the basis of solely observation and logic in a way that is completely free from any 'metaphysical' considerations. In fact, the notion of epistemological obstacle came into being in Bachelard's polemics with neo-positivism or logical empiricism.

We cannot do without 'metaphysics' in scientific understanding and this means that epistemological obstacles are unavoidable. Our beliefs about the nature of scientific knowledge, our world views, images that we hold and that are imprinted in the language that we use, schemes of thinking — all form the starting point for our dealing with scientific problems as much as they bias our approaches and solutions. They are the necessary props as well as obstacles to a 'good understanding'. Their overcoming requires a rebuilding of the fundamental understandings and this leads to philosophical considerations. It always comes to that when scientists start to reflect on the basic notions of their theories. This happens also in mathematics. Major breakthroughs in mathematics are often accompanied by discussions, within the community, about what does the result mean for mathematics as a whole, for the certainty of the mathematical knowledge, for the admissible methods of proof, etc. This is what happened with Gödel's theorems, the four-colour problem . . . In June 1993, Fermat's Last Theorem was announced proved by Andrew Wiles (June 23 in Cambridge, Wiles declared that he can prove Taniyama conjecture for semistable elliptic curves over Q, which implies Fermat's theorem). What philosophical discussions and reflections will this historic event give rise to? One interesting thing about this proof is that it is a result of an incredibly collective effort. As Ken Ribet put it: 'The method of Wiles borrows results and techniques from lots and lots of people. To mention a few: Mazur, Hida, Flach, Kolyvagin . . .', and Wiles and Ribet themselves. In December of the same year there was a rumour about there apparently being a gap in the proof: mathematicians did not take Wiles' announcement for granted, they started on a job of verifying it, probing it from various points of view. Doesn't this recent history tell the more general public about how mathematics come into being, as well as about the possibility of sharing an understanding of the most abstract ideas and being able to communicate them?

Heidegger (1962) claimed that 'the real movement of the sciences takes place when their basic concepts undergo a more or less radical revision which is transparent to itself':

The level which a science has reached is determined by how far it is capable of a crisis in its basic concepts . . . Among the various disciplines everywhere today there are freshly awakened tendencies to put research on new foundations. Mathematics, which is seemingly the most rigorous and most firmly constructed of the sciences, has reached a crisis in its 'foundations'. In the controversy between the formalists and the intuitionists, the issue is one of obtaining and securing the primary way of access to what are supposedly the objects of this science. (Heidegger, 1962, pp. 29–30)

For many practitioners of science, complying with the positivistic standards would mean resigning from understanding at all, because understanding requires harmony in thoughts and our thoughts are not divided into 'scientific' and 'philosophical'. We, as understanding subjects, are indivisible wholes. We have already referred to Heisenberg's position in this respect, in relation to essentialism. Let us come back to his illuminating comments about understanding quantum theory. What he says is that all the difficulties with understanding quantum theory appear exactly in the junction between experimenting and measuring on the one hand, and the mathematical apparatus on the other, and to overcome them 'true philosophy must be practiced' (Heisenberg, *ibidem*, p. 283).

Of course, I can agree with the requirement of the greatest possible clarity in concepts; but the prohibition of reflection on more general questions, on the grounds that there are no clear concepts there, does not appeal to me at all; such limitations would make the understanding of the quantum theory impossible . . . Physics consists not only in experimenting and measuring on the one side and the mathematical apparatus on the other, but in the place of their junction true philosophy must be practiced . . . I suspect that all difficulties in understanding quantum theory appear exactly in this place, usually passed over in silence by the positivists; and passed over exactly because it is impossible to use precise concepts there. The experimental physicist must speak about his experiments, and in doing this he is *de facto* using notions of classical physics, about which we know that they are not exactly adjusted to nature. This is a fundamental dilemma and it cannot be simply ignored . . . You know, of course, the poem of Schiller 'The allegory of Confucius' and you know that I especially like the following words there: 'Only completeness leads to light and truth lives in the deeps' (*Nur die Fülle führt zur Klarheit, und im Abgrund wohnt die Wahrheit*] Completeness here is not only the completeness of experience but also completeness of notions, various ways of thinking about our problem and phenomena. It is only thanks to the fact that one can speak about the peculiar relations between the formal laws of the quantum theory by using a variety of notions, which then illuminate them from all sides while seeming contradictions are brought to our awareness, that it is possible to bring about changes into the structures of our thinking, which changes are the very condition of understanding quantum mechanics . . . When speaking [about quantum theory] we are forced to use images and allegories which express, in an imprecise way, what we think. Sometimes we cannot avoid a contradiction, but, using images, we are able to somehow come closer to the real state of things. We must not, however, deny the existence of this state of things. (Heisenberg, 1969, pp. 283–5)

Epistemological obstacles are very likely to be found in sciences that raise questions concerning reality, and, therefore, also questions about the nature of being and our possibilities of knowing it, about which we have all sorts of preconceived ideas. It would seem, a priori, that the abstract mathematical knowledge is less prone to suffer these. That this is not exactly the case — we shall see from the example that follows.

Epistemological Obstacles in Mathematics: The Case of the Bolzano Theorem

Let us see, as an example, how epistemological obstacles have functioned in the historical process of understanding the theorem of Bolzano. We base our analysis on the historical study of Daval and Guilbaud (1945).

By the 'Bolzano theorem' we mean the following theorem: a function continuous in the closed interval $a \leq x \leq b$ passes from one value to another by all the intermediate values, i.e., for any y such that $f(a) < y < f(b)$ or $f(a) > y > f(b)$ there exists a number c between a and b such that $f(c) = y$. This theorem is also called the Darboux property theorem.

For Daval and Guilbaud the most important mental operation in mathematics was generalization. The way in which they present the history of Bolzano theorem is meant to support this claim. I hope to show here how, in fact, all four fundamental operations of understanding interact in this history, and how some of the crucial acts of understanding in it consisted in overcoming an epistemological obstacle.

From a Computational Technique to the Concept of Continuous Function

According to Daval and Guilbaud, the Bolzano theorem had its sources in an attempt to understand the technique of successive approximations used to compute radicals of various degrees in view of its generalization to a method of solving equations of the type $f(x) = c$.

The technique of finding a radical $x = \sqrt[n]{c}$ consisted in, first, guessing two natural numbers a and b such that $a^n < c < b^n$ and then continuing to find narrower and narrower intervals including x:

$$a < \ldots a_k < a_{k+1} < \ldots x \ldots < b_{k+1} < b_k < \ldots < b$$

Both sequences approached x but, most of the time, none of the approximations was the number x.

The conviction that the number $\sqrt[n]{c}$ exists, however, was based on a visual representation of the solution of equations like $x^n = c$. Both curves, $y = x^n$ and $y = c$ are 'continuous', have no gaps; therefore they must intersect in some point (x,y); x is exactly the nth radical of c.

An attempt to generalize the technique to solving equations of the type $f(x) = c$, where f is any function, must have posed the question of the conditions under which the technique really works. In particular, the intuitive notion of 'continuous' function had to be scrutinized. In the nineteenth century, at the age of 'arithmetization of analysis', of systematization of concepts, the image of a 'line without gaps' couldn't be satisfactory any more. And, from the practical point of view, this visual definition was of no help in studying the behaviour of particular functions. Cauchy had had the idea to reject all the (superfluous) visually based reasons for which mathematicians thought the technique worked. and focused his attention on the technique itself.

He probably tried to imagine situations where the technique would lead to false conclusions, i.e., situations in which the test on a_k and b_k would always work but the root of the equation $f(x) = c$ would not exist. In looking for the two sequences of approximations a, a_1, a_2, ..., and b, b_1, b_2, ... we check the consecutive terms by verifying whether c or $f(x)$ is between $f(a_k)$ and $f(b_k)$. Well, it may happen that we always get $f(a_k) < c < f(b_k)$ and nevertheless x — the common limit of a's and b's — is not the root of the equation $f(x) = c$. For example, take

$$f(x) = \begin{cases} x \text{ for } 0 \leq x < 2 \\ 4 \text{ for } 2 \leq x \leq 5 \end{cases}$$

and solve the equation: $f(x) = 3$.

It is clear that the solution does not exist. However, if we formally apply the technique of successive approximations, we may be led to the conclusion that the root is 2. But, $f(2) = 4$, and not 3.

If we think why things turned out so bad, we may notice that the crux of the matter lies in the behaviour of the sequences $f(a_k)$ and $f(b_k)$. While a_k and b_k were nicely converging to the same limit, the other two were not, and certainly they were not converging to c, which is important if we want x — the common limit of a's and b's — to satisfy the equation $f(x) = c$. For it may happen that the equation has no solution even if the sequences $f(a_k)$ and $f(b_k)$ have a common limit. This was then the idea of Cauchy: to take the strictly sufficient condition for the technique to work, i.e., the condition that, if a_k is a sequence of arguments of the function tending to an argument z, then the corresponding sequence of values must converge to $f(z) = c$, and use this as a definition of 'continuous function', 'continuous functions' being the name traditionally used relative to functions for which the technique worked.

In deciding to define (and understand) continuity as he did, Cauchy had to overcome the obstacle of thinking of functions as 'lines' and of continuity as a being a global property of such lines. Now, functions are viewed as relationships between independent and dependent variables and continuity of a function is continuity in a point: continuity is defined locally.

Bolzano theorem describes situations in which the consecutive approximations technique of solving equations of the type $f(x) = c$ is sure to work. It is a synthesis — a small theory of the technique — in which are condensed the intention to generalize the technique to a broader range of functions, the discrimination between situations in which the technique works and those in which it does not work, the identification of the sufficient condition upon which it works, the identification of an important notion of 'functions continuous in a point' distinguished from the intuitive concept of visually represented continuous lines.

Overcoming a Misinterpretation of the Bolzano Theorem

For a very long time after Cauchy announced his theorem, it was regarded as an equivalence and not as just an implication. Darboux disclosed this error but, according to Lebesgue, the faulty formulation was taught in Paris as late as in 1903. There is nothing unexpected about this error, though, if we consider all the obstacles that had to be overcome in order to understand the Bolzano theorem.

As Daval and Guilbaud explain it, in the second half of the nineteenth century, the understanding of continuous functions was based on a concept of 'continuous variable'. It was defined as a variable whose increment can be infinitely small. The continuous function was defined as a function $y = f(x)$ such that if x changes continuously, so does y.

The reason why, from this definition, it was rapidly inferred that the function $y = f(x)$ is continuous if and only if, when x continuously passes from a to b in the interval $< a, b >$, then y passes from $f(a)$ to $f(b)$ through all the intermediary values, can be found in, basically, two ideas prevailing at that time. The first was the belief that a finite continuous variable cannot pass from one value to another without passing through all the intermediary values. This is all right if this is how we think about independent real variables, or, as we say today, intervals of real numbers.

A problem arises, however, when two variables enter into play and one depends upon the other: when the variable y is a function of the variable x, then the 'continuous variation' of y is not exactly the same as the 'continuous variation' of x because the latter expression means that x is an element of an interval while the values of y may cover the most fantastic subsets of the real numbers, not necessarily intervals.

The faulty 'if and only if' version of the Bolzano theorem was a result of considering the expressions 'x varies continuously' 'and x passes from a to b through all the intermediary values' as equivalent, and of the non discrimination between the character of change of a single independent real variable and that of couples of variables, one depending on the other.

A way out of this error is in becoming aware of and rejecting the above ways of understanding. Restricting the definition of a continuous variable to only what it explicitly says, namely: that it is a variable whose increment is arbitrarily small, we obtain the following definition of a continuous function: the function $y = f(x)$ is continuous if, by varying the increase of x, the increase of y can be made arbitrarily small — which is exactly what Cauchy wanted to say in his definition of a function continuous in a point.

Further Generalizations: General Analysis

The manner of speaking about functions in terms of variables, common in the nineteenth century, led to focusing attention on 'variability' and ways in which y changes when x changes. The domains of variability of x and y remained in the background. Their determination did not seem necessary to define a function. The 'rule' or 'formula' of the function was sufficient and 'naturally' pointed to the values which could be used for x and y.

The discrimination between 'continuity' as a global property of lines representing functions and 'continuity' as a local property of functions brought about an identification of two objects: the domain and the range of function. This way, the function f is no more an attribution of particular numbers to particular numbers, but becomes a mapping of the set Dom$f$ onto the set Imf. The thinking about functions becomes more 'global' again. The domain of the function may have certain properties and one may ask the question whether the function preserves them or not.

The language used to speak about the arguments and values becomes more static: from 'variables' to 'sets'; on the other hand, the way of speaking about the function becomes more dynamic; from 'rule' or 'law' to 'mapping'.

Traditionally, it was thought that the set in which the variable x varies is always somehow naturally given. Most often it was a subset of reals. This domain was so natural that there was seemingly no point in speaking about its properties. Properties always distinguish something from something else, but here there was nothing to distinguish because real numbers were the whole world.

Now, the identification of the concepts of domain and range of function led to the question: why just the real numbers? Functions, from being defined on just real numbers, were generalized to functions or mappings defined on any set. Functions started to be seen everywhere and the 'functional thinking' (Klein's *funktionales Denken*) indeed pervaded all mathematics.

Before, variables and continuous functions were thought of in terms of 'an arbitrary increment of the variable': in the Bolzano theorem the question was of passing through all the intermediary values. Now, the generalizing movement gave birth to notions such as the neighbourhood of a point, topological space, condensation point, and generalizations of the notions of closeness, position (*situs*), limit, which were conceived so far in terms of numbers. It is enough to know, for any element of a given set, what it means to lie in its neighbourhood. This defines the topology of the set and allows for evaluation of the mutual position of the elements of the set without necessarily using the notion of number.

The property of continuity of a function can then be defined with the use of the weaker notion of the condensation point and not with convergence: the function f from A to Y, where Y is a topological space, is continuous in a condensation point a of the set A if $f(a)$ is a condensation point of the set $f(A)$.

In this new language the expression 'to pass through all the intermediary values' must be replaced by an expression free from reference to order. Order, the relation of 'lying in between', natural in the domain of real numbers may not make sense in arbitrary topological spaces. According to Daval and Guilbaud, the generalization of the Bolzano theorem to the statement that 'continuous functions preserve the property of connectedness of sets' could consist in such a generalization of the property 'to pass through all the intermediate values' that made abstraction from order or movement on the number line and preserves only the idea of 'solidarity' between the parts of the set.

It is exactly this solidarity between different parts of the set of values of y that discloses the existence, in the proof of Cauchy, of the two sequences $f(a_n)$ and $f(b_n)$ that have common limit c. Let us say the same as Cauchy but exclusively in terms of condensation points. When we had to prove that c is necessarily among the values of y, the latter were divided in two parts: the y's that are greater than c and $f(b_n)$ are among them, and the y's that are lesser than c and $f(a_n)$ are among them. But — and here is the essential argument — this classification excludes one value, namely $f(L) = c$ (L is the common limit of a_n and b_n). If we get rid of sequences and their countable character, the proof goes as follows: for the division of the set of all values of y into two (and only two) subsets to be complete, it is necessary that the condensation point c belongs to either one or the other of these categories. It is clear then that the essential feature of the set of values of y is that it cannot be divided into two parts so that no part contains none of the condensation points of the other. (Daval and Guilbaud, 1945, pp. 126–7, my translation)

i.e., the set of values of y must be 'connected'.

This is how connectedness as a property of sets is identified and, at the same time, it is distinguished from continuity as a property of mappings: 'a continuous mapping preserves the connectedness of sets.'

All this leads to a synthesis: a thought is born that, in the generalized geometry the question of invariants of mappings is important. Now, the generalized Bolzano theorem becomes a theorem of the theory of invariants of continuous mappings, i.e., topology.

The Notion of Epistemological Obstacle as a Category of Thought in Mathematics Education; Problems of Definition

The notion of epistemological obstacle, taken from Bachelard, made its appearance in mathematics education (more precisely, in the French *didactique des mathématiques*, thanks to Brousseau) around the year 1976, and very soon started to function as a 'category'. By 'category' I mean here, after Skarga (*ibidem*), a notion which, albeit not necessary in the development of a scientific domain, is sufficiently general and powerful to direct the thought and shape a field of research around itself:

> Human thought . . . tends to organize its problems around certain notions that I call categories . . . These [categories] are not invariably characteristic of our intellect and they have not a character of universality or necessity, yet they have sufficient range to direct thought. They have not a formal character, but usually a high degree of generality, that allows them to be applied in various domains. Each category is normally accompanied by other words and phrases, eagerly used, fashionable, which often in the eyes of the authors are meant to add to the scientificity, seriousness, modernity of their texts, . . . A category fulfils a double role. On the one hand, it shapes the field of theoretical research, remaining, however, in its center, and being the object of analysis itself. . . . On the other, it is for this category that the researcher reaches in trying to explain various questions . . . However, the main function of a category is that it directs the thought. (Skarga, 1989, pp. 108–9)

This is exactly what happened with the notion of epistemological obstacle: it started to 'direct the thought', a whole research programme started to develop around it, while, at the same time, heated debates were taking place among the theoreticians about the very nature of epistemological obstacles, the possible definitions, the rationale of bringing it into the field of mathematical thought, so different, after all, from the sciences of nature. This trend in mathematics education is slowly dying out, there are other questions and new words that occupy more central places, and the notion of epistemological obstacle has not grown to have a definition that would receive a wider consensus. A interdisciplinary conference that brought together psychologists, philosophers of science, and mathematics and physics educators, organized by Nadine Bednarz in Montréal in 1988 (Bednarz and Garnier, 1989), was partly meant to elucidate the notion of epistemological obstacle, but participants left with the feeling of confusion greater than ever.

It is possible that the most characteristic feature of a category is that it is hard to grasp with a definition, difficult to enclose within a rigid theory. A category does not belong to the world of theories; if it functions the way it does — by directing the thought — it is because it works somewhere between and above the vernacular and the research field. It is better described by the use that was made of it in research, what questions did it lead to, what explanations did it provide, what kind of discourse has developed around it.

Bachelard himself never gave any definition of his *obstacle épistémologique*; he only provided us with a series of examples of poignant differences between physics in the eighteenth century and the contemporary physics and the hint that this notion is useful in the 'psychoanalysis of the scientific thought'. The obstacles could be found in the human tendencies to hasty generalizations, or to explaining everything with familiar metaphors, or universal laws such as 'all bodies fall', or, still, by looking for a substance responsible for a phenomenon. Obstacles were there on the path of change from the ordinary thinking to the scientific thinking, from one kind of rationality to another kind of rationality.

For myself, the general lines of a theory of culture as described by E.T. Hall seemed to provide an appropriate framework within which not to define but somehow explicate the notion of epistemological obstacle, which seemed, first of all, a cultural phenomenon. This will be described in more detail in the next chapter. But there are other possible, and maybe even more adequate frameworks. Certainly, Michel Foucault's notion of *épistémè* and his archaeology of knowledge (1973) provides a useful basis; it is even closer to the historical-empirical methodology adopted by mathematics educationists in that it looks at culture diachronically, and not synchronically (or spatially) as Hall's theory does. Moreover, it focuses more on the taken for granted and unconscious of science — this is where epistemological obstacles are grounded — and it looks at different epochs by comparing their unconscious layers: epistemological obstacles reveal themselves in the differences. But Foucault looks at this unconscious layer in a positive way, which, again, agrees, with the philosophy of epistemological obstacles: these obstacles are, contrary to the connotations that the word 'obstacle' can bring to mind, positive. They are positive in the sense that they constituted the ground of the 'epistemological space' that determined, in a way, the kind of scientific questions and ways of approaching them, characteristic of a given epoch. In a foreword to the English edition, Foucault writes,

On the one hand, the history of science traces the progress of discovery, the formulation of problems, and the clash of controversy . . . it describes the processes and products of the scientific consciousness. But, on the other hand, it tries to restore what eluded that consciousness: the influences that affected it, the implicit philosophies

that were subjacent to it, the unformulated thematics, the unseen
obstacles; it describes the unconscious obstacles. This unconscious is
always the negative of science — that which resists it, deflects it, or
disturbs it. What I would like to do, however, is to reveal a positive
unconscious of knowledge: a level that eludes the consciousness of a
scientist and yet is part of the scientific discourse, instead of disputing
its validity and seeking to diminish its scientific nature. What was
common to the natural history, the economics, and the grammar of
the Classical period was certainly not present to the consciousness
of the scientist; . . . but unknown to themselves, the naturalists,
economists, and grammarians employed the same rules to define the
objects of their own study, to form their concepts, to build their
theories. It is these rules of formation, which were never formulated
in their own right, but are to be found only in widely differing theories,
concepts, and objects of study, that I have tried to reveal, by isolating,
as their specific locus, a level that I have called, somewhat arbitrarily
perhaps, archaeological. (Foucault, 1973, p. xi)

Foucault's theory can also be viewed as better fitting with Bachelard's
notion because both authors belong to the same philosophical tradition, while
Hall's anglo-saxon, empiricist approach seems very different in spirit with the
more rationalistic or 'Cartesian' perspective of Bachelard. Indeed, Foucault
himself points to the difference between the two approaches, at the point
when he describes the changes of conceptual schemas between the sixteenth
and the seventeenth centuries.

The sixteenth century viewed language as the mirror of the world, the
seventeenth and eighteenth centuries regarded it as a representation. In the
former period of time the prevalent ways of understanding the world were
based on the identification of resemblances of the most diffuse and general sort.
Language belonged to nature: both language and nature were networks of signs.
Knowledge was the same as interpretation of texts. For example, a 'natural-
istic' study of an animal could be a 'mixture of exact descriptions, reported
citations, uncriticized fables, non-differentiated remarks on anatomy, heraldry,
habitat, mythological values of the animal, its uses in medicine or magic'
(Foucault, 1973, p. 54). Thus, 'to know an animal or a plant or whatever in
the world is to collect all the thick layer of signs that could be deposed in them
. . .'; 'nature itself is a continuous fabric of words and marks, tales and char-
acters, discourse and forms . . . Nature is, from top to bottom, written' (*ibidem*).
The seventeenth century brought a criticism of this resemblance-based *épistémè*
both in England and France, but different perspectives were taken.

We already find a critique of resemblance in Bacon — an empirical
critique that concerns, not the relations of order and equality between
things, but the types of mind and the forms of illusion to which they
might be subject. We are dealing with a doctrine of *quid pro quo*. Bacon

does not dissipate similitudes by means of evidence and its attendant rules. He shows them, shimmering before our eyes, vanishing as one draws near, then re-forming again a moment later, a little further off. They are *idols*. The *idols of the den* and the *idols of the theatre* make us believe that things resemble what we have learned and the theories we have formed for ourselves . . . Only prudence on the part of the mind can dissipate them, if it abjures its natural haste and levity in order to become 'penetrating' and ultimately perceive the differences inherent in nature.

The Cartesian critique of resemblance is of another type. It is no longer sixteenth-century thought becoming troubled as it contemplates itself and beginning to jettison its most familiar forms; it is Classical thought excluding resemblance as the fundamental experience, and primary form of knowledge, denouncing it as a confused mixture that must be analysed in terms of identity, difference, measurement and order. (Foucault, *ibidem*, pp. 51–2)

This is the same difference of perspectives that separates the anglo-saxon analytic philosophy such as practised, for example, by Ryle and Austin, and the French structural linguistics of Lévy-Strauss and Jakobson. The former studies the use of language and claims that only the use can provide the standards; the latter constructs models of the use and study their logical implications. For Ryle, the aim of the analysis of language was 'to move conceptual roadblocks'. Austin did not believe in the 'gospel of clarity'; he would say that philosophy resolves one set of questions only to arrive at another set of questions (Cranston, 1972). This can be called an 'empiricist' approach: the studied reality is the use of language within a complex network of social relations. The French approach was more 'rationalistic': it attempted to provide a 'logically satisfying explanation of the world' (Cranston, *ibidem*). Language was viewed as a system or structure governed by rules; social structure is a theoretical model of relations between people. These structures and models are the only reality that we are able to study.

Foucault, whose works such as *The Order of Things* or *Madness and civilization* are usually classified as belonging to the French structuralist school, has nevertheless been found as having bridged the gap between the English linguistic empiricism and French structuralism in at least one point: in Foucault, *Man*, the abstract construct, the '*sujet épistémique*', becomes finally *a man*, unique, individual, only forced to accept the binding rules and categories of the *épistémè* he happens to find himself historically tied within under pain of appearing as mad (Cranston, *ibidem*; Foucault, 1973, p. xiii). Indeed, there could be even more to it than that: in points interesting for a mathematics educationist there seems to be a kind of homomorphism between Hall's 'major cultural triad' and Foucault's *épistémè*. We shall clarify this point in the next chapter. One reason, however, why I have decided to remain by Hall's theory, is that, unlike Foucault, Hall looks at many different cultures, not just the culture developed by the western civilization. This perspective raises the question of a relativity of epistemological obstacles that is not only diachronic but spreads across the different coexisting cultural backgrounds that students bring today to their classes in more and more countries. It is therefore more real, and more realistic: many of us have to face the cultural relativity of epistemological obstacles and deal with it in our daily work with students. Another reason is that the method of historico-empirical studies that we propose ourselves to develop with relation to understanding in mathematics is more empirical than rationalistic in spirit: for us the reality is the students' actual understanding, not models or theories that we build about it.

To end this section, let us only mention that the notion of epistemological obstacle, implicit under different names, forms and in different contexts and philosophical settings can be found in many philosophers before and after Bachelard. We have already recalled the Baconian 'idols'. Husserl stressed the discontinuity between the common or practical knowledge that remains unquestioned, taken for granted, and the scientific attitude. At the turn of the century, the awareness of social and cultural determinants of scientific knowledge appeared in the works of Durkheim, Granet, Halbwachs, Scheeler and others. Without reference to Bachelard, similar ideas appear in the works of Schütz, Garfinkel, Cicourel. A Polish philosopher, Florian Znaniecki (1882–1958), in his *Social roles of scientists* (in Polish), occupied himself with the sociology of scientists and distinguished such historical types of roles they played as sages, technicians, scholars, researchers, determining very different standards of what is and what is not scientific and significant. Kuhn's theory of scientific revolutions shows how changing can be the scientific truth, how the fundamental categories of thought and rules of rationality can vary from one paradigm to another. It is needless to recall the role and works of Popper and Lakatos in this area. All this — to mention but a few.

Chapter 5

Developmental and Cultural Constraints of Understanding

In analysis to-day there is no longer anything but whole numbers, or finite or infinite systems of whole numbers, bound together by a network of equalities and inequalities. Mathematics, as it has been said, has been arithmetized.

But we must not imagine that the science of mathematics has attained to absolute exactness without making any sacrifice. What it has gained in exactness it has lost in objectivity. It is by withdrawing from reality that it has acquired this perfect purity. We can now move freely over its whole domain, which formerly bristled with obstacles. But these obstacles have not disappeared; they have only been removed to the frontier, and will have to be conquered again if we wish to cross the frontier and penetrate into the realms of practice. (Henri Poincaré, 1952)

Understanding is both developmentally and culturally bound. What a person understands and how he or she understands is not independent from his or her developmental stage, from the language in which he or she communicates, from the culture into which he or she has been socialized. His or her beliefs, his or her 'cognitive norms', his or her world view can all be sources of obstacles to understanding the theoretical frameworks of contemporary scientific knowledge. His or her conceptions cannot be more elaborate than his or her developmental stage allows for, even if the level of his or her speech and technical skills have already superseded this stage.

In the sequel, while trying to support this thesis, we shall be interested in finding the developmental and cultural roots of epistemological obstacles. Two theories turn out to be of help here: L.S. Vygotski's theory of development of concepts from early childhood to adolescence and E.T. Hall's theory of culture (Sierpinska, 1988; 1993). Vygotski's experimental studies into the development of concepts will guide us towards an idea of how the child's first understandings of mathematical notions constitute themselves into obstacles in the adolescent's thinking. Hall's theory of culture will explain how epistemological obstacles come into being, how they function in scientific communities and how they are being transmitted through socialization and education.

These two sources of obstacles: 'development' and 'culture' are closely interrelated. We start by an explication of this relationship.

The Relationship Between Development and Culture

Development and Instruction

In considering the question of relationship between development and instruction, or between spontaneous concepts that develop through physical and mental maturation and informal socialization out of school, and scientific concepts that are a product of culture and can only emerge in the process of instruction, Vygotski claims that, while there is 'a certain element of truth' in the theory that 'development must complete certain cycles or stages or bear certain fruits before instruction is possible' (Vygotski, 1987, p. 195), this theory does not contain the whole truth. He even says that this one-sided dependence is of secondary importance.

> Instruction can give more to development than is present in its direct results. Applied to one point in the child's thought, it alters and restructures many others . . . Instruction is not limited to trailing after development or moving stride for stride along it. It can move ahead of development, pushing it further and eliciting new formations. (Vygotski, 1987, p. 198)

But the relationship between development and instruction is not straightforward; it is very complex (*ibidem*, p. 201). Instruction does influence development, but not in a direct way.

> It would be a mistake to think that a pupil's failure in arithmetic in a given semester necessarily represents the progress in his internal [developmental] semester. If we represent both the educational process and the development of the mental functions that are directly involved in that process as curves . . . we find that these curves never coincide. Their relationship is extremely complex. We usually begin the teaching of arithmetic with addition and end with division. There is an internal sequence in the statement of all arithmetic knowledge and information. From the developmental perspective, however, the various features and components of this process may have an entirely different significance. It may be that the first, second, third and fourth components of arithmetic instruction are inconsequential for the development of arithmetic thinking. Some fifth component may be decisive. At this point, the developmental curve may rise sharply and begin to run ahead of the instructional process. What is learned thereafter may be learned in an entirely different way. Here there is a

sudden shift in the role of instruction in development. The child has finally understood something, finally learned something essential; a general principle has been clarified in this 'aha experience'. (Vygotski *ibidem*, p. 207)

And here Vygotski says something very important, indeed he gives a crucial argument against both disregarding instruction in development as well as saying that instruction should go hand in hand with development:

> If the course of development coincided completely with that of instruction, every point in the instructional process would have equal significance for development. . . . [But] in both instruction and development there are critical moments. These moments govern those that precede it and those that follow it. These points of transition on the two curves do not coincide but display complex interrelationships. Indeed, as we said before, there could be no relationship between instruction and development if the two curves were to fuse. (*ibidem*, p. 207)

Instruction cannot always wait for the development to be fully accomplished; often it must pull it. Teaching interventions must be wisely dosed, they must be used at appropriate time and on the right level: they must be within what Vygotski has called the 'zone of proximal development'. This zone — the close domain of the child's potential development — has more significance, he says, for the dynamics of intellectual development and for the success of instruction than does the actual level of development (*ibidem*, p. 209).

This has important consequences: if the instruction does not intervene at the right moment then some intellectual abilities may not have the chance to develop. For example, if, at the time of the development of conceptual thinking (usually around adolescence), the student is not given the opportunity and is not guided to engage in more formal reasonings, deductions and inferences in which the premises or reasons are made explicit and whose rules are agreed upon, he or she may never become able to develop the style and level of thinking that is necessary to understand and construct mathematical proofs. At the age of 20 or more, when the student comes to study mathematics at the university level, the propitious developmental moment would have passed, and it may be too late for the teaching intervention to have any effects.

Development As a Social Affair

Instruction, knowledge, scientific knowledge are cultural notions; they are always embedded in a certain culture while creating and conveying a certain culture themselves. According to Vygotski, development is a cultural affair.

Thus it is also a social affair. Social psychologists, W. Doise and G. Mugny (1984) claim that 'different cultural systems all indicate that systems of social interaction influence individual cognitive development while at the same time social interactions in different cultures have common elements influencing the initiation of cognitive development'. Indeed, statistical researches have shown a relationship between the school failures of students and the socio-economic status of their parents. Efforts to explain this state of affairs led some psychologists to the conclusion that it is not the low degree of intelligence that is responsible for the students' failures but the psycho-social conditions in which these children are tested (see, e.g., Vial *et al.*, 1974, cited by Perret-Clermont, 1980): the very situation of test is a social situation and a social relation between the experimenter and the child which may not be interpreted in the same way by children from different social classes (Perret-Clermont, *ibidem*, p. 4; Tort, 1974, pp. 266–7, quoted by Perret-Clermont). The test may not measure the intellectual abilities of the child but his or her social abilities to defend himself or herself in an unfriendly and threatening situation.

The 'Social Handicaps' Influencing Mathematical Development

How the socio-economic backgrounds of students can affect their mathematical development is an important problem in mathematics education. Research findings show that not only this background has an impact on the students spontaneous development, but often teachers adjust their attitudes and teaching so that the condition of the students be perpetuated. Very often mathematics teachers conceive of mathematics as a 'crucial subject for reproducing existing social values' and modify curriculum material according to the social class and gender of their pupils (Atweh and Cooper, 1992). It is hypothesized that the socio-economic context of the school and its culture as well as the gender of the students will determine to a large degree the teacher's behaviour towards the students, what and how he or she will teach as well as what the students will be expected to learn and understand. Also the students' view of their chances to succeed in mathematics is biased by the place they think they occupy in the society. This affects their participation. The phenomenon of resistance of students to learning can be partially caused by such beliefs. In such case classes turn into meaningless 'rituals' of activities that have nothing in common neither with mathematics nor learning or are constantly interrupted by the 'bad behaviour' of students. Atweh and Cooper claim that the study of how students resist learning might be crucial for designing intervention studies intending to increase the participation and success of under-represented groups in mathematics.

These findings are supported by older psychological research into the fundamental question whether psycho-sociological factors only interfere in an explicit expression of cognitive abilities or if indeed they determine the course of the development of cognitive processes in childhood (Perret-Clermont, *ibidem*, p. 5). Psychologists were led to the conclusion that, since communication and motivation play such an important role in the development of cognitive processes, then it is not the social background in itself that hinders the intellectual development but a kind of 'social handicap'. The development is retarded if, in the social environment of the child, too little time is devoted to social and verbal interactions and the degree of elaboration of these verbalizations is not very high. It also depends on the home situation and parents' aspirations with respect to the child. For a normal intellectual development the child must feel the need and motivation to communicate on higher and higher levels.

Cultural Values in Psychological and Educational Research; 'Ethnomathematics'

The above reasoning implicitly admits that the culture of socially and economically privileged classes is something better and higher valued than the culture of the working class or poor people. The point is only how, by making the knowledge of privileged classes accessible to the child, to create conditions that will help him or her to make his or her way to this class. The laudable result is when the child rejects his or her own culture and starts to think and speak like the experimenter or the teacher. But research into the actual ways of knowing and understanding of children who, to survive, have to work (as, for example, the street candy vendors), has shown quite plainly that the intelligence of these children is indeed very highly developed and their sense of numbers imposing (Carraher *et al.*, 1985; Saxe, 1990).

There is a whole movement in mathematics education now, called 'ethnomathematics' which studies mathematical thinking in different cultures and proposes to ground the teaching of mathematics in schools in such problems and contexts that are familiar and meaningful in the cultural environments of students and to allow the students to use whatever means they like to approach these problems.

Of course, there is the risk, then, that this will result in following too closely the students' spontaneous development, which can be disastrous for their development indeed — this is at least what Vygotski seems to be saying.

My interest in Vygotski's theory of conceptual development started during my cooperation with Monika Viwegier (Sierpinska and Viwegier, 1989; 1992). It resulted in a certain interpretation of this theory (Sierpinska, 1993) of which I give an account below (with the permission of the publisher).

The Genesis of Understanding and the Developmental Roots of Epistemological Obstacles

Introduction

The genesis of concepts in a child, according to Vygotski, is the genesis of his or her intellectual operations such as generalization, identification of features of objects, their comparison and differentiation, and synthesis of thoughts in the form of systems. The very same operations lie at the foundations of understanding. This explains why I have been attracted by Vygotski's theory of the development of concepts. The various genetic forms of these operations, discovered and described by Vygotski, seemed to provide, almost immediately, the possible genetic forms of understanding. Moreover, the theory can be used to explain some of the curious ways in which students understand mathematical notions, and why, at certain stages of their construction of these notions, they simply cannot understand in a different or more elaborate or more abstract way.

Generalization of mathematical objects and situations, identification of certain elements or features of these objects and situations as objects in themselves, or as more important than others, discrimination between objects and features of objects, synthesis of various judgments about objects and relations between objects, are the elementary operations both in understanding, and concept formation, and in thinking, in general. But, from a qualitative point of view, these operations are by no means the same in a child and in an adult. From early childhood through elementary school years through adolescence and adulthood, the operation of generalization, for example, undergoes an evolution from simple formation of chaotic aggregates of objects linked by various subjective and affective relations, to connection of objects on the basis of their playing a role in some common situation, to connection of objects linked by some common and abstract feature.

The reason why a mathematics educator at any level of teaching may be interested in this theory is that the general pattern of development of conceptual thinking from early childhood to adolescence seems to be recapitulated each time a student embarks on the project of understanding something new or to construct a new concept. 'Different genetic forms of thinking coexist', Vygotski says, and an adolescent or even an adult, when confronted with a new situation or concept, often starts with an understanding which is at a very low level of generalization and synthesis, with very vague discrimination between the relevant and the irrelevant features.

Vygotski distinguishes several stages and two processes of development of concepts in a child from early childhood till adolescence, where the changing roles and levels of sophistication of the elementary intellectual operations are clearly seen. The first of these processes starts very early: this is mainly the process of the development of generalization. Identification and discrimination are there too, of course, but, at the beginning, they operate only on the level of material, concrete objects. This process is composed of two main stages: the stage of 'syncretic images' and the stage of 'complexes', the latter falling into five phases.

The second process starts later, in the last phase of the first (7–8 years of age). This is where begins the development of identification of more and more abstract features of objects and relations. Some features are distinguished from others as more important. Hierarchies of features are built. This process starts later because it requires an already well developed operation of generalization.

When these two processes finally merge at the threshold of adolescence, the child is in possession of 'pre-concepts' or 'potential concepts' and the ground is set for the operation of synthesis necessary for the construction of concepts which cannot exist otherwise but as elements of a system.

This section is composed of two main parts. The first presents the development of the operations of generalization, discrimination, identification and synthesis according to Vygotski. The second derives from it the genetic roots of epistemological obstacles. The first is split into the discussion of three paths of development: the development of generalization in children between the age of 2 and 7 or 8, the development of identification and discrimination in elementary-school children; the development of synthesis in adolescents.

The Development of Generalization

Vygotski distinguishes two important steps in the development of the operation of generalization in experimental conditions before the age of adolescence: 'syncretization' and 'complexization', or formation of 'syncretic images', and 'complexes' which are surrogates of concepts in the child's thinking. 'Syncretization' and 'complexization' differ by the kind of criteria by which, implicitly, the child decides that an object belongs to the same group of objects.

Syncretization uses loose criteria: objects are brought together in a random, unsystematic way. The choice is made on the basis of various subjective impressions of closeness or contiguity. In real life, a 2-year-old will generalize objects on the basis of subjective, and very often affective, impressions. A shop, for example, can be understood as something pleasant (it is a place where people buy candy for kids); a dog as something terrible, if the child happened to be bitten by one (Luria, 1981, p. 51).

The product of syncretization is a 'chaotic heap' of subjectively linked objects (Vygotski, *ibidem*, p. 135). The subjectivity of relations on which the syncretic image is built makes this kind of generalization very unstable, labile.

In 'complexization' subjective impressions of kinship between concrete objects are replaced by connections that actually exist between objects. In spite, however, of being built on more objective connections, a complex is not yet a concept. The difference lies in the character of these connections.

In a concept, these connections are logically of the same type. Connections that bring objects together in a complex, are more often than not logically heterogeneous, factual, randomly discovered in direct experience. In fact, any connection between an object and the model can be a sufficient reason for including the former into the complex (Vygotski, p. 137).

If a name is given to a complex of objects, it does not function as a term covering a certain range of objects (its referential meaning) and a certain set of logically coherent criteria that allow for deciding whether a given object may or may not be termed that way (its categorical meaning), as it happens in the case of scientific concepts (Luria, 1981, pp. 34–9). Rather, as Vygotski metaphorically expresses it (*ibidem*, p. 164), the name functions as a family name for a group of objects. Just as members of, say, the Pietrov family, enter the group of family members on many different grounds (as, for example, being the son of a Pietrov, or the wife or the mother of a Pietrov, etc.), elements of a complex are there for just as many various reasons. For example, one object can be taken because it is of the same colour as the model, another because it is of the same shape, still another because it can be used together with the model for some practical purpose in the same situation (for example, a spoon will be added to a saucer), etc.

The metaphor of 'family name' has also been used by Wittgenstein (see Chapter 1) in his distinction between ordinary language and the more formal languages of mathematics and sciences. What Wittgenstein seems to be saying is that 'complexive thinking' pervades the use of ordinary language. He also considered it as being 'all right': 'ordinary language is in order as it is.' Unlike Russell, he was not proposing, in his later works, to correct the propositions of ordinary language but simply to understand it. Vygotski had a more Russellian ideal in mind: for him, 'concept' meant 'scientific concept' furnished with a definition; the goal of education is to bring children to a level where they would be able to think in terms of scientific concepts.

One symptom of 'complexive thinking' is that, in the sorting out of objects, there is a lack of a logically homogeneous set of criteria. Objects are put together in classes on the basis of some resemblance which can differ from one class to another. Foucault in *The Order of Things* reminds us that the way in which people ordered their world in the sixteenth century in Europe was obviously based on a kind of complexive rather than conceptual thinking: factual and heterogeneous resemblances were the basis on which things were brought together. There were many kinds of resemblances: contingency in space, various analogies (e.g., the analogy of the human body to the earth, man's flesh resembling the soil, blood veins resembling rivers, etc.). Moreover, the resemblance of one thing to another had always to be marked by some more or less visible sign on one of the things, representing the other in some iconic way. Walnuts were considered as good for headaches because the kernel of the nut resembles human brain. There had to be some resemblance between the illness and the remedy. Also words were regarded as signs that were not arbitrary; they bore a resemblance to things that it was necessary to decipher in order to understand.

> Words offer themselves to men as things to be deciphered . . . Language partakes in the world-wide dissemination of similitudes and signatures. It must, therefore, be studied itself as a thing in nature. (Foucault, 1973, p. 35)

This kind of thinking can also be detected in students' first experiences with algebra. They seem indeed to be looking at the strange algebraic aggregates of letters and numerals as hieroglyphs or magic 'signs' to decipher. Having no logical or methodological tools, they look for sameness, associations with class activities to put some order into this new world. Let us have an example of such behaviour.

Example: **complexive thinking about equations**

The example originates from an interview conducted in 1992 by a Concordia University in Montréal graduate student in mathematics education, Marino Discepola. In the interview, a successful 15-year-old high-school student ('Jane') was given a set of algebraic expressions and asked to sort them out according to her own criteria. She formed the following groups:

(1) $y = 5/8x$	$y = 2p/x$	$y = ax + b$	$y = 2x$
(2) $2x = 0$	$2x - 5 = 0$	$2a - 5 = 0$	
(3) $A = bh/2$	$h = 2A/b$	$P = xy/2$	$g = 5/8h$
(4) $4 = 5 - 1$	$8 = 8$	$2 = 3$	$Cx + D = Ax + B$
	$x + 13 = x$	$3/4 = 2/3$	$1/a + 1/b = 1/c$
(5) $2x - x$	$x = 5/8$		

Jane explained that she took together the expressions in (1) because 'you are showing here what y is going to equal to'. In group (2) 'they are all equal zero'. Group (3) are 'formulas'; initially the group contained only the first three expressions; after some hesitation, $g = 5/8h$ was added and Jane explained that this is the formula for gravity. Group (4) was called 'arithmetic'; she explained her inclusion of '$Cx + D = Ax + B$' by saying: 'you don't know what Cx is, so it could be like $7 + 3 = 10$ or $5 + 5$. Four is equal to four and eight is equal to eight and same thing here, same thing here and here.' Group (5) was composed of items she hadn't noticed and thus did not include them anywhere before.

Asked to go over again her groupings and asked for the particular reasons of including items like $2 = 3$, and $3/4 = 2/3$ together with other items in group (4) she used the following arguments: '[$2 = 3$] Well, you have in problem . . . you have to figure if there is something missing out of it and you have to figure out . . . because we used to have problems like that where you have to figure out why maybe 2 is equal to 3'; '[$3/4 = 2/3$] Well, sometimes when solving for x . . . if this was 3x and you want to find out for x . . . you do 4 times 2 over 3 times 3x which is 9x so 8 over 9 . . .'; '[$x + 13 = x$] assuming the same principle as this where you don't know what x is, so it could be $1 + 13 = 14$ just like $4 = 5 - 1$.' For the group (5) she said that 'each x could be replaced by 5/8'.

Obviously Jane has not been using a single criterion to classify the whole set of expressions. Rather, she went by various associations, on the basis, sometimes, of the external appearance of the expressions (groups 1 and 2, mainly), and, at other times, on the basis of association with a domain of class activities in which the expressions appeared (solving for x, figuring out why there is a contradiction). '$3/4 = 2/3$' is not a false statement — it is a part of an equation, it can be completed to be an equation. Anyway, the expressions are neither statements nor conditions for her, they are not finished mathematical objects. They are tasks to perform, computations to be done. Variables are not names of an arbitrary element of a set; they are numbers awaiting an operation (note that an x on the left side of the equation may be assigned a different value than the x on the right side of it). [End of example]

One form of complexization is that of forming 'chain-complexes'. Vygotski used this term when referring to the behaviour of a child who, in an experimental situation of adding objects or pictures of objects to a given model, focuses on the last object added and is satisfied with any link between the new object and this last one, disrespectful of any contradiction that may occur with regard to the previously added objects. For example,

> . . . the child may select several objects having corners or angles when a yellow triangle is presented as a model. Then, at some point, a blue object is selected and we find that the child subsequently begins to select other blue objects that may be circles or semicircles. The child then moves on to a new feature and begins to select more circular objects. In the formation of the chained complex, we find these kinds of transitions from one feature to another. (Vygotski, *ibidem*, p. 139)

Example: **complexive thinking about equations** (continued)
Symptoms of chain-complexization, mixed (as it often happens in reality) with other forms of complexive thinking, could also be observed in Jane. Asked to arrange the given set of expressions into fewer groups she formed four groups of which the first was:

$$x = 5/8, \quad y = 5/8x, \quad y = 2x, \quad y = 2P/x, \quad 2x = 0, \quad 2x - x,$$
$$2x - 5 = 0, \quad x + 13 = x.$$

Let us speculate on how she could have been thinking: she first took x = 5/8, then y = 5/8x because 5/8 is in both; y = 2x and y = 2P/x are added because the previous was y equals something as well; then 2x = 0 because 2 and x were in the previous expressions; 2x − x also has a 2x in it; so does 2x − 5 = 0; x + 13 = x has similar shape. When asked later why she put all these expressions together, she said: 'supposing x = 5/8 we could solve all these equations . . . by replacing x by 5/8.' This could have been an afterthought. She might have thus transformed her chain-complex into a complex by associations, where the core object would be 'x = 5/8'. Anyway, it is rather clear that Jane has not developed a concept of equation yet. For her, 'to solve an equation' does not mean to find values that satisfy the condition given in it, but to compute something, to produce a number, by whatever means.

In the interview, Jane complained that the task she was given was difficult; she said she 'could not get started'. Here is an excerpt from the interview:

Marino:	Why is it harder?
Jane:	Well, because . . . sometimes I don't see the relation, what they have in common.
M.:	So it is much easier to see the differences?
J.:	Yeah!
M.:	So now you are looking for things that they have in common?
J.:	Ha, ha.
M.:	And which parts do you focus on?
J.	Now I am going to focus on the whole equation.

Jane's behaviour here is characteristic of the very first phase of conceptual thinking, the phase of crisis and maturation, full of hesitation, and many returns to the most primitive complexive thinking, but also with emerging self-awareness, dissatisfaction with one's own thinking, search for consistency. [End of example]

Chain-complexization may carry very far away from the original model. There is no focus on one single feature in building such a generalization. Within a complex, an object preserves all its features; neither is distinguished as the one that is essential for the complex. Even if there was a feature that connected an object to a complex and made it similar to objects that were already there, there is no reason whatsoever for the person who forms the complex to make abstraction from other features that the object objectively possesses.

> No single feature abstracted from others plays a unique role. The significance of the feature that is selected is essentially functional in nature. It is an equal among equals, one feature among many others that define the object. (Vygotski, *ibidem*, p. 141)

For Vygotski, this 'equity' of features is a strongly discriminating characteristic of complexization with respect to the kind of generalization that is at the basis of concept formation. The latter is founded on a hierarchy of connections and a hierarchy of relations between features. It creates a qualitatively new object which goes beyond just the union of its elements — it is a system, and it is a system within other systems. On the other hand, the complex is a conglomerate of its elements, and its relations with other conglomerates are not relevant.

> The complex is not a superordinate to its elements in the way the concept is a superordinate to the concrete objects that are included within it. The complex merges empirically with the concrete elements which constitute it. This merging of the general and the particular, of the complex and its element . . . constitutes the essential feature of complexive thinking generally and of the chained complex in particular. (Vygotski, *ibidem*, p. 140)

It is possible to take a slightly different point of view on the fact that, in a complex, the relations that connect the various elements can be of so many various kinds, each taking into account different features. It is not so much that the child takes all the features of an object on equal terms but rather that the child is unstable in distinguishing the features of the object he or she is considering. At one moment it can be, for example, the colour, at another, the shape. The child may not be able to focus on one feature for a longer time.

At the level of complexes, and, *a fortiori*, syncretic images, processes of understanding are very short. The object of understanding (i.e., that which is being understood) changes all the time. In these conditions, the synthesis of a concept on the basis of a couple of features that have been well identified and distinguished from others in an interrelated chain of acts of understanding, cannot be possible.

At some point in their pre-school life children come to form the so-called 'diffuse complexes' which allow them to transcend the world of their immediate experience. This kind of generalization develops when the child goes beyond just stating facts and starts to draw conclusions, make inferences. It often strikes us how unexpected and original or 'impossible' the child's conclusions are 'in domains of thinking that are not subordinated to practical verification' (Vygotski, p. 141). We usually explain it by the children's natural tendency to mix up their dreams and fantasies with reality. The fact is that children base their inferences on a very wide basis; they do not feel bound by any logical or empirical constraints. Absolutely any connection between the premise and the conclusion would do. This leads to very 'diffuse', expanding complexes characterized by unexpected associations, strange leaps of thought. But, however striking the originality of these boundless complexes might be, the principle of their construction is the same as that which underlies the more restricted concrete complexes: they rely on factual connections between different objects. Taking an analogy with art, they resemble forms such as 'collage' in which various parts and pieces of ready-made real objects or pictures of objects are assembled in an often unexpected fashion to form a certain whole — an object of art.

Diffuse-complexes are not something specific just to the kindergarten children. They were common in the sixteenth century *épistémè* as described by Foucault. They may also occur in adolescents and adults today. Here is an example.

Example: **diffuse-complexive thinking about the numerical continuum in adolescents**

The humanities students described in (Sierpinska, 1987) were a little bit lost in such diffuse-complexization when they extended the problem of whether the equality $0.999 \ldots = 1$ holds true or not to questions about the existence of the smallest particle of matter, the limits of the universe, the limits of human knowledge, to questions of truth and convention in science. Strictly speaking, all these questions have nothing to do with the equality $0.999 \ldots = 1$ regarded as a simple, easy to prove fact of the theory of real numbers, a consequence of the assumption that real numbers are an Archimedean do-main. But, for these students, the concept of relative validity of a statement within a theory was not yet something they would know and agree with. This concept was still to be developed and the above mentioned 'diffuse com-plex' was one step towards this goal, reached, finally, at the end of a three-week period of discussions and serious thinking. [End of example]

Pseudo-conceptualization is a form of generalization that normally starts developing in a child at the age of 3. Results of this activity of the mind resemble concepts in that the objects they refer to are the same as those referred to by concepts bearing the same name (i.e., the referential meanings of a pseudoconcept and a concept with the same name are the same). This means that the child and the adult would use the same name for the same objects. However, and this is the major difference, the criteria they would use to decide whether a given object belongs to the given name will be of com-pletely different nature. While the child would be guided by concrete factual features and connections, the adult, in conceptualizing, will guide himself or herself by an abstract and logically coherent set of criteria.

In experimental conditions,

> the child forms a pseudoconcept when he selects objects to match a model which are like those that would be selected and united with one another on the basis of an abstracted concept. Thus this general-ization could arise on the basis of a concept. In fact, however, it arises on the basis of the child's complexive thinking. It is only in terms of the final result that this complexive generalization corresponds with a generalization constructed on the basis of a concept. (*ibidem*, p. 142)

For example, given a triangle, the child will select all triangles from the experimental material, just as an adult would probably do. But, in doing so, the child makes up his or her decisions on the basis of the general appearance of the concrete material pieces of plastic or wood and not on the basis of, for example, the thought that the object given at the start is a model of the geometrical abstract concept of triangle defined as a three sided polygon.

Vygotski claims that, at the kindergarten age, the pseudoconcept form of generalization dominates over other forms of complexive thinking. The rea-son for this overlapping of referential meaning in children and adults, accord-ing to Vygotski, is that the child is not on his or her own in constructing the referential meanings of words but is very strongly oriented by the stability and consistency of meanings in the language of adults that communicate with the child. The child is more or less left to his or her own devices in the choice of the categorical meaning, i.e., the criteria upon which one decides what object should be called what name: 'as he moves along this predetermined path the child thinks as he can on the given level of development of his intellect . . . The adult cannot transmit their own mode of thinking to the child' (Vygotski, p. 115).

Let me add here that, if the child uses a wrong word to name something he or she is immediately corrected. And the child wants to be taught the names of things; children do not rebel against being corrected. Parents know how importunate children can be in asking for names of things and how they take delight in repeating each new name and trying it on new objects, seeking the approval of parents or other adults.

This readiness of the child to accept adults' suggestions as to what and how to generalize weakens significantly at the threshold of conceptual thinking. This may be linked, as we shall see later, with the fact that conceptual thinking is systemic in nature: concepts are systems that are parts of a system. Accepting to change the meaning of one word often means that a whole system of meanings has to be fundamentally reconstructed. This is costly from the point of view of both the emotional and the intellectual investments.

It is the most striking behavioural difference between elementary-school children and adolescents that the former are more open to what the adults tell them about the meanings of words. Adolescents seem to have their own views on what words should mean and are able to defend them with passion (Sierpinska, 1987, 1993; Sierpinska and Viwegier, 1989, 1992).

The reason for this difference of attitude may lie in that complexes and concepts have completely different structures. In a complex, which is a conglomerate of objects linked by various non-homogeneous, concrete and factual connections, contradictions, inconsistencies are something normal. But concepts are supposed to be consistent systems of relations and the discovery of a contradiction is a disaster that must be repaired. Martha, a 14-year-old student described in (Sierpinska and Viwegier, 1989, or Sierpinska, 1993) desperately defended her conviction that a set cannot have more elements than its proper subset: the set of all natural numbers couldn't have 'as many elements' as the set of all even numbers. For her, 'to be a subset' partly meant 'to have less elements' and she strived to preserve this concept which the newly introduced concept of equipotence threatened to overthrow. But when she discovered a logical gap in her arguments, this was a sufficient reason for her to give up and to accept her defeat. She could not bear an inconsistency in her thoughts.

The Development of the Mental Operations of Identification and Discrimination

Along with pseudoconceptualization, the child starts to develop the operations of identification and discrimination on the level of features of objects and relations between features of objects.

In constructing pseudoconcepts on the basis of maximum similarity between features of objects, the child must sort out the features and identify some of them as more important than other (in a given situation), because similarity between objects can never be complete. It is in the phase of pseudoconceptualization that

> . . . we encounter a situation, very interesting from the point of view of psychology, that the child does not attach equal importance to all the features of an object. The features that, for the child, are the most similar to the object given as a model in the task, come into the focus of the child's attention and thus are, in a way, singled out, abstracted from other features which, thereby, shift to the peripheries of attention. It is here that the process of abstraction appears for the first time in all its clarity. This abstraction is frequently poorly differentiated in nature because it is a whole group of inadequately differentiated features that is abstracted (often based only on a confused impression of commonality) rather than sharply isolated features. Nonetheless, the child's integral perception has been overcome. Features have been differentiated into two unequal groups . . . The concrete object with all its features, in all its empirical completeness, no longer enters into the complex; it is no longer included into the generalization. As it enters the complex, it now leaves some of its features on the threshold. As a result, it is impoverished. Those features that serve as a foundation for its inclusion in the complex emerge in special relief in the child's thinking. (Vygotski, *ibidem*, p. 147)

Thus, at some point of his or her pre-school life, the child starts to identify features of objects and to discriminate between the more and the less significant in view of some generalization.

The same phenomenon may occur at an older age, when the child — a student — builds up his or her understanding of abstract concepts. For example, at some point in the process of understanding the topic of equations at the high-school level, the student must identify the simultaneous occurrence of variables and the equals sign as features characteristic of equations before he or she starts to conceptually think of equations as equality conditions on variables.

It is such identification of the 'characteristic' features of objects that further leads to the development of the categorical meaning of words (connotations).

After the preliminary phase of identification, in the aim of generalization, of whole groups of features, poorly discriminated from one another, there comes the phase of building up generalizations on the basis of an identification of a single common feature.

Generalizations thus constructed are called 'potential concepts'. They are still pseudoconcepts from the point of view of the kind of criteria that make up their categorical meaning: the above mentioned 'single common feature' remains concrete and factual. Very often this common feature is related to the function of the object or its role in a particular situation. And thus, for example, a dog would be that who guards the house, and an equation — something you solve for x, a function — something you find the values of, put them in a table and draw a graph.

In the phase of potential conceptualizations

to define an object or meaning of word means for the child to say what it does, or, more frequently, what can be done with it. When the issue is the definition of abstract concepts, it is the active situation, the equivalent of the child's word meaning, that advances to the fore-front. In a study of thinking and speech, Messer gives a typical ex-ample of a definition of an abstract concept that was elicited from one of his subjects who was in the first year of instruction. The child said: 'Intelligence is when I am thirsty but do not drink from a dirty pond.' This type of concrete functional meaning is the sole mental founda-tion of the potential concept. (Vygotski, *ibidem*, p. 159)

As, in generalizing, the child becomes more and more able of founding the thinking on the same single feature, he or she goes beyond complexization and approaches true conceptualization via the intermediary phase of 'potential concepts'.

'Potential concepts' are called potential because they contain in them-selves the possibility of becoming fully fledged concepts, once the feature that lies at their basis detaches itself from the concrete, the factual, the situational.

A remark that occurs to me at this point is that what the so-called 'con-textual' or 'situational' mathematics movement in mathematics education proposes to do is, in fact, to engage students in constructing pseudo-concepts and potential concepts (or, rather, I should say, 'pre-concepts' because we are speaking of real and not of experimental concepts), that is, in generalizations that are already based on an identification of a single feature but are still very closely linked to concrete situations. This is not a bad idea, altogether, if we admit that, in constructing a new concept, the student has to pass through syncretization and complexization and that pre-concepts is the necessary phase in the transition to conceptual thinking.

Moreover, not much more than pre-concepts can be expected before the age of adolescence. Students may not be able to focus their attention on the definitional single and abstract feature of objects, taking them in all their actual and situational richness. But, it is important to be aware that one can-not expect that older students will develop conceptualizations spontaneously by themselves, through some 'necessary, natural law of evolution'. It is the teachers' and adults' role to provide the youth with challenging theoretical questions and problems in and out of school setting to open the 'gate to conceptual thinking' for them (Vygotski, *ibidem*, pp. 191, 212).

The Development of the Operation of Synthesis: Conceptual Thinking

The construction of a concept involves a substantial use of the operation of abstraction of features and the synthesis of these features into a coherent whole. One can speak of conceptual thinking when such abstract syntheses become the fundamental form of thought with which the subject perceives and inter-prets reality (*ibidem*, p. 159). The synthesis itself is a culmination of a series of identifications, discriminations and generalizations. The crucial role in this operation is played by the 'functional use of the word'.

> The concept arises in the intellectual operation. It is not the play of associations that leads at its construction. In a unique combination, all the elementary intellectual functions participate in its formation. The central feature of this operation is the functional use of word as a means of voluntarily directing attention, as a means of abstracting and isolating features, and as a means of the synthesizing and symbolizing these features through the sign. (Vygotski, *ibidem*, p. 164)

The formation of a concept involves not only the synthesis that allowed to isolate the necessary and sufficient criterion of its meaning; this synthesis must also grasp the concept's relations with other concepts, ideas, judgments. Concepts do not exist in isolation. A concept is immediately embedded into a system of ideas and judgments.

> The concept actually does find its natural place in judgements and conclusions, acting as a constituent of them. The child who responds with the word 'big' when presented with the word 'house', or with the phrase 'apples hang from it' when presented with the word 'tree' proves that the concept exists only within a general structure of judgements, that it exists only as an inseparable part of that structure. (*ibidem*, pp. 163–4)

Vygotski claims that having judgments, being able to formulate judgments about objects precedes the ability to define concepts involved in these judgments.

Adolescence does not automatically trigger conceptual thinking in children. As in other areas of their mental and physical development, early adolescence is a very stormy time of transition and change: 'the period of crisis and maturation' (*ibidem*, p. 160).

Several clashes characterize this beginning phase of conceptual thinking. Among them is the discrepancy between the ability to 'do things with' a concept, i.e., use it, make it work, and the ability to think and speak about it, in particular, to define it in general terms.

> In the concrete situation, the adolescent forms the concept and applies it correctly. However, when it comes to the verbal definition of this concept, the adolescent's thinking encounters extreme difficulty. The concept's definition is significantly narrower than the concept as it is actually used. This indicates that the concept arises as the result of processes other than the logical processing of certain elements of experience. Moreover, it comes into conscious awareness and acquires a logical character at a comparatively late stage of its development . . .

In our experiments we often observed a situation where the child or adolescent correctly resolved the task involved in the formation of the concept. However, in providing a definition of the concept he had formed the same child sank to a more primitive level and began to enumerate the concrete objects grasped by the concept in a particular situation. Thus, the adolescent uses the word as a concept but defines it as a complex. This type of oscillation between thinking in complexes and thinking in concepts is characteristic of the transitional age. (*ibidem*, p. 161)

Another difficulty experienced by adolescents is that of transfer of concept from one concrete situation to another. However, this difficulty is quite quickly overcome. A more serious problem is related to the transfer of a concept from abstract definition to concrete situations (i.e., when it comes to its interpretations and applications). But even that should normally be overcome by the end of the transitional age.

Rather early, children are able to use words in their correct meanings; they may not always be aware of their own thinking in making the choice of the right word. They are not able to use a word 'intentionally'.

Vygotski gives an example of 7–8-year-old children, who when asked to explain what does the word 'because' mean in the sentence: 'I am not going to school tomorrow because I am ill', would give answers like: 'this means that he is ill', 'this means he will not go to school'. Or, when asked to complete the sentence 'This man fell off his bike, because . . .', they would answer: 'he fell off his bike because he fell and then he hurt himself', 'because he broke his leg, his arm'.

For Vygotski, an awareness of one's own thinking processes, a conscious and intentional (and not just spontaneous or imitative) use of words is exactly that which founds the conceptual thinking. Now, because awareness and intentional use of one's own thinking processes presupposes their generalization, and generalization is nothing but a constitution of a hierarchy, then conceptual thinking must be systemic. Indeed, for Vygotski, awareness of concepts and their systemic character are synonymous (*ibidem*, p. 192).

One important consequence of this, and Vygotski stresses it very strongly, is that the system of concepts cannot be given (transmitted) to the child from outside. The systemic character of thought is synonymous with awareness and awareness is always an awareness of one's own thought. In order to be aware of one's own thoughts and thinking processes one must first have these thoughts and experience these thinking processes.

> . . . the system — and the conscious awareness that is associated with it — is not brought into the domain of the child's concepts from without; it does not simply replace the child's own mode of forming and using concepts. Rather, the system itself presupposes a rich and mature form of concept in the child. This form of concept is necessary

so that it may become the object of conscious awareness and systematization. (*ibidem*, p. 192)

The domain *par excellence* of systematization is the domain of scientific concepts (*ibidem*, p. 212). This is why learning at school is so important. Scientific concepts precede the spontaneous concepts in the development of the child, and in fact, foster their development.

The Spiral Development of Real Concepts in a Child

The systemic character of generalizations is more visible in the real processes of concept formation than in the experimental setting, where the child is usually given the task of forming some artificial concept independently from his or her previous knowledge and experience. A generalization is always built on some previous generalizations. The development of generalizations resembles a spiral and not a series of concentric circles (*ibidem*, p. 229).

In an example taken from research on the development of mathematical ideas Vygotski shows how algebraic thinking develops upon the arithmetic thinking and transcends it through generalization.

> An analysis of the development of preschooler's general representations (which correspond to the experimental concepts that we call complexes) indicated that general representations — as a higher stage in the development of word meaning — emerge not from generalization of isolated representations but from general perceptions. That is they emerge from the generalizations that dominated the previous stage . . . In our study of arithmetic and algebraic concepts we established an analogous relationship between new generalizations and those that precede them. Here, in studying the transition from the school child's preconcepts to the adolescent's concepts, we were able to establish what is in essence the same thing that we established in previous research on the transition from generalized perception to general representations (i.e., from syncretic images to complexes). (*ibidem*, p. 230)

Vygotski describes the preconcept of number as 'an abstraction of number from the object and a generalization of the quantitative features of the object' (*ibidem*). The concept of number, on the other hand, is 'an abstraction from the number [of things] and a generalization of any relation between numbers' (*ibidem*).

Thus, the concept is an abstraction and generalization of *thoughts about thoughts*, while the preconcept is an abstraction and generalization of *thoughts about things*. The concept is not an evolution of the pre-concept; it is a leap to a new and higher level of thought; it is thinking about the thoughts of the previous levels.

Vygotski seems to be saying that the concept of number belongs to algebraic thinking; arithmetic thinking is concerned with at most the preconcept of number. Algebraic thinking is based on a generalization of one's own arithmetical operations and thoughts and is, therefore, characterized by free acting in and on the arithmetical domain. In algebra, arithmetic expressions can be transformed, combined according to the general laws of arithmetic operations and not just calculated, 'executed' like in the frame of arithmetic thinking. Operations are independent from the particular arithmetic expressions they are involved in. 2 + 3 for an arithmetically thinking school child is 5, period. 2 + 3 for the algebraically thinking adolescent is a particular case of a + b, where a, b are any real numbers. For the algebraically thinking adolescent arithmetical operations are special cases of the more general algebraic notions.

As long as one works within a system without being aware of its laws, one is tied up in it. Awareness brings about freedom and control over the system. Once the system is seen as one of the possible systems, a way is open to new systems, new generalizations and syntheses, new understanding.

The Psycho-genetic Roots of Epistemological Obstacles

In the experiment with the notion of equipotence involving children 10–12 and 14-year-olds (Sierpinska and Viwegier, 1992), it appeared less difficult for the 10-year-old Agnès to accept the equipotence of given infinite sets than for the 14-year-old Martha, who never accepted the equipotence unconditionally. Also, Agnès was swift in grasping the main argument for the equipotence of natural and even numbers while Martha argued very strongly against it and it took her a long while to discover an inconsistency in her reasoning. But: she discovered it! She was able to reflect on and judge her own thinking and was certainly more aware of the difficulties inherent in the notion of equipotence, of its non-intuitiveness.

While Agnès' thinking was still very complex in nature, Martha certainly thought conceptually of infinity and subsets although her concepts were not exactly those we know from studying *Mengenlehre*. For her, 'infinity' was something 'as large as we wish' and therefore impossible to count, and a subset was a part with less elements than the whole. These concepts, embedded in a whole system of her other concepts and beliefs (also about the nature of scientific knowledge) functioned as obstacles to her acceptance of the proposed definition of 'as many as' and, even more so, to its logical consequences (especially to the equipotence of natural and even numbers) and Martha was aware of it.

Systemic thinking cannot bear inconsistencies and Martha struggled to remove hers from her system, first, by trying to undermine the above mentioned consequence of the definition of 'as many as'. When she failed — and she admitted it by discovering an inconsistency in her arguments — she proposed to reject the definition itself. She would rather change the axioms of the theory than any of what she considered as fundamental truths or 'basic statements' (to use the term of Popper and Lakatos, see Lakatos, 1978b). Informed that, in the mathematical theory, 'as many as' is understood in very much the proposed way and the equipotence of natural and even numbers is accepted as a theorem, she fell into frustration and dramatically declared herself disappointed with mathematics. In spite of this frustration or maybe exactly because of it we may say that, by the end of the experiment, Martha's understanding of mathematics was much deeper than in any of the younger children.

We say that, in Martha, her concepts of infinity and subset functioned as epistemological obstacles because, first of all, they were concepts (not complexes), parts of a system of concepts, ways of thinking and beliefs and therefore they could not be removed or changed without injuring the whole system. Second, they belonged to the sphere of scientific thinking and its foundations; they were linked with beliefs about what knowledge is and what makes it valid.

It seems that one cannot sensibly speak of epistemological obstacles in children before they reach the age of conceptual thinking.

Things went easier with the younger children because they did not have to *overcome* epistemological obstacles. The epistemological obstacles still remained to be *constructed*.

And constructed they are in the child's development and socialization, gradually, on the basis of the child's experiences with, first, the concrete sets and concrete numbers of things, small numbers of things, and then, inferences about large numbers and the inner invisible structure of things — thus transcending the immediate experience and the possibilities of actual counting.

First generalizations are built on images of the concrete and the finite. No wonder they resemble so much their archetypes. A point is a very tiny dot, infinity is 'so many that you cannot count' etc. Concepts cannot be given to the child, ready made, in the verbalized form or symbolic representation. The child has to construct them as generalizations of his or her previous generalizations and it is quite natural that the adolescent's first concepts may bear little resemblance to the fully fledged ones developed by generalizations made by mathematicians in their adult, mature, and often genius lives. And thus they become obstacles to understanding the theories.

In our experiment, younger children, too, experienced difficulties in understanding why some of the given sets could be regarded as having 'as many elements one as the other'. But these difficulties were not a consequence of an epistemological obstacle. If they could not understand the statement it was not because it didn't fit into what they already knew. They would not bother about fitness or consistency. They just struggled for finding a way to explain it to themselves, for finding a way to make it acceptable from their own point of view. And, in the frame of complexive thinking, this meant finding some concrete way of actually matching the elements of the two sets together in pairs. It was not necessary, for these children, to actually perform the matching. Not any more. They were much too far advanced in their complexive thinking. It was enough to be able to imagine how this can be done, and to show it with a vague gesture. Arguments why the method of pairing would work were not felt as necessary by the children in the case of two lines. If argumentation appeared in the case of natural and even numbers it is because the elements could not be represented on a sheet of paper in a way that would show all their elements matched simultaneously. The problem was much more abstract and it was not obvious that the method of matching 1 with 2, 2 with 4 etc., would indeed work. A verbal argument was necessary and Agnès was able to find it: the sets are infinite and infinity is something that never ends, so you never run short of these even numbers to match with the natural numbers. The challenge of the situation was so big that it almost pulled Agnès beyond her complexive thinking. Of course, the chances of her staying there were probably minimal. It could be seen, however, that rational and deductive argumentation, and good understanding of unboundedness of the set of natural numbers were all within Agnès' zone of proximal development.

This is how, according to Vygotski, the child is able to transcend his or her actual ways of thinking. The challenging questions posed by the adult lead the child's thinking beyond the forms he or she is using and sometimes force it into forms that are much more elaborate. Concepts develop this way, but, simultaneously, the seeds are thrown of future epistemological obstacles. The obstacles grow on the soil of complexive, childish, thinking — they have genetic roots. But the fertilizers (the challenges that make them grow) come from the surrounding culture, from the implicit and explicit ways in which the child is socialized and brought up at home, in the society, in the school institution.

It is to the cultural roots of epistemological obstacles that we turn now.

The Cultural Roots of Epistemological Obstacles

What the child will 'complexize' and the adolescent 'conceptualize', or, to put it differently, what each of them will attempt to understand and how will they understand it depends not only on the particularities of the human brain and on the constraints of the genetic development but also and foremost on the culture into which the child is socialized. The language used in the child's environment may favour certain images rather than other. For example, certainly the abundance of nouns in some languages and the way abstract constructs are spoken about inspire a way of understanding that 'reify' the world, fills it up with stable and fixed 'things' rather than with processes, dynamic changes and different forms of energy constantly changing from one to another (Lakoff and Johnson, *ibidem*). Atoms like little billiard balls, geometrical points like little dots, arranged as beads in a necklace — these are the images conveyed to the child by the way these concepts are spoken about.

An object of understanding must be noticed to become an object of understanding. But what to notice, and what are the noticed things signs of

— this is learned, acquired through the processes of socialization and education. A mother will teach her child to eat with a spoon — to notice this object and identify it as a tool for bringing the food to the mouth and not to throw it at the dog. In a mathematics class, when teaching word-problem solving, the teacher will point to information that is relevant from the mathematical point of view, and discard that which is irrelevant. In a 'buying and selling' problem, it is not relevant whether the apples bought were McIntosh or Golden Delicious, or whether the buyer's name was Yi-Ching or Eddy. What counts is the price and the quantity of purchased goods. This teaching to attend to numbers only is so successful that when asked the now legendary problem: 'There are 5 goats and 7 sheep aboard a boat. How old is the captain?' the students almost unanimously respond: '35'.

In different cultures, different things are attended to. Numbers and counting are important in certain cultures. Children are trained in memorizing the sequence of numerals and a child who 'can count up till 100' at the age of 4 is praised by everybody around. Some cultures have not found it worthwhile to invent numerals above a certain small number, and do not bother to think about numbers as objects in themselves.

The child learns by imitating the behaviour of adults. He or she learns also what the adults would wish him or her not to learn, in the hope that the child will be a better and 'revised' version of themselves. Schemes of behaviours induce schemes of thinking. The child acquires, without knowing it, certain schemes of approaching problems and solving them.

Cultures determine their own epistemological obstacles — things that are so obvious, so natural that nobody would think of questioning them [lest he or she be branded a blasphemist!]. First, one would have to be aware of them being obstacles indeed. And being aware of an obstacle can be very close to its overcoming.

Anthropologists have tried to make us more aware of the implicit, the unspoken, the 'hidden dimension' of our culture (Hall, 1969, 1976, 1981; Hook, 1969). They have tried to explain the difficulty of communication between different ethnic groups. But there may be similar difficulties in communication between the scientific community and the laymen, the teachers and the learners, the scientific thinking and the everyday thinking.

The cultural dimension of mathematics learning is more and more taken into account in mathematics educational research (Bishop, 1988, 1991; Chevallard, 1990, 1992; Keitel *et al.*, 1989; Mellin-Olsen, 1987; Vasco, 1986, to name but a few). In a review of a book devoted to the relationship between the cultural development and the development of arithmetical skills, strategies and concepts in young street candy sellers in Brazil (Saxe, 1990), Alan Bishop writes:

> These are fascinating and challenging times in mathematics education, as the influences from anthropology are forcing us to reshape our constructs and our methodologies. Research like Lave's is making us

reexamine our problem solving research ideas to take full account of the social situation in which the problem is framed. The ethnographic research approach and its associated assumptions are becoming more acceptable within our research community. Ethnomathematics is an ever growing field with enormous implications for both curriculum development and pedagogical practice in all countries. The developing field of cultural psychology . . . is going to have a profound influence on psychological theory and will also, in my view, have challenging implications for all of us in mathematics education. (Bishop, 1991)

These words were written in 1991. One might get the impression that the 'cultural' trend in mathematics education is very recent. In fact, the cultural dimension in the study of the teaching and learning processes in mathematics appeared at least as far back as in the mid-1970s in the French and German didactics of mathematics under the influence of sociologists of education such as, for example, Basil Bernstein. Education started to be viewed as 'transmission of culture', and a means for its 'reproduction' (e.g., Bernstein, 1971; also, Marody, 1987). Guy Brousseau's concepts of *'contrat didactique'* and *'situation didactique'*, Yves Chevallard's *'transposition didactique'*, Heinrich Bauersfeld's studies of the invisible culture of the mathematics classroom — the discovery of patterns and routines of the classroom communication — are all based on a holistic view of institutionalized learning as part of a certain culture and a culture itself.

What I personally have reached for in the anthropological thought are the theoretical considerations of E.T. Hall (1981) — his 'theory of culture' — which appears to quite convincingly explain epistemological obstacles as a cultural phenomenon.

The 'Cultural Triad'

Hall describes culture as a 'form of communication' (Hall, *ibidem*, p. 49) or as 'a learned and shared way of behaviour' (p. 66). Teaching and learning are crucial in a culture. Hall claims that ways of teaching determine, in a sense, all other components of culture, and learning is an activity just as important for survival as sleep, water and food.

He speaks of the 'fundamental triad': three levels of experiencing the world by man, three ways of transmission of this experience to children, three types of consciousness, three types of emotional relations to things: the 'formal', the 'informal', the 'technical'.

The 'formal' level is the level of traditions, conventions, unquestioned opinions, sanctioned customs and rites that do not call for justification. The transmission of this level of culture is based on direct admonition, explicit correction of errors without explanation ('don't say "I goed", say "I went" '). Built up over generations, the formal systems are normally very coherent. For people living in cultural communities, they play a role analogous to that which instinct has for animals.

The informal level is the level of the often unarticulated schemes of behaviour and thinking. Our knowledge of typing, or skiing, or biking belongs to this level of culture if we do not happen to be instructors of these skills. This level of culture is acquired through imitation, practice and participation in a culture, and not by following a set of instructions. Very often neither the imitated nor the imitating know that some teaching–learning process is taking place.

At the technical level, knowledge is explicitly formulated. This knowledge is analytical, aimed to be logically coherent and rationally justified.

> The process of teaching [at this level] has a planned, coherent form . . . Knowledge belongs to the instructor. His skills are function of his knowledge and analytical abilities. If he has clearly and conscientiously analysed the material, his presence is not even necessary. He can write it on paper or record on tape . . . [Like the formal education] the technical education starts with errors and correction of errors, but a different tone is used here and the student is being explained his error. (*ibidem.*, pp. 82, 84–5)

In terms of the triad, Hall then defines culture, taken at any given point, as 'made up of formal behavior patterns that constitute a core around which there are certain informal adaptations. The core is also supported by a series of technical props' (*ibidem*, p. 91).

It is necessary to stress that the contents of the levels of culture are not something stable and fixed once and for all; not only these contents change considerably from one culture to another, they also change within one culture. Elements of the formal level can be pushed into the implicit and informal. Sometimes an idea is born within the technical sphere which contradicts the common beliefs of the formal level and is being publicly rejected by those who consider themselves responsible for the standards, whether scientific or moral or religious or other. But with time, use and thoughtless repetition the idea may shift to the formal level and become a new kind of belief. Indeed, 'every really significant scientific idea is born as a heresy and dies as a prejudice' (Cackowski, 1992).

I promised, in Chapter 4, to show how one can establish a 'homomorphism' between Hall's cultural triad and Foucault's *épistémè*. Here is a suggestion: Foucault's *épistémè* can be regarded as related categories, rules of sense and rules of rationality prevalent in a given epoch and culture (Skarga, op.cit.). These three pillars seem to correspond to the three levels of culture: the formal, the informal and the technical. Categories normally function without much justification, directing the thought, determining the important questions; it is around them that a whole world view is built up. When they start to be questioned, the society is ready for a change. The rules of sense are usually not fully articulated and can be unconscious, but they are what guides the way of making sense of events, phenomena, texts; they order the world. We can say that they belong to Hall's 'informal level'. The rules of rationality, in their turn, are more appropriately placed on the 'technical level' of culture. Different epochs characterize rationality in different ways, but explicitness, articulation of meanings, justification of statements, generality are probably the common features. Differences appear in the standards of this articulation, justification, generality.

In the sequel we shall use the language of Hall's 'triad' to speak about the cultural constraints of epistemological obstacles in mathematics.

The Mathematical Culture

Mathematics can be regarded as a developing system of culture and a sub-culture of the overall culture in which it develops (Wilder, 1981).

Also in the mathematical culture three levels of experiencing mathematical thoughts, three ways of transmission of this experience to others, three types of consciousness, three types of emotional relations can be distinguished: 'the formal', the 'informal', and the 'technical'.

Let us assume that the 'technical' level of a mathematical culture is the level of mathematical theories, of knowledge that is verbalized and justified in a way that is widely accepted by the community of mathematicians. In the following, the formal and the informal levels of culture will be discussed in more detail — they are the hotbed of epistemological obstacles.

At the 'formal' level, our understanding is grounded in beliefs; at the 'informal' level — in schemes of action and thought; at the 'technical' level — in rationally justified, explicit knowledge.

In a mathematical culture the fundamental role is played by the 'informal' level. This role is both positive and negative. The 'informal' level of a mathematical culture is the level of tacit knowledge (Polanyi, 1964), of unspoken ways of approaching and solving problems. This is also the level of canons of rigour and implicit conventions about, for example, how to justify and present a mathematical result. Today, for example, to write in a mathematical paper that a certain theorem has exceptions would be exhilarating. But, as we already mentioned, in the nineteenth century, it was perfectly acceptable for N.H. Abel to write such a sentence with respect to the well-known Cauchy's theorem that the limit of a convergent sequence of continuous functions is a continuous function (Lakatos, 1978a).

Example: **culturally bound notions of rigour in mathematics**

Another example of a historical difference in viewing mathematical rigour is given by Kvasz (1990). It is related to the problem of convergence of power series. At the time when the expansion of real functions in power series had known its apogee, mathematicians did not find it necessary to prove the convergence of the series. For example, in the expansion:

$$\sin x = x - 1/3!x^3 + 1/5!x^5 - \ldots$$

the existence of the sine was guaranteed by its geometrical meaning. Series were just a computational tool. If the tool works then the series must converge to sin x. This was, as Kvasz calls it, a realistic approach to mathematical objects.

> The realistic point of view is based on the belief in the existence of some reality — geometrical, physical or other, which solves all questions of existence. So the mathematician needs not to take care of them, and not because he is not rigorous enough but because it does not make sense. (Kvasz, 1990)

This realistic approach became untenable when complex functions started to be studied. For example, the equation

$$e^{ix} = 1 + ix + 1/2!(ix)^2 + \dots$$

cannot be regarded as a description of e^{ix}, otherwise well defined as an object. Its existence can only be guaranteed by a proof of convergence of the series.

> We came from the realistic to the nominalistic point of view. Here the symbols refer to no reality. They are mere abbreviations for other syntactical expressions. So the question of convergence becomes very important. Only if the convergence of the series has been proved, we have the right to use the symbol e^{ix}. (Kvasz, *ibidem*)

[End of example]

The 'formal' level of mathematical culture could be regarded as the level of beliefs, convictions and attitudes towards mathematics, ideas about its nature, relation to reality, etc. The belief in the absolute infallibility of mathematical theories, the conviction that mathematics is rigorous, or, on the other hand, the conviction that mathematical proofs rely on formal and conventional tricks, and that, therefore, mathematics is completely useless from the point of view of knowledge about the world and reality, are examples of elements of the 'formal' level.

Another element of this level is what is usually called the 'mathematical folklore', i.e., what is 'known', what is so obvious, that nobody bothers to prove it any more. In particular, the so called 'cultural intuition' belongs here (Wilder, *ibidem*, p. 133). What Wilder calls 'cultural intuition' are the convictions concerning the basic mathematical notions, which are taken for granted by mathematicians in a given epoch. The existence of such 'cultural intuition' at each moment of the development of mathematics has been formulated as a law of this development (law 9) by Wilder. Here are some examples of such 'cultural intuitions':

- the belief of the early Greek mathematical community in the commensurability of all line segments;

- the pre-Grassmann-Hamilton belief that all algebras and operations on numbers must be commutative;
- the pre-Bolzano-Weierstrass intuition concerning real continuous functions; in particular, that any such function can be non-differentiable in at most a finite number of points;
- the conviction that the unit sphere cannot be decomposed into a finite number of parts, from which two unit spheres could be composed (a conviction refuted by Banach and Tarski in 1924, with the help of the Axiom of Choice).

Let us remark that the way in which Wilder presents his examples of cultural intuitions shows his own, rather platonistic, attitude towards the nature of mathematics. Mathematical ideas seem to pre-exist, and the task of mathematics is to discover them, give them names, find relations between them. First experiences in a given domain allow to formulate certain guesses (or 'intuitions' in Wilder's terminology) that can be refuted in the course of further research into the nature of mathematical objects. But isn't it rather that what we make research into are the logical consequences of definitions and assumptions we have deliberately chosen ourselves? We might have chosen a definition of function that would not let in the plague of functions without derivatives. We might have not accepted the Axiom of Choice into the foundations of mathematics. Didn't we have the Choice?

In a 'formal' or 'technical' way we can acquire certain knowledge about mathematics, we can learn algorithms, some methods of proof (mathematical induction, *reductio ad absurdum*, etc.), solving some 'typical' problems, ready and written parts of a theory. We can be passive users of mathematics. But it is only on the 'informal' level, by working with mathematicians, through 'imitation and practice' as Polya used to say, that we can learn to pose sensible questions, put up hypotheses, propose generalizations, synthesize concepts, explain and prove.

'Informal' knowledge and understanding is thus an indispensable support of any creative thinking in mathematics. On the other hand, however, this same knowledge and ways of understanding, as not fully conscious, and unquestioned, and drawn from experience in concrete situations, can guide our thinking in new situations in a way that will make the resolution impossible. Reiterating attempts, we may unconsciously always apply the same schema of thought or action, bewildered by the fact, that what has always worked so well suddenly fails us completely. It is only an awareness of what was the 'obstacle' that allows us to overcome the impasse and change our ways of understanding .

The Interplay Between the Three Levels of Mathematical Culture

The formal, the informal and the technical, albeit autonomous from the point of view of their identity, are in constant mutual interaction. This feature of culture makes possible the cultural changes, the downfall of world views, the rise of theories that bring about changes in our representations of the structure of matter, of time and space, of number . . . This feature of culture makes understanding possible.

On the one hand, the formal and the informal affect the technical; on the other — the technical 'creates very quickly its own formal system' (Hall, *ibidem*, p. 81). As Bachelard said:

> Knowledge acquired through a scientific effort can decline itself: the abstract and sincere question gets used, the concrete answer remains. At this point the spiritual activity inverts and blocs itself. An episte-mological obstacle encrusts itself on the unquestioned knowledge. Intellectual habits, once healthy and useful, can, at the long term, impede the research. 'Our mind — rightly says Mr Bergson — has an irresistible tendency to consider as clearer the idea that serves it more often'. (Bachelard, 1983, pp. 14–15)

What is considered as obvious and natural, what is unquestioned, will, in some measure, determine what will be considered as problematic: what questions and hypotheses will be posed and what will be the ways of attacking them.

On the other hand, the problems will determine the results that will be obtained, i.e., what will be considered as the 'justified body of scientific or technical knowledge'.

The way in which the 'technical sphere' can affect the 'formal' sphere is described by Hall as follows:

> Science, whose nature is, as we think, technical, has developed a series of formal systems that nobody puts into question. They are linked with the methodology of scientific research, with the stress put on the objectivism of members of the scientific community, on their loyalty to their own work and the work of others. In fact, a part of what is being called science, should be classified as a new formal system, which quickly takes the place or replaces the older formal systems, concentrated around popular beliefs and religions . . . The so-called social sciences or the behavioral sciences are saturated with the ritualized procedure transmitted by professors to those who will later transmit it to their students. Rumour has it that a certain zealant of scientific sociology has elaborated an index, with the help of which one can evaluate the degree of 'scientificity' of a given publication. The scale is based on the ratio main text — annotations, and on the number of statistical data in the text. (Hall, 1981, p. 81)

Example: **beliefs related to Hilbert's programme of finitistic proofs**

In the history of mathematics, the successes of formalization at the turn of the century have encouraged Hilbert to formulate a programme full of optimistic belief in the possibility of carrying through finitistic proofs of consistency of the fundamental mathematical theories. This belief had driven mathematicians' and logicians' 'technical' activity for several decades and reached its culmination, in 1930, with Gödel's proofs of the impossibility of proving the consistency of arithmetics with the methods of arithmetic.

This result has caused confusion among philosophers of mathematics. The myth of absolute infallibility of mathematics was seriously shaken.

Morris Kline (1980) writes,

> The logicists, formalists and set theorists rely on axiomatic foundations. In the first few decades of this century this type of foundation was hailed as the choice basis on which to build mathematics. But Gödel's theorem that no one system of axioms embraces all of the truths that belong to any one structure, and the Löwenheim-Skolem theorem shows that each embraces more than was intended. Only the intuitionists can be indifferent to the problems posed by the axiomatic approach.
>
> To top all the disagreements and uncertainties about which foundation is the best, the lack of proof of consistency still hangs over the heads of all mathematicians like the sword of Damocles. No matter which philosophy of mathematics one adopts, one proceeds at the risk of arriving at a contradiction. (Kline, 1980, p. 310)

After Gödel some philosophers tried to find a way out of this feeling of uncertainty. In fact, some of them proceeded to build their certainty on this uncertainty. This is how the philosophy of Lakatos could be described, perhaps. In the years 1960–70 Lakatos started to promote a philosophy of fallibilistic mathematics: mathematics as a 'quasi-empirical science'. According to Lakatos (1978b), the basic logical flow in mathematics is not the transmission of truth through the channels of deduction from axioms to theorems, but rather the retransmission of falsity from the special statements (the socalled 'basic statements') towards the axioms. In this approach, axioms are but 'working hypotheses', and if it turns out, on the basis of the axioms, that one of the basic statements does not hold, then one would rather change the axioms than reject the statement.

The idea of mathematics presented by Lakatos in his *Proofs and refutations*, is well rendered by Kline (*ibidem*) when he writes:

> [mathematics] is a series of great intuitions carefully sifted, refined and organised by the logic men are willing and able to apply at any time. The more they attempt to refine the concepts and systematize the deductive structure of mathematics, the more sophisticated are its intuitions. But mathematics rests upon certain intuitions that may be the product of what our sense organs, brains and the external world are like. It is a human construction and any attempt to find an absolute basis for it is probably doomed to failure.

Mathematics grows through a series of great intuitive advances, which are later established not in one step but a series of corrections of oversights and errors until the proof reaches the level of accepted proof for that time. No proof is final. New counterexamples undermine old proofs. The proofs are then revised and mistakenly considered proven for all time . . . Actually the mathematician does not rely upon rigorous proof to the extent that is normally supposed. His creations have a meaning for him that precedes any formalization, and this meaning gives the creations an existence or reality *ipso facto*. The attempt to determine precise metes and bounds of a result by deriving it from an axiomatic structure may help in some ways but does not actually enhance its status. (Kline, *ibidem*, p. 313)

Today's mathematicians (when they care to bother about it) remain perplexed between the awareness of lack of absolute proofs of consistency and the strong feeling of the soundness of the mathematics they create. [End of example]

Another example of flow of elements of culture from the technical to the formal level is supplied by the history of the so-called 'principle of homogeneous quantities'.

Example: **the principle of homogeneity: an axiom turned norm of rigour**

The Definition V, 3 of the 'Elements' says: 'Ratio is a quantitative relation between two homogeneous quantities'. This definition has led to the rule: it is impossible to speak about the ratio of two non-homogeneous quantities. This rule became a kind of unquestioned dogma, very difficult to overcome. One symptom of this obstacle was the reluctance, in kinematics, to consider the ratio of distance to time as an expression of velocity. As the historians Dedron and Itard remarked: 'It is perhaps of interest to note that in none of the work of seventeenth century applied mathematicians, except perhaps in that of Wallis, do we find the modern definition of velocity as the quotient of distance travelled divided by time, or the limit of this quotient as the time interval tends to zero. Even for Euler, in *Letters to a German Princess*, 'Velocity is that well-known property whereby one says that in a certain time a body travels a greater or less distance in space' (Dedron and Itard, 1973, p. 192).

Of course, the life of the principle of homogeneity would not be as long as it was, were it not consistent with other elements of the formal level of mathematical culture. The principle of homogeneity is closely related to the idea of discrimination between the discrete and the continuous quantities, proposed in the 'Elements'. Numbers could only be coefficients in equations involving magnitudes. They showed how many times a given quantity has to be taken. Quantities were represented geometrically as line segments (lengths), parallelograms (areas), parallelepipeds (volumes). It does not make sense to add a length and a volume, and even less to divide a length into a volume. The expression a/b where a and b are quantities, could not be replaced by a number — result of division of the measure of a by the measure of b. A ratio carried in itself the information about the quantities of the two magnitudes a and b, the information about what is being compared to what. In a/b regarded as a number this information is lost. [End of example]

The flow of elements of culture from one level to another has a dialectic character: something that, on the technical level, is an achievement that pushes the research forward, may become, on the formal level, a dogma that nobody dares to shake. On the informal level — it may imprint itself as a scheme of thought, a habit so natural that it becomes a part of ourselves.

A progress on the technical level always requires a certain overcoming of our intellectual habits and of what we have considered as infallible truths — the sacred cows of our minds.

At the same time, deprived from our beliefs, convictions and schemes of thought, we would be totally helpless in front of any intellectual task. Einstein wrote: '. . . if the researcher went about his work without any preconceived opinion, how should he be able at all to select out those facts from the immense abundance of the most complex experience, and just those which are simple enough to permit lawful connections to become evident' (cited in Holton, 1978, p. 99). Laws are not derived by induction from observation of particular facts. Indeed, the very notion of 'fact' does not make much sense prior to theory. However, these pre-suppositions are not taken at random — they are guided by what is called the scientist's 'intuition' which, in case of individuals such as Einstein, means a global vision of the past and future developments of a domain.

The situation is not very different in mathematics. Mathematicians do incline themselves under the logical necessities of their proofs and verifications and sometimes unexpected or paradoxical results are obtained. But the very fact that some results are considered paradoxical proves the existence, also in mathematicians, of what Holton calls 'thematic presuppositions', i.e., 'the unverifiable, unfalsifiable and yet not arbitrary conceptions and hypotheses'.

NIHIL NOVI

The vision of 'good' understanding in mathematics presented in this book, full of metaphors of struggle, 'overcoming' obstacles, 'breaking' with a scheme of thought, etc., is nothing new. This is just another way of saying that 'there is no royal road to geometry'. However, this seems to be more true today than 2500 years ago. Haven't we less and less royal roads on Earth anyway?

References

AJDUKIEWICZ, K. (1934) 'Sprache und Sinn', *Erkenntnis IV*, pp. 100–38.

AJDUKIEWICZ, K. (1946) 'O tzw. neopozytywizmie', *Mysl Wspolczesna 6–7*, pp. 155–76.

AJDUKIEWICZ, K. (1974) *Pragmatic logic*, Dortrecht, Boston, D. Reidel Publishing Co., Warszawa, Polish Scientific Publishers.

AJDUKIEWICZ, K. (1985) 'Klasyfikacja rozumowan', in *Jezyk i poznanie*, 2, pp. 206–25.

ARENDT, H. (1978) *The life of the mind: 1. Thinking*, New York, Harcourt Brace Jovanovitch, Inc.

ARISTOTLE (1932) 'Rhetoric', in Cooper, L. *The Rhetoric of Aristotle. An Expanded Translation with Supplementary Examples for Students of Composition and Public Speaking*, New York, Appleton-Century-Crofts, Educational Division, Meredith Corporation.

ARZARELLO, F. (1989) 'The role of conceptual models in the activity of problem solving', Proceedings of the XIIIth Psychology of Mathematics Education Conference, Paris, pp. 93–100.

ATWEH, B. and COOPER, T. (1992) 'The effect of gender and social class on classroom communication in secondary school mathematics', A contribution to *ICME7, Working Group 7: Language and Communication*, Québec, Canada.

AUSTIN, J.L. (1961) *Philosophical Papers*, Oxford, Clarendon Press.

BACHELARD, G. (1970) *La philosophie du non*, Paris, Presses Universitaires de France (First published in 1949).

BACHELARD, G. (1975) *Le nouvel esprit scientifique*, Paris, Presses Universitaires de France (First published in 1934).

BACHELARD, G. (1983) *La formation de l'esprit scientifique,* Paris, Presses Universitaires de France (First published in 1938).

BALACHEFF, N. (1986) 'Cognitive versus situational analysis of problem solving behaviors', *For the Learning of Mathematics*, 6, 3, pp. 10–12.

BAR-HILLEL, Y. (1971) *Pragmatics of natural language*, Dortrecht, Reidel.

BARTOLINI-BUSSI, M. (1990) 'Mathematics knowledge as a collective enterprise', Paper read at the 4th conference on Systematic Cooperation between Theory and Practice, Brakel, Germany, September.

BARTOLINI-BUSSI, M. (1992) 'Verbal interaction and mathematical knowledge: Methodologies for transcript analysis', A contribution to *ICME7, Working Group 7: Language and Communication,* Québec, Canada.

BATTISTA, M.T. (1983) 'A complete model for operations on integers', *Arithmetic Teacher,* 30, 9, pp. 26–31.

BAUERSFELD, H. (1983) 'Subjektive Erfahrungsberiche als Grundlage einer Interactionstheorie des Mathematiklernens und lehrens', in BAUERSFELD, H. u.a., *Lernen und Lehren von Mathematik* (Analysen zu Unterrichtshandeln II), Köln, Germany, pp. 1–56.

BAUERSFELD, H. (1990) 'Activity theory and radical constructivism' (Manuscript).

BAUERSFELD, H. and ZAWADOWSKI, W. (1987) 'Metafory i metonimie w nauczaniu matematyki', *Dydaktyka Matematyki,* 8, pp. 155–86.

BEDNARZ, N. and GARNIER, C. (Eds) (1989) *Construction des savoirs: Obstacles et conflits,* Montréal, Agence d'ARC.

BEDNARZ, N., JANVIER, B., MARY, C. and LEPAGE, A. (1992) *L'Algèbre comme outil de résolution de problèmes: une réflexion sur les changements nécessaires dans le passage d'un mode de traitement arithmétique à un mode de traitement algébrique* (Actes du Colloque portant sur l'émergence de l'algèbre), Montréal, 10 April 1992, Publications of CIRADE, UQAM, November.

BERGERON, J. and HERSCOVICS, N. (1982) 'Levels in the understanding of the function concept', in VAN BARNEVELD, G. and VERSTAPPEN, P. (Eds) *Proceedings of the Conference on Functions,* Enschede, The Netherlands, National Institute of Curriculum Development.

BERGSON, H. (1975) *Creative evolution,* Westport, Conn., Greenwood Press.

BERNSTEIN, B. (1971) *Class, codes and control,* London, Routledge and Kegan Paul.

BETH, E.W. and PIAGET, J. (1961) *Epistémologie mathématique et psychologie* (Etudes d'épistémologie génétique publiées sous la direction de Jean Piaget, XIV), Paris, Presses Universitaires de France, pp. 328–9.

BISHOP, A.J. (1988) *Mathematics enculturation: a cultural perspective on mathematics education,* Dortrecht, Kluwer.

BISHOP, A.J. (1991) 'Toward a cultural psychology of mathematics — A review of "Culture and cognitive development: Studies in mathematical understanding" by Geoffrey, B. Saxe', *Journal for Research in Mathematics Education,* 22, 1, pp. 76–80.

BOHM, D. and PEAT, D.F. (1987) *Science, order and creativity,* London, Routledge.

BORASI, R. and ROSE, B. (1989) 'Journal writing and mathematics instruction. *Educational Studies in Mathematics,* 20, 4, pp. 347–65.

BOYER, C. (1968) *A history of mathematics,* New York, Wiley and Sons.

BREIDENBACH, D., DUBINSKY, E., HAWKES, J. and NICHOLS, D. (1992) 'Development of the process conception of function', *Educational Studies in Mathematics,* 23, 3, pp. 247–86.

BRITTON, J., BURGESS, T., MARTIN, N., McLEOD, A. and ROSEN, H. (1975) *The development of writing abilities (11–18),* London, Macmillan Education.

BROUSSEAU, G. (1986) 'Fondements et méthodes de la didactique des mathématiques', *Recherches en Didactique des Mathématiques,* 7, 2, pp. 33–115.

BROUSSEAU, G. (1989) 'Le contrat didactique: Le milieu', *Recherches en Didactique des Mathématiques*, 9, 3, pp. 309–36.

BRUNER, J.S. (1973) 'The growth of representational processes in childhood', in ANGLIN, J.M. (Ed) *Beyond the information given. Studies in the psychology of knowing*, New York, W.W. Norton and Co.

CACKOWSKI, Z. (1979) 'The continuity and discontinuity of human cognition', *Dialectics & Humanism*, 2, pp. 125–36.

CACKOWSKI, Z. (1987) Article 'Fenomenalizm', in *Filozofia a Nauka — Zarys Encyklopedyczny*, Warszawa, Poland, Zaklad Narodowy im. Ossolinskich.

CACKOWSKI, Z. (1992) 'Przeszkoda epistemologiczna', *Kwartalnik Pedagogiczny* 1, 141, pp. 3–14.

CAJORI, F. (1929) *A history of mathematical notation, II*, Chicago, Open Court Publications Co.

CARRAHER, T., CARRAHER, D. and SCHLIEMANN, A. (1985) 'Mathematics in the streets and in the schools', *British Journal of Developmental Psychology*, 3, pp. 21–9.

CAUCHY, A.L. (1821) *Cours d'Analyse de l'Ecole Polytechnique*, le Partie, Analyse Algébrique, Paris, De l'Imprimerie Royale.

CAVAILLÈS, J. (1962) *Philosophie Mathématique*, Paris, Hermann.

CESTARI, M.L. (1983) *A assimetria na relaçao professor/alumno, um dos pilares da dependencia cultural, social e economica*, Federal University of Rio Grande do Sul, Brazil.

CHEVALLARD, Y. (1985a) *La transposition didactique: du savoir savant au savoir enseigné*, Grenoble, La Pensée Sauvage Éditions.

CHEVALLARD, Y. (1985b) 'Le passage de l'arithmétique à l'algèbre dans l'enseignement des mathématiques au collège', *Petit x # 5*, pp. 51–94.

CHEVALLARD, Y. (1990) 'On mathematics education and culture: critical afterthoughts', *Educational Studies in Mathematics*, 21, pp. 3–27.

CHEVALLARD, Y. (1992) 'Concepts fondamentaux de la didactique: perspectives apportées par une approche anthropologique', *Recherches en Didactique des Mathématiques*, 12, 1, pp. 73–112.

CHILVERS, P. (1985) 'A consistent model for operations on directed numbers', *Mathematics in School*, 14, 1, pp. 26–8.

CIVIL, M. (1992) 'Preservice teachers communicating mathematics', A contribution to *ICME7, Working Group 7: Language and Communication*, Québec, Canada.

CLEMENTS, K. (1981–1982) 'Visual imagery and school mathematics', *For the Learning of Mathematics*, 2, 2, pp. 2–9; 2, 3, pp. 33–9.

CONNOLLY, P. and VILARDI, T. (Eds) (1989) *Writing to learn mathematics and science*, New York, Teachers' College.

CORNU, B. (1981) 'Apprentissage de la notion de limite: modèles spontanés et modèles propres', Proceedings of the Vth Psychology of Mathematics Education Conference, Grenoble, pp. 322–6.

CORNU, B. (1983) 'Quelques obstacles à l'apprentissage de la notion de limite', *Recherches en Didactique des Mathématiques*, 4, pp. 236–68.

CRANSTON, M.W. (1972) *Philosophy and language*, Toronto, CBC Learning Systems.

CURCIO, F.R. and ARTZT, A.F. (1992) 'The effects of small group interaction on graph comprehension of fifth graders', A contribution to *ICME7, Working Group 7: Language and Communication*, Qúebec, Canada.

CZEZOWSKI, T. (1959) *Glówne zasady nauk filozoficznych*, Wroclaw, Poland, Zaklad Narodowy im. Ossolinskich.

DANTO, A. (1969) 'Semantic vehicles, understanding and innate ideas', in HOOK, S. (Ed) *Language and Philosophy. A Symposium*, New York, New York University Press.

DAVAL R. and GUILBAUD, G.T. (1945) *Le raisonnement mathématique*, Paris, Presses Universitaires de France.

DAVIS, R.B. (1984) *Learning mathematics: the cognitive science approach to mathematics education*, New Jersey, Ablex Publishing Corporation.

DAVYDOV, V.V. (1990) 'The content and unsolved problems of activity theory', Paper presented at the 2nd International Congress for Research on Activity Theory, Helsinki, May 21–5.

DAVYDOV, V.V. and RADZIKHOVSKII, L.A. (1985) 'Vygotski's theory and the activity-oriented approach in psychology', in WERTSCH, J.V. (Ed) *Culture, communication and cognition. Vygotskian Perspectives*, London, Cambridge University Press.

DEDEKIND, R. (1963) *Essays on the theory of numbers: I. Continuity and irrational numbers. II. The nature and meaning of numbers*. (authorized translation by Wooster Woodruff Beman), New York: Dover Publications.

DEDRON, P. and ITARD, J. (1973) *Mathematics and Mathematicians*, Milton Keynes, The Open University Press.

DEWEY, J. (1971) *How We Think? A Restatement of the Relation of Reflective Thinking to the Educative Process*, Chicago, Henry Regnery Co., A Gateway Edition (first published in 1910).

DOISE, W. and MUGNY, G. (Eds) (1984) *The Social Development of Intellect*, Oxford, Pergamon Press.

DORIER, J.L. (1991) 'Sur l'enseignement des concepts élémentaires d'algèbre linéaire à l'université', *Recherches en Didactique des Mathématiques*, 11, 2.3, pp. 325–64.

DOUADY, R. (1986) 'Jeu de cadres et dialectique outil-objet', *Recherches en Didactique des Mathématiques*, 7, 2, pp. 5–31.

DÖRFLER, W. (1991) 'Forms and means of generalization in mathematics', in BISHOP, A.J., MELLIN-OLSEN, S. and VAN DORMOLEN, J. (Eds) *Mathematical Knowledge: Its Growth Through Teaching*, Dortrecht/Boston/London, Kluwer Academic Publishers.

DUBINSKY, E. and HAREL, G. (1992b) 'The nature of the process conception of function', in DUBINSKY, E. and HAREL, G. (Eds) *The Concept of Function: Elements of Pedagogy and Epistemology*, Notes and Reports Series of The Mathematical Association of America.

DUBINSKY, E. and LEWIN, P. (1986) 'Reflective abstraction and mathematics education: the genetic decomposition of induction and compactness', *Journal of Mathematical Behavior*, 5, pp. 55–92.

DUMMETT, M. (1991) *Frege: Philosophy of Mathematics*, Cambridge, Mass., Harvard University Press.

DURKIN, K. and SHIRE, B. (1991) *Language in Mathematics Education — Research and Practice*, Milton Keynes, Philadelphia, Open University Press.

DYRSZLAG, Z. (1972) 'O poziomach rozumienia pojec matematycznych', *Zeszyty Naukowe WSP w Opolu, Studia i Monografie*, 32.

DYRSZLAG, Z. (1978) 'O poziomach i kontroli rozumienia pojec matematycznych w procesie dydaktycznym', *Zeszyty Naukowe WSP w Opolu, Seria B: Studia i Monografie*, 65.

DYRSZLAG, Z. (1984) 'Sposoby kontroli rozumienia pojec matematycznych', *Oswiata i Wychowanie*, 9, B, pp. 42–3.

EGRET, M.A. and DUVAL, R. (1989) 'Comment une classe de quatrième a pris conscience de ce qu'est une démarche de démonstration', *Annales de Didactique et de Sciences Cognitives*, Université Louis Pasteur, IREM de Strasbourg.

FEYNMAN, R.P. (1965) *The Feynman Lectures on Physics*, 1, Reading, Mass., Addison-Wesley.

FOUCAULT, M. (1973) *The Order of Things. An Archeology of Human Sciences*, New York, Vintage Books.

FREUDENTHAL, H. (1973) *Mathematics as an Educational Task*, Dortrecht, Holland, D. Reidel.

FREUDENTHAL, H. (1983) *Didactical Phenomenology of Mathematical Structures*, Dortrecht, Holland, D. Reidel.

FRIEDMAN, M. (1988) 'Explanation and scientific understanding', in PITT, J.C. (Ed) *Theories of explanation*, New York, Oxford University Press.

GAGATSIS, A. (1985) 'Questions soulevées par le test de closure', *Revue Française de Pédagogie*, 70, January-February-March, pp. 41–50.

GIBSON, J.J. (1986) *The Ecological Approach to Visual Perception*, Hillsdale, NJ, Lawrence Erlbaum Associates.

GOLDSTEIN, M. and GOLDSTEIN, I.F. (1978) *How We Know. An Exploration of the Scientific Process*, New York and London, Plenum Press.

GREENO, J.G. (1991) 'Number sense as situated knowing in a conceptual domain', *Journal for Reseach on Mathematics Education*, 22, 3, pp. 170–218.

GRICE, H.P. (1981) 'Presupposition and conversational implicature', in COLE, P. (Ed) *Radical pragmatics*, New York, Academic Press.

GUTTIÉREZ, A., JAIME, A. and FORTUNY, J.M. (1991) 'An alternative paradigm to evaluate the acquisition of the Van Hiele levels', *Journal for Reseach on Mathematics Education*, 22, 3, pp. 237–51.

HACKING, I. (1975) *Why Does Language Matter to Philosophy*, Cambridge, UK, Cambridge University Press.

HADAMARD, J. (1945) *An Essay on the Psychology of Invention in the Mathematical Field*, New York, Dover Publications Inc.

HALL, E.T. (1969) *The Hidden Dimension*, New York, Anchor Press, Doubleday.

HALL, E.T. (1976) *Beyond Culture*, New York, Anchor Press, Doubleday.

HALL, E.T. (1981) *The Silent Language*, New York, Anchor Press, Doubleday (First edition: 1959).

HANSON, N.R. (1961) *Patterns of Discovery*, Cambridge, UK, Cambridge University Press.

HART, K. (1981) *Children's Understanding of Mathematics: 11–16*, London, John Murray.

HEFENDEHL-HEBEKER, L. (1991) 'Negative numbers: obstacles in their evolution from intuitive to intellectual constructs', *For the Learning of Mathematics*, 11, 1, pp. 26–32.

HEIDEGGER, M. (1962) *Being and time*, New York, Harper and Row.

HEISENBERG, W. (1969) *Der Teil und das Ganze*, Munich, R. Piper and Co. Verlag.

HEMPEL, C.G. and OPPENHEIM, P. (1948) 'Studies in the logic of explanation', *Philosophy of Science*, 15, pp. 567–79.

HERSCOVICS, N. and BERGERON, J.C. (1989) 'A model to describe the construction of mathematical concepts from an epistemological perspective', Proceedings of the 13th Meeting of the CMESG, St. Catharine's, Ont., May 26–31.

HIRSCH, E.D. JR (1967) *Validity in Interpretation*, New Haven, Yale University Press.

HOFFER, A. (1983) 'Van Hiele-based research', in LANDAU, M. and LESH, R. (Eds) *Acquisition of Mathematical Concepts and Processes*, New York, Academic Press.

HOFFMAN, M.R. and POWELL, A.B. (1989) 'Mathematical and commentary writing: vehicles for student reflection and empowerment', *Mathematics Teaching*, 126, pp. 55–7.

HOFSTADTER, D.R.H. (1985) *Metamagical Themas: Questing for the Essence of Mind and Pattern*, New York, Bantam Books.

HOLTON, G. (1978) *The Scientific Imagination: Case Studies*, Cambridge, Cambridge University Press.

HOOK, S. (Ed) (1969) *Language and Philosophy. A Symposium*, New York, New York University Press.

JANVIER, C. (1978) 'The interpretation of complex cartesian graphs representing situations — studies and teaching experiments', Doctoral dissertation, University of Nottingham, Shell Centre for Mathematics Education and Université du Québec à Montréal.

JOHNSON M. (1980) 'A philosophical perspective on the problems of metaphor: A model of metaphoric comprehension', in HONECK, R.P. and HOFFMAN, R.R. (Eds) *Cognition and Figurative Language*, Hillsdale, NJ, Lawrence Erlbaum Associates.

JUSZKIEWICZ, A.P. (1976) *Historia Matematyki*, (2), Warszawa, Poland, Panstwowe Wydawnictwo Naukowe.

KEITEL, C., DAMEROW, P., BISHOP, A.J. and GERDES, P. (Eds) (1989) *Mathematics, Education and Society*, Paris, UNESCO.

KLAKLA, M., KLAKLA, M., NAWROCKI, J. and NOWECKI, B.J. (1992) 'Pewna koncepcja badania rozumienia pojec matematycznych i jej weryfikacja na przykladzie kwantyfikatorow', *Dydaktyka Matematyki*, 13, pp. 181–223.

KLINE, M. (1980) *Mathematics: The loss of Certainty*, New York, Oxford University Press.

KORZYBSKI, A. (1950) *Science and Sanity*, Lakeville, Conn., International Neo-Aristotelian Publishing Co.

KOTARBINSKI, T. (1961) *Elementy teorii poznania, logiki formalnej i metodologii nauk*, Wydanie II, przejrzane, Wroclaw, Poland, Zaklad Narodowy im. Ossolinskich.

KRUMMHEUER, G. (1991) 'Argumentations-formate in Mathematikunterricht', in MAIER, H. and VOIGT, J. (Eds) *Interpretative Unterrichtsforschung*, Köln, Germany, Aulis.

KRYGOWSKA, Z. (1969) 'Le texte mathématique dans l'enseignement', *Educational Studies in Mathematics*, 2, pp. 360–70.

KVASZ, L. (1990) 'On understanding as standing under', Proceedings of the BISME-2, Bratislava, August 23–5, pp. 152–5.

LABORDE, C. (1990) 'Language and mathematics', in NESHER, P. and KILPATRICK, J. (Eds) *Mathematics and Cognition*, Cambridge (England), New York, Cambridge University Press.

LACOMBE, D. (1984) 'Spécificités du langage mathématique et difficultés pédagogiques résultantes', in *Signes et discours dans l'éducation mathématique* (Actes des Neuvièmes Journées de l'Éducation Mathématique), UER Didactique, Université Paris VII.

LAKATOS, I. (1978a) 'Cauchy and the continuum', in Lakatos, I. *Philosophical Papers of I. Lakatos. Mathematics, Science & Epistemology*, Cambridge, Mass., Cambridge University Press.

LAKATOS, I. (1978b) *The Methodology of Scientific Research Programmes*, Cambridge, Mass., Cambridge University Press.

LAKOFF, G. and JOHNSON, M. (1980) *Metaphors We Live By*, Chicago, University of Chicago Press.

LAMPERT, M. (1988) 'The teacher's role in reinventing the meaning of mathematical knowing in the classroom', in BEHR, M.J., LACAMPAGNE, C.B. and WHEELER, M.M. (Eds) *Proceedings of the Xth North American chapter of the Psychology in Mathematics Education Conference (NAPME)*, DeKalb, Il, pp. 433–80.

LANGE, JZN, J. DE (1984) 'Mathematics for all is no mathematics at all', in DAMEROW, P. (Ed) *Mathematics for All*, Paris, UNESCO, pp. 66–72.

LEGRAND, M. (1988) 'Genèse et étude sommaire d'une situation co-didactique: le débat scientifique en situation d'enseignement', in LABORDE, C. (Ed) *Actes du Premier Colloque Franco-Allemand de Didactique des Mathématiques et de l'Informatique*, Grenoble, La Pensée Sauvage.

LEIBNIZ, W.G. (1765) *New Essays on Human Understanding* (The 1982 edition: translated and edited by Peter Remnant and Jonathan Bennett), Cambridge, Cambridge University Press.

LEONT'EV, A.N. (1981) 'The problem of activity in psychology', in WERTSCH, J.V. (Ed) *The Concept of Activity in Soviet Psychology*, Armonk, NY, Sharpe.

LESH, R., LANDAU, M. and HAMILTON, E. (1983) 'Conceptual models and applied mathematical problem-solving research', in LANDAU, M. and LESH, R. (Eds) *Acquisition of Mathematical Concepts and Processes*, New York, Academic Press.

LOCKE, J. (1690) *An Essay Concerning Human Understanding* (The 1961 edition: edited with an introduction by John W. Yolton) Oxford, Clarendon Press.

LOSKA, R. (1992) 'Teaching without instruction: the Socratic method', A contribution to *ICME7: Working Group 7: Language and Communication*, Québec, Canada.

LUBOMIRSKI, A. (1983) *O uogolnianiu w matematyce*, Wroclaw, Poland, Zaklad Narodowy im. Ossolinskich.

LURIA, A.R. (1981) *Language and Cognition*, New York, John Wiley and Sons.

MACE, W.M. (1977) 'James J. Gibson's strategy for perceiving: Ask not what's inside your head, but what your head is inside of', in SHAW, R. and BRANSFORD. J. (Eds) *Perceiving, Acting and Knowing: Toward an Ecological Psychology*, Hillsdale, NJ, Lawrence Erlbaum Associates.

MAIER, H. (1986) 'Empirische Arbeiten zum Problemfeld Sprache im Mathematikunterricht', *Zentralblatt für Didaktik der Mathematik*, 18, 4, pp. 137–47.

MAIER, H. (1992) 'On verbal communication in mathematics classroom. How does the character of language affect understanding', A contribution to *ICME7: Working Group 7: Language and Communication*, Québec, Canada.

MALLE, G. (1990) 'Semantic problems in elementary algebra', Proceedings of the BISME-2, Bratislava, August 23–5, pp. 37–57.

MARODY, M. (1987) *Technologie intelektu*, Poland PWN.

MASLOW, A.H. (1966) *The Psychology of Science. A Reconnaissance*, New York, Harper and Row.

MASON, J. (1982) 'Attention', *For the Learning of Mathematics*, 2, 3, pp. 21–3.

MASON, J. (1989) 'Mathematical abstraction as the result of a delicate shift of attention', *For the Learning of Mathematics*, 9, 2, pp. 2–8.

MASON, J. and DAVIS, J. (1990) 'On noticing in the mathematics classroom', Proceedings of the 4th Systematic Cooperation between Theory and Practice Conference, September, Brakel, Germany.

MELLIN-OLSEN, S. (1987) *The Politics of Mathematics Education*, Dortrecht, Holland, Reidel.

MERLEAU-PONTY, M. (1973) *The Prose of the World*, Evanston, Northwestern University Press.

MILL, J.S. (1843) 'System of Logic ratiocinative and inductive, being a connected view of the principles of evidence and the methods of scientific investigation', in ROBSON, J.M. (Ed) (1973) *Collected works of J.S. Mill*, 7, Toronto, University of Toronto Press, Routledge and Kegan Paul.

MINSKY, M. (1975) 'A framework for representing knowledge', in WINSTON, P. (Ed) *The Psychology of Computer Vision*, New York, McGraw-Hill.

177

MORGAN, C. (1991) 'Mathematics coursework: towards common understanding', Paper presented at the Group for Research into Social Perspectives of Mathematics Education, London.

MORGAN, C. (1992) 'Written reports of mathematical problem solving', A contribution to *ICME7, Working Group 7: Language and Communication*, Québec. Canada.

NANTAIS, N. and HERSCOVICS, N. (1989) 'Epistemological analysis of early multiplication', Proceedings of the XIIIth Psychology of Mathematics Education Conference, Paris, pp. 93–100.

NEISSER, U. (1991) 'Direct perception and other forms of knowing', in HOFFMAN R.R. and PALERMO, D.S. (Eds) *Cognition and the Symbolic Processes. Applied and ecological perspectives*, Hillsdale, NJ, Lawrence Erlbaum Associates.

NEWTON, I. (1969) *Mathematical principles of natural philosophy*. Translated into English by Andrew Motte in 1729. The translation revised and supplied with an historical account and explanatory appendix by Florian Cajori, New York, Greenwood Press.

OAKS, A. and ROSE, B. (1992) 'Writing as a tool for expanding student conception of mathematics', A contribution to *ICME7, Working Group 7: Language and Communication*, Québec. Canada.

OGDEN, C.K. and RICHARDS, I.A. (1946) *The Meaning of Meaning*, New York, Harcourt, Brace and Company (first published in 1923).

PEIRCE, C.S. (1906) 'Prolegomena to an apology for pragmaticism', *The Monist*, 16, pp. 492–546.

PEIRCE, C.S. (1955) *Philosophical writings of Peirce, Selected and edited with an introduction by Justus Buchler*, New York; Dover Publications.

PEIRCE, C.S. (1984) Notes for lectures on logic to be given 1st term 1870–71, MS 171: Spring 1870, In MOORE, E.C. *et al.* (Eds) *Writings of Ch. S. Peirce. A Chronological Edition*, Bloomington, Indiana University Press, 2, pp. 1867–1871.

PEIRCE, C.S. (1986) 'On the nature of signs, MS 214: Winter-Spring 1873', in FISCH, M.H. *et al.* (Eds) *Writings of Ch. S. Peirce. A Chronological Edition*, Vol 3. Bloomington, Indiana University Press, 3, pp. 1872–78.

PELED, I. (1991) 'Levels of knowledge about signed numbers: effects of age and ability', Proceedings of the XVth Psychology of Mathematics Education Conference, Assissi, Italy, pp. 145–52.

PENROSE, R. (1990) *The Emperor's New Mind. Concerning Computers, Minds and the Laws of Physics*, London, Vintage.

PERRET-CLERMONT, A.N. (1980) *Social Interaction and Cognitive Development in Children*, London, Academic Press.

PERRET-CLERMONT, A.N. (1990) 'Social psychology of transmission: negotiation of knowledge and relationship between teachers and students', Paper presented at the Symposium on Research on Effective and Responsible Teaching. University of Fribourg, Switzerland.

PETRIE, H.G. (1979) 'Metaphor and learning', in ORTONY, A. (Ed) *Metaphor and thought*, Cambridge, Mass, Cambridge University Press.

PIAGET, J. (1958) 'Problèmes de la psychosociologie de l'enfance', in GURVITCH, G. (Ed) *Traité de sociologie*, 2, Paris, Presses Universitaires de France.

PIAGET, J. (1975a) *The equilibration of cognitive structures: the central problem of intellectual development*, Chicago, University of Chicago Press.

PIAGET, J. (1975b) *To understand is to invent. The future of education*, New York, The Viking Press (esp. the first chapter: A structural foundation for to-morrow's education. First published in 'Prospects', Unesco 1972).

PIAGET, J. (1978) *Success and Understanding*, London and Henley, Routledge and Kegan Paul.

PIAGET, J. and GARCIA, R. (1989) *Psychogenesis and the history of science*, New York, Columbia University Press.

PIMM, D. (1988) 'Mathematical metaphor', *For the Learning of Mathematics*, 8, 1, pp. 30–4.

PIMM, D. (1990) 'Certain metonymic aspects of mathematical discourse', Proceedings of the XIVth Psychology of Mathematics Education Conference, Vol. III, Mexico. July, pp. 129–36.

PIMM, D. (1992) 'Metaphoric and metonymic discourse in mathematics class-rooms', A contribution to *ICME7, Working Group 7: Language and Communication*, Québec, Canada.

PIRIE, S. and KIEREN, T. (1989) 'A recursive theory of mathematical under-standing', *For the Learning of Mathematics*, 9, 3, pp. 7–11.

PIRIE, S. and SCHWARZENBERGER, R.L.E. (1988) 'Mathematical discussion and mathematical understanding', *Educational Studies in Mathematics*, 19, pp. 459–70.

POINCARÉ, H. (1952) *Science and Method*, New York, Dover (Translated by Francis Maitland).

POINCARÉ, H. (1970) *La valeur de la science*, Paris, Flammarion.

POLANYI, M. (1964) *Personal Knowledge. Towards a Post-Critical Philosophy*, London, Routledge and Kegan Paul.

POLLAK, H.O. (1968) 'On some of the problems of teaching applications of mathematics', *Educational Studies in Mathematics*, 1, pp. 24–30.

PYCIOR, H.M. (1984) 'Internalism, externalism and beyond: 19th century British algebra', *Historia Mathematica*, 11, pp. 424–41.

RICHARDS, J. (1991) 'Mathematical discussion', in VON GLASERSFELD, E. (Ed) *Radical Constructivism in Mathematics Education*, Kluwer Academic Publishers.

RICŒUR, P. (1976) *Interpretation Theory: Discourse and the Surplus of Meaning*, Fort Worth, Tex., The Texas Christian University Press.

RICŒUR, P. (1977) *The Rule of Metaphor: Multidisciplinary Studies of the Creation of Meaning in Language*, Toronto, Buffalo, University of Toronto Press.

RICŒUR, P. (1981) *Hermeneutics and the Human Sciences*, Cambridge, Cambridge University Press (Edited, translated and introduced by J.B. Thompson).

SAXE, G.B. (1990) *Culture and Cognitive Development: Studies in Mathematical understanding*, Hillsdale, NJ, Lawrence Erlbaum Associates.

SCHANK, R.C. and ABELSON, R. (1977) *Scripts, Plans, Goals and Understanding*, Hillsdale, NJ, Lawrence Erlbaum Associates.

SCHOENFELD, A.H. (1987) 'What's all the fuss about metacognition?', in SCHOENFELD, A.H. (Ed) *Cognitive Science and Mathematics Education*, Hillsdale, NJ, Lawrence Erlbaum Associates.

SFARD, A. (1991) 'On the dual nature of mathematical conceptions: Reflections on processes and objects as different sides of the same coin', *Educational Studies in Mathematics*, 22, 1, pp. 1–36.

SFARD, A. (1992) 'Operational origins of mathematical objects and the quandary of reification — the case of function', in HAREL, G. and DUBINSKY, E. (Eds) *The Concept of Function: Aspects of Epistemology and Pedagogy*, Notes and Reports Series of The Mathematical Association of America.

SFARD, A. (1994) 'Reification as the birth of a metaphor', *For the Learning of Mathematics*, 14, 1, pp. 44–45.

SIERPINSKA, A. (1985a) 'La notion d'obstacle épistémologique dans l'enseignement des mathématiques', Actes de la 37e Rencontre CIEAEM, pp. 73–95.

SIERPINSKA, A. (1985b) 'Obstacles épistémologiques relatifs à la notion de limite', *Recherches en Didactique des Mathématiques*, 6, 1, pp. 5–68.

SIERPINSKA, A. (1987) 'Humanities students & epistemological obstacles related to limits', *Educational Studies in Mathematics*, 18, pp. 371–97.

SIERPINSKA, A. (1988) 'Sur un programme de recherche lié à la notion d'obstacle épistémologique', in BEDNARZ, N. and GARNIER, C. (Eds) *Construction des savoirs, Obstacles et conflits*, Montréal, Agence d'ARC.

SIERPINSKA, A. (1989) *On 15–17 Years Old Students' Conceptions of Functions, Iterations of Functions and Attractive Fixed Points*, Preprint 454, Institute of Mathematics, Pol. Acad. Sci. Warszawa, Poland.

SIERPINSKA, A. (1990a) 'Epistemological obstacle and understanding — two useful categories of thought for research into teaching and learning mathematics', Proceedings of the 2nd Bratislava International Symposium on Mathematics Education, pp. 5–20.

SIERPINSKA, A. (1990b) 'Some remarks on understanding in mathematics', *For the Learning in Mathematics*, 10, 3, pp. 24–36.

SIERPINSKA, A. (1991) 'Quelques idées sur la méthodologie de la recherche en didactique des mathématiques liée à la notion d'obstacle épistémologique', *Cahiers de Didactique des Mathématique*, 7 (Tetradia didaktikes ton matematikon), Thessalonique.

SIERPINSKA, A. (1992a) 'On understanding the notion of function', in DUBINSKY, E. and HAREL, G. (Eds) *The Concept of Function: Elements of Pedagogy and Epistemology*, Notes and Reports Series of The Mathematical Association of America.

SIERPINSKA, A. (1992b) 'The diachronic dimension in research on understanding in mathematics — usefulness and limitations of the concept of epistemological obstacle', Talk given at the conference: Interaction between History of Mathematics and Mathematics learning, Essen, November 2–5.

SIERPINSKA, A. (1992c) 'What stands under understanding', *Acta Didactica Universitatis Comenianae, Mathematics*, 1, pp. 1–28.

SIERPINSKA, A. (1993) 'On the development of concepts according to Vygotski', *FOCUS on Learning Problems in Mathematics*, 15, pp. 2–3.

SIERPINSKA, A. and VIWEGIER, M. (1989) 'How & when attitudes towards mathematics and infinity become constituted into obstacles in students', Proceedings of the XIIIth Psychology of Mathematics Education Conference, Paris.

SIERPINSKA, A. and VIWEGIER, M. (1992) 'O powstawaniu przeszkod epistemologicznych zwiazanych z pojeciem nieskonczonosci u dzieci 10–12 i 14 letnich, *Dydaktyka Matematyki*, 13, pp. 253–311.

SKARGA, B. (1989) *Granice historycznosci*, Warsaw, Poland, Panstwowy Instytut Wydawniczy.

SKEMP, R.K. (1978) 'Relational and instrumental understanding', *Arithmetic Teacher*, 26, 3, pp. 9–15.

STEINBRING, H. (1993) 'Problem in the development of mathematical knowledge in the classroom: the case of a calculus lesson', *For the Learning of Mathematics*, 13, 3, pp. 37–50.

STERRET, A. (Ed) (1990) 'Using writing to teach mathematics', *The Mathematical Association of America.*

THOMAS, R.S.D. (1991) 'Meanings in ordinary language and in mathematics', *Philosophia Mathematica*, 6, 1, pp. 3–38.

TORT, M. (1974) *Le quotient intellectuel*, Cahiers libres, Paris, Maspero.

VAN HIELE, D. and P. (1958) *Report on methods of initiation into geometry*, in FREUDENTHAL, H. (Ed) *Gröningen*, J.B. Wolters.

VASCO, C.E. (1986) 'Learning elementary school mathematics as a culturally conditioned process', in WHITE, M.I. and POLLAK, S. (Eds) *The Cultural Transition: Human Experience and Social Transformation in the Third World and Japan*, Boston, Routledge and Kegan Paul, pp. 141–73.

VIAL, M., STAMBAK, M., and BURGVIERE, E. *et al.* (1974) 'Charactéristiques psychologiques individuelles, origine sociale et échecs scolaires', in 'Pourquoi les échecs scolaires dans la première année de la scolarité', *Recherches Pédagogiques*, 68, Paris, INRDP.

VOIGT, J. (1985) 'Patterns and routines in classroom interaction', *Recherches en Didactique des Mathématiques*, 6, 1, pp. 69–118.

VYGOTSKI, L.S. (1987) 'Thinking and speech', in RIEBER, R.W. and CARTON, A.S. (Eds) *The Collected Works of L.S. Vygotski* (Translations by Norris Minick), New York, Plenum Press.

WILDER, R.L. (1981) *Mathematics as a Cultural System*, Pergamon Press.

WILLIAMS, S.R. (1991) 'Models of limit held by college calculus students', *Journal for Research in Mathematics Education*, 22, 3, pp. 219–36.

WITTGENSTEIN, L. (1958) *Philosophical Investigations* (Translated by G.E.M. Anscombe), Oxford, Basil Blackwell.

WITTGENSTEIN, L. (1969) *The Blue and the Brown Books*, Oxford, Basil Blackwell.

YACKEL, E. (1987) 'A year in the life of a second grade class: a small group perspective', Proceedings of the XIth Psychology of Mathematics Education Conference in Monréal, Canada, pp. 208–14.

YOUNG, J.Z. (1960) *Doubt and Certainty in Science*, New York, Oxford University Press.

Index

understandings 2
unifying principle: and understanding
 33–4

values, set of: solidarity in 132
variability 131
variables: continuous 130–1, 132
vectors 96
 linear independence of 46–7, 48, 51
 and T-invariance 115–16

verbalization: of understandings 66, 68
Viète's algebraic notation 8
Vygotski, L.S. xiii
 and development of generalization
 144–51, 159
 and pre-concept of number 156
 theory of development of concepts
 138–44

zone of proximal development 140